ATS-112   ADMISSION TEST SERIES

This is your
PASSBOOK for...

Differential Aptitude Tests (DATS)

Test Preparation Study Guide
Questions & Answers

NATIONAL LEARNING CORPORATION®

COPYRIGHT NOTICE

This book is SOLELY intended for, is sold ONLY to, and its use is RESTRICTED to individual, bona fide applicants or candidates who qualify by virtue of having seriously filed applications for appropriate license, certificate, professional and/or promotional advancement, higher school matriculation, scholarship, or other legitimate requirements of education and/or governmental authorities.

This book is NOT intended for use, class instruction, tutoring, training, duplication, copying, reprinting, excerption, or adaptation, etc., by:

1) Other publishers
2) Proprietors and/or Instructors of "Coaching" and/or Preparatory Courses
3) Personnel and/or Training Divisions of commercial, industrial, and governmental organizations
4) Schools, colleges, or universities and/or their departments and staffs, including teachers and other personnel
5) Testing Agencies or Bureaus
6) Study groups which seek by the purchase of a single volume to copy and/or duplicate and/or adapt this material for use by the group as a whole without having purchased individual volumes for each of the members of the group
7) Et al.

Such persons would be in violation of appropriate Federal and State statutes.

PROVISION OF LICENSING AGREEMENTS – Recognized educational, commercial, industrial, and governmental institutions and organizations, and others legitimately engaged in educational pursuits, including training, testing, and measurement activities, may address request for a licensing agreement to the copyright owners, who will determine whether, and under what conditions, including fees and charges, the materials in this book may be used them. In other words, a licensing facility exists for the legitimate use of the material in this book on other than an individual basis. However, it is asseverated and affirmed here that the material in this book CANNOT be used without the receipt of the express permission of such a licensing agreement from the Publishers. Inquiries re licensing should be addressed to the company, attention rights and permissions department.

All rights reserved, including the right of reproduction in whole or in part, in any form or by any means, electronic or mechanical, including photocopying, recording, or by any information storage and retrieval system, without permission in writing from the Publisher.

Copyright © 2024 by
National Learning Corporation

212 Michael Drive, Syosset, NY 11791
(516) 921-8888 • www.passbooks.com
E-mail: info@passbooks.com

PUBLISHED IN THE UNITED STATES OF AMERICA

PASSBOOK® SERIES

THE *PASSBOOK® SERIES* has been created to prepare applicants and candidates for the ultimate academic battlefield – the examination room.

At some time in our lives, each and every one of us may be required to take an examination – for validation, matriculation, admission, qualification, registration, certification, or licensure.

Based on the assumption that every applicant or candidate has met the basic formal educational standards, has taken the required number of courses, and read the necessary texts, the *PASSBOOK® SERIES* furnishes the one special preparation which may assure passing with confidence, instead of failing with insecurity. Examination questions – together with answers – are furnished as the basic vehicle for study so that the mysteries of the examination and its compounding difficulties may be eliminated or diminished by a sure method.

This book is meant to help you pass your examination provided that you qualify and are serious in your objective.

The entire field is reviewed through the huge store of content information which is succinctly presented through a provocative and challenging approach – the question-and-answer method.

A climate of success is established by furnishing the correct answers at the end of each test.

You soon learn to recognize types of questions, forms of questions, and patterns of questioning. You may even begin to anticipate expected outcomes.

You perceive that many questions are repeated or adapted so that you can gain acute insights, which may enable you to score many sure points.

You learn how to confront new questions, or types of questions, and to attack them confidently and work out the correct answers.

You note objectives and emphases, and recognize pitfalls and dangers, so that you may make positive educational adjustments.

Moreover, you are kept fully informed in relation to new concepts, methods, practices, and directions in the field.

You discover that you are actually taking the examination all the time: you are preparing for the examination by "taking" an examination, not by reading extraneous and/or supererogatory textbooks.

In short, this PASSBOOK®, used directedly, should be an important factor in helping you to pass your test.

DIFFERENTIAL APTITUDE TESTS

What Does the DAT Measure?

The DAT is a series of tests that measure your ability to learn or to succeed in a number of different areas. The scores that tell how you did on each test are called percentile ranks.

Differential Aptitude Tests

Verbal Reasoning - Measures your ability to see relationships among words. It is important for success in academic courses, as well as in many occupational fields including business, law, and education.

Numerical Reasoning - Measures your ability to perform mathematical reasoning tasks. It is important for success, in such courses as mathematics and chemistry, as well as in many occupational fields including engineering and carpentry.

Abstract Reasoning - Measures your ability to see the relationships among things rather than among words or numbers. It is important in such occupational fields as drafting, mathematics, and computer programming.

Perceptual Speed and Accuracy – Measures how quickly and correctly you can compare and mark written lists. It is important for success in jobs requiring careful record keeping and the use of technical scientific data.

Mechanical Reasoning - Measures how well you can understand basic mechanical principles as applied to machines, tools, and motion. It is important in such occupational fields as carpentry, engineering, and machine operation.

Space Relations - Measures your ability to visualize the shape and position of objects when you are shown only pictures or patterns. It is important in such occupational fields as carpentry, engineering, automobile design, and art.

Spelling - Measures how well you can spell common English words. It is important for success in academic courses, as well as in many occupational fields including business, law, journalism, and education.

Language Usage - Measures how well you can detect errors in grammar, punctuation, and capitalization. It is important for success in school, as well as in such occupational fields as journalism, business, and law.

Scholastic Aptitude - Your Scholastic Aptitude score stands for a combined Verbal Reasoning plus Numerical Reasoning score. The scores on these two tests measure your ability to learn from books and teachers and to master school subjects

Your Individual Report may include several kinds of scores. These scores are briefly described below.

Raw Score (RS) - The number of questions you answered correctly. NP stands for the number possible.

Percentile Ranks (PR) - Your percentile rank scores on the DAT are presented in two ways: one that compares your performance with the performance of females in your grade; and one that compares your performance with that of males in your grade. On some of the tests, the two percentile ranks may be very close; on others, the percentile ranks may be further apart. This is because males and females tend to score about the same on some tests and differently on others.

National Percentile Bands - Since you might earn a slightly different score on any given day, the National Percentile Bands show the range of scores that you might earn if you were to take the test many times. The middle score in each band is your actual percentile rank. It is based upon your same-sex percentile rank.

Stanines (S) - Stanines, like percentile ranks, allow you to compare your aptitudes to those of other students your own age. They range from 1 (low) to 9 (high), with 5 representing average performance.

Normal Curve Equivalent (NCE) - This score may be used by your counselor for research purposes.

Scaled Score (SS) - Scaled scores can be used by your counselor to examine score changes over time.

What Does the Career Interest Inventory Measure?

The Career Interest Inventory provides information about your interest in a variety of fields of work and school subjects and/or activities.

Career Interest Inventory
Occupational Groups

Social Science - Workers in this field are concerned about the social needs of people. Examples of jobs include counselor, social worker, psychologist, sociologist, and historian.

Clerical Services - Workers in this field do a variety of things, such as prepare and keep records and operate office machines. Examples of jobs include secretary, clerk typist, cashier, and bookkeeper.

Health Services - Workers in this field provide a variety of services for the sick, injured, and disabled. Examples of jobs include nurse, doctor, physical therapist, and veterinarian.

Agriculture - This field involves working with plants and animals. Examples of jobs include farmer, forest ranger, gardener, horse trainer.

Customer Services - Workers in this field perform a variety of tasks, such as guard and clean buildings, prepare and serve food, cut and style hair. Examples of jobs include cook, police officer, and flight attendant.

Fine Arts - Workers in this field use special skills in creative arts and entertainment. Examples of jobs include writer, artist, editor, news reporter, musician, singer, and photographer.

Mathematics and Science - Workers in this field like to do research that often involves observing things and doing experiments. Examples of jobs include engineer, computer scientist, and chemist.

Building Trades - Jobs in this field involve highly skilledwork. They include carpenter, bricklayer, plumber, painter, welder, and roofer.

Educational Services - Workers in this field enjoy helping people learn. Examples of jobs include teacher, librarian, museum worker, college professor.

Legal Services - Workers in this field advise people about legal matters. Examples of jobs include lawyer, judge, and paralegal.

Transportation - The majority of the workers in this field operate vehicles such as trucks, tractors, buses. Examples of jobs include ambulance driver, truck driver, and service station attencant.

Sales - Sales work involves buying and selling products or services. Examples of jobs include salesperson, fund raiser, real estate sales agent.

Management - Workers in this field establish goals, direct operations, and control activities within an organization. Examples of jobs include manager, accountant, and banker.

Benchwork - Workers in this field often use handtools to make or repair small products. Examples of jobs include jewelry repairer, locksmith, and video repairer.

Machine Operation - Workers in this field use and operate machines to work with such materials as metal, paper, or wood. Examples of jobs include press operator, band saw operator, and furnace operator.

GLOSSARY OF DIFFERENTIAL APTITUDES

Specific capacities and abilities required of an individual in order to learn or perform adequately a task or job duty:

G   INTELLIGENCE - General learning ability. The ability to "catch on" or understand instructions and underlying principles. Ability to reason and make judgments. Closely related to doing well in school

V   VERBAL - Ability to understand meanings of words and ideas associated with them, and to use them effectively. To comprehend language, to understand relationships between words, and to understand meanings of whole sentences and paragraphs. To present information or ideas clearly.

N   NUMERICAL - Ability to perform arithmetic operations quickly and accurately.

S   SPATIAL - Ability to comprehend forms in space and understand relationships of plane and solid objects. May be used in such tasks as blueprint reading and in solving geometry problems. Frequently described as the ability to "visualize" objects of two or three dimensions, or to think visually of geometric forms.

P   FORM PERCEPTION - Ability to perceive pertinent detail in objects or in pictorial or graphic material. To make visual comparisons and discriminations and see slight differences in shapes and shadings of figures and widths and lengths of lines.

Q   CLERICAL PERCEPTION - Ability to perceive pertinent detail in verbal or tabular material. To observe differences in copy, to proofread words and numbers, and to avoid perceptual errors in arithmetic computation.

K   MOTOR COORDINATION - Ability.to coordinate eyes and hands or fingers rapidly and accurately in making precise movements with speed. Ability to make a movement response accurately and quickly.

F   FINGER DEXTERITY - Ability to move the fingers and manipulate small objects with the fingers rapidly or accurately.

M   MANUAL DEXTERITY - Ability to move the hands easily and skillfully. To work with the hands in placing and turning motions.

E   EYE-HAND-FOOT COORDINATION - Ability to move the hand and foot coordinately with each other in accordance with visual stimuli.

C   COLOR DISCRIMINATION - Ability to perceive or recognize similarities or differences in colors, or in shades or other values of the same color; to identify a particular color, or to recognize harmonious or contrasting color combinations, or to match colors accurately.

HOW TO TAKE A TEST

You have studied long, hard and conscientiously.

With your official admission card in hand, and your heart pounding, you have been admitted to the examination room.

You note that there are several hundred other applicants in the examination room waiting to take the same test.

They all appear to be equally well prepared.

You know that nothing but your best effort will suffice. The "moment of truth" is at hand: you now have to demonstrate objectively, in writing, your knowledge of content and your understanding of subject matter.

You are fighting the most important battle of your life—to pass and/or score high on an examination which will determine your career and provide the economic basis for your livelihood.

What extra, special things should you know and should you do in taking the examination?

I. YOU MUST PASS AN EXAMINATION

A. WHAT EVERY CANDIDATE SHOULD KNOW
Examination applicants often ask us for help in preparing for the written test. What can I study in advance? What kinds of questions will be asked? How will the test be given? How will the papers be graded?

B. HOW ARE EXAMS DEVELOPED?
Examinations are carefully written by trained technicians who are specialists in the field known as "psychological measurement," in consultation with recognized authorities in the field of work that the test will cover. These experts recommend the subject matter areas or skills to be tested; only those knowledges or skills important to your success on the job are included. The most reliable books and source materials available are used as references. Together, the experts and technicians judge the difficulty level of the questions.
Test technicians know how to phrase questions so that the problem is clearly stated. Their ethics do not permit "trick" or "catch" questions. Questions may have been tried out on sample groups, or subjected to statistical analysis, to determine their usefulness.
Written tests are often used in combination with performance tests, ratings of training and experience, and oral interviews. All of these measures combine to form the best-known means of finding the right person for the right job.

II. HOW TO PASS THE WRITTEN TEST

A. BASIC STEPS

1) Study the announcement

How, then, can you know what subjects to study? Our best answer is: "Learn as much as possible about the class of positions for which you've applied." The exam will test the knowledge, skills and abilities needed to do the work.

Your most valuable source of information about the position you want is the official exam announcement. This announcement lists the training and experience qualifications. Check these standards and apply only if you come reasonably close to meeting them. Many jurisdictions preview the written test in the exam announcement by including a section called "Knowledge and Abilities Required," "Scope of the Examination," or some similar heading. Here you will find out specifically what fields will be tested.

2) Choose appropriate study materials

If the position for which you are applying is technical or advanced, you will read more advanced, specialized material. If you are already familiar with the basic principles of your field, elementary textbooks would waste your time. Concentrate on advanced textbooks and technical periodicals. Think through the concepts and review difficult problems in your field.

These are all general sources. You can get more ideas on your own initiative, following these leads. For example, training manuals and publications of the government agency which employs workers in your field can be useful, particularly for technical and professional positions. A letter or visit to the government department involved may result in more specific study suggestions, and certainly will provide you with a more definite idea of the exact nature of the position you are seeking.

3) Study this book!

III. KINDS OF TESTS

Tests are used for purposes other than measuring knowledge and ability to perform specified duties. For some positions, it is equally important to test ability to make adjustments to new situations or to profit from training. In others, basic mental abilities not dependent on information are essential. Questions which test these things may not appear as pertinent to the duties of the position as those which test for knowledge and information. Yet they are often highly important parts of a fair examination. For very general questions, it is almost impossible to help you direct your study efforts. What we can do is to point out some of the more common of these general abilities needed in public service positions and describe some typical questions.

1) General information

Broad, general information has been found useful for predicting job success in some kinds of work. This is tested in a variety of ways, from vocabulary lists to questions about current events. Basic background in some field of work, such as sociology or economics, may be sampled in a group of questions. Often these are principles which have become familiar to most persons through exposure rather than through formal training. It is difficult to advise you how to study for these questions; being alert to the world around you is our best suggestion.

2) Verbal ability

An example of an ability needed in many positions is verbal or language ability. Verbal ability is, in brief, the ability to use and understand words. Vocabulary and grammar tests are typical measures of this ability. Reading comprehension or paragraph interpretation questions are common in many kinds of civil service tests. You are given a paragraph of written material and asked to find its central meaning.

IV. KINDS OF QUESTIONS

1. Multiple-choice Questions

Most popular of the short-answer questions is the "multiple choice" or "best answer" question. It can be used, for example, to test for factual knowledge, ability to solve problems or judgment in meeting situations found at work.

A multiple-choice question is normally one of three types:
- It can begin with an incomplete statement followed by several possible endings. You are to find the one ending which best completes the statement, although some of the others may not be entirely wrong.
- It can also be a complete statement in the form of a question which is answered by choosing one of the statements listed.
- It can be in the form of a problem – again you select the best answer.

Here is an example of a multiple-choice question with a discussion which should give you some clues as to the method for choosing the right answer:

When an employee has a complaint about his assignment, the action which will best help him overcome his difficulty is to
  A. discuss his difficulty with his coworkers
  B. take the problem to the head of the organization
  C. take the problem to the person who gave him the assignment
  D. say nothing to anyone about his complaint

In answering this question, you should study each of the choices to find which is best. Consider choice "A" – Certainly an employee may discuss his complaint with fellow employees, but no change or improvement can result, and the complaint remains unresolved. Choice "B" is a poor choice since the head of the organization probably does not know what assignment you have been given, and taking your problem to him is known as "going over the head" of the supervisor. The supervisor, or person who made the assignment, is the person who can clarify it or correct any injustice. Choice "C" is, therefore, correct. To say nothing, as in choice "D," is unwise. Supervisors have and interest in knowing the problems employees are facing, and the employee is seeking a solution to his problem.

2. True/False

3. Matching Questions

Matching an answer from a column of choices within another column.

V. RECORDING YOUR ANSWERS

Computer terminals are used more and more today for many different kinds of exams.

For an examination with very few applicants, you may be told to record your answers in the test booklet itself. Separate answer sheets are much more common. If this separate answer sheet is to be scored by machine – and this is often the case – it is highly important that you mark your answers correctly in order to get credit.

VI. BEFORE THE TEST

YOUR PHYSICAL CONDITION IS IMPORTANT

If you are not well, you can't do your best work on tests. If you are half asleep, you can't do your best either. Here are some tips:

1) Get about the same amount of sleep you usually get. Don't stay up all night before the test, either partying or worrying—DON'T DO IT!
2) If you wear glasses, be sure to wear them when you go to take the test. This goes for hearing aids, too.
3) If you have any physical problems that may keep you from doing your best, be sure to tell the person giving the test. If you are sick or in poor health, you relay cannot do your best on any test. You can always come back and take the test some other time.

Common sense will help you find procedures to follow to get ready for an examination. Too many of us, however, overlook these sensible measures. Indeed, nervousness and fatigue have been found to be the most serious reasons why applicants fail to do their best on civil service tests. Here is a list of reminders:

- Begin your preparation early – Don't wait until the last minute to go scurrying around for books and materials or to find out what the position is all about.
- Prepare continuously – An hour a night for a week is better than an all-night cram session. This has been definitely established. What is more, a night a week for a month will return better dividends than crowding your study into a shorter period of time.
- Locate the place of the exam – You have been sent a notice telling you when and where to report for the examination. If the location is in a different town or otherwise unfamiliar to you, it would be well to inquire the best route and learn something about the building.
- Relax the night before the test – Allow your mind to rest. Do not study at all that night. Plan some mild recreation or diversion; then go to bed early and get a good night's sleep.
- Get up early enough to make a leisurely trip to the place for the test – This way unforeseen events, traffic snarls, unfamiliar buildings, etc. will not upset you.
- Dress comfortably – A written test is not a fashion show. You will be known by number and not by name, so wear something comfortable.
- Leave excess paraphernalia at home – Shopping bags and odd bundles will get in your way. You need bring only the items mentioned in the official notice you received; usually everything you need is provided. Do not bring reference books to the exam. They will only confuse those last minutes and be taken away from you when in the test room.

- Arrive somewhat ahead of time – If because of transportation schedules you must get there very early, bring a newspaper or magazine to take your mind off yourself while waiting.
- Locate the examination room – When you have found the proper room, you will be directed to the seat or part of the room where you will sit. Sometimes you are given a sheet of instructions to read while you are waiting. Do not fill out any forms until you are told to do so; just read them and be prepared.
- Relax and prepare to listen to the instructions
- If you have any physical problem that may keep you from doing your best, be sure to tell the test administrator. If you are sick or in poor health, you really cannot do your best on the exam. You can come back and take the test some other time.

VII. AT THE TEST

The day of the test is here and you have the test booklet in your hand. The temptation to get going is very strong. Caution! There is more to success than knowing the right answers. You must know how to identify your papers and understand variations in the type of short-answer question used in this particular examination. Follow these suggestions for maximum results from your efforts:

1) Cooperate with the monitor

The test administrator has a duty to create a situation in which you can be as much at ease as possible. He will give instructions, tell you when to begin, check to see that you are marking your answer sheet correctly, and so on. He is not there to guard you, although he will see that your competitors do not take unfair advantage. He wants to help you do your best.

2) Listen to all instructions

Don't jump the gun! Wait until you understand all directions. In most civil service tests you get more time than you need to answer the questions. So don't be in a hurry. Read each word of instructions until you clearly understand the meaning. Study the examples, listen to all announcements and follow directions. Ask questions if you do not understand what to do.

3) Identify your papers

Civil service exams are usually identified by number only. You will be assigned a number; you must not put your name on your test papers. Be sure to copy your number correctly. Since more than one exam may be given, copy your exact examination title.

4) Plan your time

Unless you are told that a test is a "speed" or "rate of work" test, speed itself is usually not important. Time enough to answer all the questions will be provided, but this does not mean that you have all day. An overall time limit has been set. Divide the total time (in minutes) by the number of questions to determine the approximate time you have for each question.

5) Do not linger over difficult questions

If you come across a difficult question, mark it with a paper clip (useful to have along) and come back to it when you have been through the booklet. One caution if you do this – be sure to skip a number on your answer sheet as well. Check often to be sure that you have not lost your place and that you are marking in the row numbered the same as the question you are answering.

6) Read the questions

Be sure you know what the question asks! Many capable people are unsuccessful because they failed to read the questions correctly.

7) Answer all questions

Unless you have been instructed that a penalty will be deducted for incorrect answers, it is better to guess than to omit a question.

8) Speed tests

It is often better NOT to guess on speed tests. It has been found that on timed tests people are tempted to spend the last few seconds before time is called in marking answers at random – without even reading them – in the hope of picking up a few extra points. To discourage this practice, the instructions may warn you that your score will be "corrected" for guessing. That is, a penalty will be applied. The incorrect answers will be deducted from the correct ones, or some other penalty formula will be used.

9) Review your answers

If you finish before time is called, go back to the questions you guessed or omitted to give them further thought. Review other answers if you have time.

10) Return your test materials

If you are ready to leave before others have finished or time is called, take ALL your materials to the monitor and leave quietly. Never take any test material with you. The monitor can discover whose papers are not complete, and taking a test booklet may be grounds for disqualification.

VIII. EXAMINATION TECHNIQUES

1) Read the general instructions carefully. These are usually printed on the first page of the exam booklet. As a rule, these instructions refer to the timing of the examination; the fact that you should not start work until the signal and must stop work at a signal, etc. If there are any special instructions, such as a choice of questions to be answered, make sure that you note this instruction carefully.

2) When you are ready to start work on the examination, that is as soon as the signal has been given, read the instructions to each question booklet, underline any key words or phrases, such as least, best, outline, describe and the like. In this way you will tend to answer as requested rather than discover on reviewing your paper that you listed without describing, that you selected the worst choice rather than the best choice, etc.

3) If the examination is of the objective or multiple-choice type – that is, each question will also give a series of possible answers: A, B, C or D, and you are called upon to select the best answer and write the letter next to that answer on your answer paper – it is advisable to start answering each question in turn. There may be anywhere from 50 to 100 such questions in the three or four hours allotted and you can see how much time would be taken if you read through all the questions before beginning to answer any. Furthermore, if you

come across a question or group of questions which you know would be difficult to answer, it would undoubtedly affect your handling of all the other questions.

4) If the examination is of the essay type and contains but a few questions, it is a moot point as to whether you should read all the questions before starting to answer any one. Of course, if you are given a choice – say five out of seven and the like – then it is essential to read all the questions so you can eliminate the two that are most difficult. If, however, you are asked to answer all the questions, there may be danger in trying to answer the easiest one first because you may find that you will spend too much time on it. The best technique is to answer the first question, then proceed to the second, etc.

5) Time your answers. Before the exam begins, write down the time it started, then add the time allowed for the examination and write down the time it must be completed, then divide the time available somewhat as follows:
   - If 3-1/2 hours are allowed, that would be 210 minutes. If you have 80 objective-type questions, that would be an average of 2-1/2 minutes per question. Allow yourself no more than 2 minutes per question, or a total of 160 minutes, which will permit about 50 minutes to review.
   - If for the time allotment of 210 minutes there are 7 essay questions to answer, that would average about 30 minutes a question. Give yourself only 25 minutes per question so that you have about 35 minutes to review.

6) The most important instruction is to read each question and make sure you know what is wanted. The second most important instruction is to time yourself properly so that you answer every question. The third most important instruction is to answer every question. Guess if you have to but include something for each question. Remember that you will receive no credit for a blank and will probably receive some credit if you write something in answer to an essay question. If you guess a letter – say "B" for a multiple-choice question – you may have guessed right. If you leave a blank as an answer to a multiple-choice question, the examiners may respect your feelings but it will not add a point to your score. Some exams may penalize you for wrong answers, so in such cases only, you may not want to guess unless you have some basis for your answer.

7) Suggestions
   a. Objective-type questions
      1. Examine the question booklet for proper sequence of pages and questions
      2. Read all instructions carefully
      3. Skip any question which seems too difficult; return to it after all other questions have been answered
      4. Apportion your time properly; do not spend too much time on any single question or group of questions
      5. Note and underline key words – all, most, fewest, least, best, worst, same, opposite, etc.
      6. Pay particular attention to negatives
      7. Note unusual option, e.g., unduly long, short, complex, different or similar in content to the body of the question
      8. Observe the use of "hedging" words – probably, may, most likely, etc.

9. Make sure that your answer is put next to the same number as the question
10. Do not second-guess unless you have good reason to believe the second answer is definitely more correct
11. Cross out original answer if you decide another answer is more accurate; do not erase until you are ready to hand your paper in
12. Answer all questions; guess unless instructed otherwise
13. Leave time for review

b. Essay questions
   1. Read each question carefully
   2. Determine exactly what is wanted. Underline key words or phrases.
   3. Decide on outline or paragraph answer
   4. Include many different points and elements unless asked to develop any one or two points or elements
   5. Show impartiality by giving pros and cons unless directed to select one side only
   6. Make and write down any assumptions you find necessary to answer the questions
   7. Watch your English, grammar, punctuation and choice of words
   8. Time your answers; don't crowd material

8) Answering the essay question

Most essay questions can be answered by framing the specific response around several key words or ideas. Here are a few such key words or ideas:

M's: manpower, materials, methods, money, management
P's: purpose, program, policy, plan, procedure, practice, problems, pitfalls, personnel, public relations

a. Six basic steps in handling problems:
   1. Preliminary plan and background development
   2. Collect information, data and facts
   3. Analyze and interpret information, data and facts
   4. Analyze and develop solutions as well as make recommendations
   5. Prepare report and sell recommendations
   6. Install recommendations and follow up effectiveness

b. Pitfalls to avoid
1. Taking things for granted – A statement of the situation does not necessarily imply that each of the elements is necessarily true; for example, a complaint may be invalid and biased so that all that can be taken for granted is that a complaint has been registered
2. Considering only one side of a situation – Wherever possible, indicate several alternatives and then point out the reasons you selected the best one
3. Failing to indicate follow up – Whenever your answer indicates action on your part, make certain that you will take proper follow-up action to see how successful your recommendations, procedures or actions turn out to be
4. Taking too long in answering any single question – Remember to time your answers properly

EXAMINATION SECTION

GENERAL AND MENTAL ABILITY
COMMENTARY

No matter what the level of the examination tested for, be it for trainee or administrator, whether a specific substantive examination is drawn up *ad hoc* for the position announced or whether a brief, simple qualifying test is given, keen analysis of current testing practices reveals that the type of question indicative of general or mental ability or aptitude, or *intelligence*, is an inevitable component and/or element of most examinations.

In other words, the examiners assume that all candidates must possess, or show, a certain level of understanding or *good sense* in matters or situations that may be considered common or general to all. This, then, is the purpose of the general-or-mental-type question: it seems to delimn, in objective terms, the basic, clearly definable, mental or intellectual status of the examinee, no matter what his education or his training or his experience of his present position or reputation.

In some cases, and for certain whole fields of job positions, tests of general and mental ability have even supplanted the specialized subject-area or position-information examination.

Moreover, even in the latter type of examination, e.g., the specific position-type, it will be found that questions testing general qualities study the examination at point after point.

This section should be of inestimable value to the candidate as he prepares not only for the job-examination, but also for any other examination that he may take at this time or in the future.

Now the candidate should *take* the tests of general and mental ability that follow, because of this special importance. These, particularly, portray the extended and rounded examination of general and/or mental ability.

The *Tests* that follow also serve to focus the candidate's attention on the variety and types of questions to be encountered, and to familiarize him with answer-patterns-and-nuances.

EXAMINATION SECTION
TEST 1

DIRECTIONS: Each question or incomplete statement is followed by several suggested answers or completions. Select the one that BEST answers the question or completes the statement. *PRINT THE LETTER OF THE CORRECT ANSWER IN THE SPACE AT THE RIGHT.*

1. Which one of the five things below does NOT belong with the others?
   A. Horse   B. Dog   C. Camel   D. Fish   E. Bear

   1.____

2. Which one of the five words below tells BEST what a sword is?
   A. Cut   B. Weapon   C. Officer   D. Tool   E. Fight

   2.____

3. Which one of the five words below means the OPPOSITE of south?
   A. West   B. Arctic   C. North   D. Tropics   E. Pole

   3.____

4. A banana is to the peeling and an ear of corn is to the husk as an egg is to
   A. omelet   B. shell   C. cob   D. hen   E. food

   4.____

5. A person who shares what he has with his friends is said to be
   A. kind   B. generous   C. courteous
   D. meek   E. loyal

   5.____

6. Which one of the five things below is the LARGEST?
   A. Knee   B. Toe   C. Leg   D. Ankle   E. Foot

   6.____

7. Feathers are to a bird as fur is to a(n)
   A. coat   B. swan   C. rabbit   D. glove   E. ostrich

   7.____

8. Which word means the OPPOSITE of fail?
   A. Lose   B. Rise   C. Succeed
   D. Recede   E. Give up

   8.____

9. Which one of the things below is MOST like these three: carrot, bean, cabbage?
   A. Bush   B. Apple   C. Lettuce   D. Salad   E. Cherry

   9.____

10. Which one of the ten numbers below is the LARGEST?
    A. 4456   B. 6968   C. 2265   D. 3061   E. 2108
    F. 5549   G. 1335   H. 7472   I. 1286   J. 6970

    10.____

11. Parasol is to sunshine as umbrella is to
    A. rain   B. night   C. promenade
    D. winter   E. black

    11.____

12. If the below words were rearranged to make a good sentence, with what letter would the LAST word of the sentence begin?
usually   are   on   hung   walls   pictures

12._____

13. At 4 cents each, how many pencils can be bought for 32 cents?

13._____

14. Which expression tells BEST just what a floor is?
    A. Part of a house
    B. An inverted wall
    C. It is made of wood
    D. The lower part of a room
    E. Something to step on

14._____

15. A knee is to a leg the same as an elbow is to a(n)
    A. arm   B. shoulder   C. bone   D. wrist   E. hand

15._____

16. If I find a kind of plant that was never seen before, I have made a(n)
    A. invention   B. adoption   C. creation
    D. novelty   E. discovery

16._____

17. 5 10 15 20 25 30 35 41 45 50
One number is wrong in the above series.
What should that number be? (Write the CORRECT number in the space at the right.)

17._____

18. What is the MOST important reason that airplanes were invented?
    A. Trains were unsafe.
    B. Roads were crowded.
    C. There was a demand for more rapid transportation.
    D. Airplanes furnish work for mechanics.
    E. Trains were getting too crowded.

18._____

19. Railroad tracks are to a locomotive as _____ is to an automobile.
    A. tires   B. steam   C. speed   D. road   E. gasoline

19._____

20. Which one of the words below would come FIRST in the dictionary?
    A. Trail   B. Salt   C. Raving
    D. Quarry   E. Grave   F. Naught
    G. Padded

20._____

21. 7 1 7 2 7 3 7 4 7 5 7 6 7 8
One number is wrong in the above series.
What should that number be?

21._____

22. A bicycle is to a motorcycle as a wagon is to
    A. an engine   B. an airplane   C. a horse
    D. slower   E. an automobile

22._____

23. A boy who often tells stories he knows are not true is said to
    A. brag   B. cheat   C. lie
    D. exaggerate   E. lie

23._____

24. Which one of the five words below means the OPPOSITE of easy? 24.____
    A. Simple   B. Slow   C. Tough
    D. Difficult   E. Baffling

25. Which one of the five things below is MOST like these three: eagle, giraffe, lizard? 25.____
    A. Wing   B. Neck   C. Sparrow
    D. Grass   E. Spots

KEY (CORRECT ANSWERS)

1.	D	11.	A
2.	B	12.	W
3.	C	13.	8
4.	B	14.	D
5.	B	15.	A
6.	C	16.	E
7.	C	17.	40
8.	C	18.	C
9.	C	19.	D
10.	H	20.	E

21.	7
22.	E
23.	E
24.	D
25.	C

TEST 2

DIRECTIONS: Each question or incomplete statement is followed by several suggested answers or completions. Select the one that BEST answers the question or completes the statement. *PRINT THE LETTER OF THE CORRECT ANSWER IN THE SPACE AT THE RIGHT.*

1. A church is to a preacher as a school is to
   A. study
   B. pupils
   C. religion
   D. a teacher
   E. a choir

   1.____

2. Which tells BEST just what a cat is?
   A. Something that walks quietly
   B. It has soft fur
   C. A thing that climbs trees
   D. A small domestic animal
   E. It drinks milk

   2.____

3. October   June   December   August   April
   If the above words were arranged in order, with what letter would the middle word begin?

   3.____

4. Which one of the words below would come FIRST in the dictionary?
   A. Brass
   B. Button
   C. Broad
   D. Bully
   E. Breakable
   F. Brush
   G. Buckle
   H. Bright

   4.____

5. Worse is to bad as better is to
   A. very bad
   B. medium
   C. good
   D. much better
   E. worst

   5.____

6. Which tells BEST just what a colt is?
   A. An animal with hoofs
   B. An awkward little beast
   C. An animal that runs fast
   D. A young horse
   E. A little animal that eats hay

   6.____

7. houses   stone   built   of   men   wood   and
   If the above words were rearranged to make a good sentence, with what letter would the third word of the sentence begin? (Make the letter like a printed capital.)

   7.____

8. There is a saying, *All's well that ends well.*
   This means:
   A. All comes out well in the end.
   B. The success of anything is judged by the final result.
   C. Stick to a job until it is finished.
   D. Don't worry how things will turn out.

   8.____

9. Bread is to man as hay is to
   A. wheat   B. barn   C. grass   D. horse   E. flour

   9.____

10. Which tells BEST just what a guess is?
    A. A mistaken idea
    B. A statement we think is most likely correct
    C. A statement we know is correct
    D. A statement that is almost correct
    E. Something we cannot find out

11. The daughter of my mother's brother is my
    A. niece   B. aunt   C. cousin
    D. stepsister   E. granddaughter

12. If Harry is shorter than Arthur and Arthur is shorter than Tom, then Harry is _____ Tom.
    A. shorter than   B. taller than
    C. just as tall as   D. cannot say which

13. A king is to a kingdom as _____ is to a republic.
    A. a democrat   B. a monarchy   C. a president
    D. laws   E. a voter

14. 9 6 4 6 9 3 4 9 6 7 9 9 3 6 9 4 5 9 9 6 3 1 9 6
    9 0 4 9 3 6 2 9 1 7 6 9
    Count each 6 above that has a 9 next after it. Tell how many 6's you count.

15. An event which might happen is said to be
    A. doubtful   B. possible   C. certain
    D. probable   E. unreasonable

16. Which one of the five things below is MOST like these three: king, general, dictator?
    A. War   B. Power   C. President
    D. Order   E. Monarchy

17. Loud is to sound as bright is to
    A. noise   B. shiny   C. dull   D. quiet   E. light

18. Eleven   Thirteen   Nine   Twelve   Ten
    If the above words were arranged in order, with what letter would the middle word begin?

19. A quantity which grows larger is said to
    A. prosper   B. increase   C. fatten
    D. rise   E. burst

20. In a foreign language:
    boy = Puero
    good boy = Puero Duko
    The word that means GOOD begins with what letter?

21. A governor is to a state as a general is to   21._____
    A. a king   B. war   C. an army
    D. a captain   E. a commander

22. 4 3 4 2 4 3 4 2 4 2   22._____
    One number is wrong in the above series.
    What should that number be?

23. If Frank is younger than George and George is just as old as James, then   23._____
    James is _____ Frank.
    A. younger than   B. older than
    C. just as old as   D. cannot say which

24. alphabet the letter Write twenty-third the of   24._____
    Do what this mixed-up sentence tells you to do.

25. Clothes are to a man as _____ are to a bird.   25._____
    A. nests   B. colors   C. wings
    D. trees   E. feathers

KEY (CORRECT ANSWERS)

1.	D	11.	C
2.	D	12.	A
3.	A	13.	C
4.	A	14.	4
5.	C	15.	B
6.	D	16.	C
7.	H	17.	E
8.	B	18.	E
9.	D	19.	B
10.	B	20.	D

21. C
22. 3
23. B
24. W
25. E

TEST 3

DIRECTIONS: Each question or incomplete statement is followed by several suggested answers or completions. Select the one that BEST answers the question or completes the statement. *PRINT THE LETTER OF THE CORRECT ANSWER IN THE SPACE AT THE RIGHT.*

1. If Carl is younger than Edward and Carl is older than John, then John is _____ Edward.
   A. younger than
   B. older than
   C. just as old as
   D. cannot say which

   1._____

2. What is the MOST important reason that glass is used in windows?
   A. It is cheaper than wood.
   B. It permits light to pass through the window.
   C. It keeps out the rain and snow.
   D. It does not collect dust and germs.
   E. The people inside can watch their friends go by outside.

   2._____

3. cook   chocolate   the   a   cake   made   layer
   If the above words were rearranged to make a good sentence, with what letter would the third word of the sentence begin? (Make the letter like a printed capital.)

   3._____

4. A person who is sure he can accomplish a task is said to be
   A. successful   B. confident   C. proud
   D. fearless   E. brave

   4._____

5. Minute   Month   Day   Second   Hour   Year   Week
   If the above words were arranged in order, with what letter would the middle word begin?

   5._____

6. If a man has walked west from his home 8 blocks and then walked east 5 blocks, how many blocks is he from home?

   6._____

7. In a foreign language, very hot = Sano Gur, very cold = Fros Guro.
   The word that means VERY begins with what letter?

   7._____

8. Which one of the five things below is MOST like these three: skate, baseball, jump-rope?
   A. Shoe   B. Club   C. String   D. Ice   E. Scooter

   8._____

9. There is a saying: *Any port in a storm.*
   This means:
   A. Ships should not venture out to sea in storms.
   B. Stormy weather causes large waves in harbors.
   C. In emergencies any aid is acceptable.
   D. Ships usually sink in storms.

   9._____

10. sum five Write two the one and of
    Do what this mixed-up sentence tells you to do.

11. An object or institution that will last only a short time is said to be
    A. temporary   B. changeable   C. unsound
    D. worthless   E. unstable

12. In a foreign language, some bread = Pani Anko, some milk = Lecha Anko, some bread and milk = Pani Oto Lecha Anko.
    With what letter does the word that means AND begin?

13. Which word means the OPPOSITE of humility?
    A. Joy   B. Pride   C. Dry
    D. Funny   E. Recklessness

14. Tree Limb Twig Trunk Bud
    If the above words were arranged in order, with what letter would the middle word begin?

15. There is a saying, *Birds of a feather flock together*.
    This means:
    A. Birds fly in large flocks.
    B. Some birds can't fly.
    C. People associate with others like themselves.
    D. Birds in a flock have the same color.
    E. People settle inn cities to be near others.

16. Which tells BEST just what a neck is?
    A. It is something to wear a collar on.
    B. It is that which joins the head to the body.
    C. A giraffe has a long one.
    D. It is something to fasten a necklace on.
    E. It is the connecting part of the body.

17. 1 2 4 8 24 32 64
    One number is wrong in the above series.
    What should that number be?

18. Write the letter that precedes the letter that comes next before *O* in the alphabet.

19. State Park Nation City Yard
    If the above words were arranged in order, with what letter would the middle word begin?

20. There is a saying, *Kill not the goose that lays the golden eggs.*
    This means:
    A. Geese that lay golden eggs are too touch to eat.
    B. Don't destroy the things that do you good.
    C. Don't kill birds.
    D. Not many geese can lay golden eggs.
    E. Golden eggs are valuable.

21. If I have a large box with 3 small boxes in it and 3 very small boxes in each small box, how many boxes are there in all?

22. If a boy can run 200 feet in 10 seconds, how many feet can he run in 1/4 of a second?

23. Which one of the following words would come LAST in the dictionary?
    A. Health B. Juggle C. Grateful
    D. Never E. House F. Normal
    G. Latin

24. 4 5 8 9 12 13 16 18 20 21
    One number is wrong in the above series.
    What should that number be?

25. A feeling that each of two persons has for the other is said to be
    A. friendship B. mutual C. incompatible
    D. contemporary E. deference

KEY (CORRECT ANSWERS)

1.	A		11.	A
2.	B		12.	O
3.	M		13.	B
4.	B		14.	L
5.	D		15.	C
6.	3		16.	B
7.	G		17.	16
8.	E		18.	M
9.	C		19.	C
10.	8		20.	B

21. 13
22. 5
23. F
24. 17
25. B

EXAMINATION SECTION
TEST 1

DIRECTIONS: Each question or incomplete statement is followed by several suggested answers or completions. Select the one that BEST answers the question or completes the statement. *PRINT THE LETTER OF THE CORRECT ANSWER IN THE SPACE AT THE RIGHT.*

1. Which one of the five things below does NOT belong with the others?
   A. Rose B. Violet C. Pansy
   D. Grape E. Morning-glory

2. Which one of the five words below tells BEST what a gun is?
   A. Shoot B. A weapon C. A tool
   D. An apparatus E. A thing

3. Which one of the five words below means the OPPOSITE of north?
   A. East B. Star C. South
   D. Pole E. Equator

4. A boy is to a man and a lamb as to a sheep as a kitten is to a
   A. girl B. cat C. dog D. wolf E. son

5. A child who accidentally hurts another child should
   A. hurt himself B. say he didn't do it
   C. run away D. do nothing
   E say *I'm sorry*

6. Which one of the five things below is the SMALLEST?
   A. ankle B. leg C. toe D. knee E. foot

7. Which one of the five thins below is MOST like these three: a chair, a bed, and a stove?
   A. Iron B. Steps C. Wood
   D. A table E. A floor

8. Which one of the five words below means the OPPOSITE of thin?
   A. Strong B. Fat C. Healthy
   D. Tall E. Large

9. An elbow is to an arm as a knee is to
   A. a leg B. an ankle C. trousers
   D. a bone E. a man

10. Which word means the OPPOSITE of joy?
    A. Sickness B. Bad C. Happiness
    D. Sorrow E. Cry

1.____
2.____
3.____
4.____
5.____
6.____
7.____
8.____
9.____
10.____

11. Which one of the nine numbers below is the SMALLEST?
    A. 5084   B. 4160   C. 3342   D. 6521   E. 2918
    F. 3296   G. 6475   H. 2657   I. 7839

12. Which word means the OPPOSITE of ugly?
    A. Witch   B. Pretty   C. Colored
    D. Deformed   E. Mean

13. If the following numbers were arranged in order, what would the middle number be?
    A. 5   B. 9   C. 1   D. 7   E. 3

14. If you are sure you are right, you have
    A. pride   B. confidence   C. doubt
    D. confusion   E. safety

15. A sculptor is to a statue as an author is to a
    A. book   B. man   C. name
    D. bookcase   E. pen

16. Which is the MOST important reason we use money?
    A. It is made of silver.
    B. It makes goods cheaper.
    C. It makes exchanging goods easier.
    D. We have used it for a long time.
    E. It is fun to jingle.

17. Which one of the five things below is MOST like these three: a saw, a hammer, and a file? A
    A. bottle   B. pen   C. screwdriver
    D. fork   E. carpenter

18. At 3 cents each, how many pencils can be bought for 27 cents?

19. If a person sleeping quietly is awakened by a sudden cry, he is likely to be
    A. sick   B. dreaming   C. startled
    D. paralyzed   E. asleep

20. A seed is to a plant as a _____ is to a bird.
    A. tree   B. egg   C. feather   D. nest   E. flying

21. 6 1 6 2 6 3 6 4 6 5 6 7
    One number is wrong in the above series.
    What should that number be?

22. Which one of the five things below is MOST like these three: a goat, a frog, and a dove?
    A. A flower   B. A nest   C. Grass
    D. A snake   E. A tree

23. usually cans made tin of are   23._____
    If the above words were rearranged to make the best sentence, with what letter
    would the LAST word of the sentence begin? (Make the letter like a printed
    capital.)

24. A man who acquires the property of others by deceit is called a   24._____
    A. traitor   B. swindler   C. burglar
    D. prisoner   E. lawyer

25. Steam is to a locomotive as _____ is to a sailboat.   25._____
    A. the ocean   B. the wind   C. a rudder
    D. a whistle   E. a mast

KEY (CORRECT ANSWERS)

1.	D		11.	H
2.	B		12.	B
3.	C		13.	A
4.	B		14.	B
5.	E		15.	A
6.	C		16.	C
7.	D		17.	C
8.	B		18.	9
9.	A		19.	C
10.	D		20.	B

21. 6
22. D
23. T
24. B
25. B

TEST 2

DIRECTIONS: Each question or incomplete statement is followed by several suggested answers or completions. Select the one that BEST answers the question or completes the statement. *PRINT THE LETTER OF THE CORRECT ANSWER IN THE SPACE AT THE RIGHT.*

1. Which tells BEST what a cup is?
   A. A small drinking vessel
   B. Something to hold coffee
   C. A thin, breakable object
   D. It is used on a table
   E. It has a hand

2. If John is older than Peter, and Peter is older than Harry, then John is _____ Harry.
   A. older than
   B. younger than
   C. just as old as
   D. cannot say which

3. 5 3 1 8 7 5 1 5 6 3 5 2 0 9 5 3 5 1 0 2 5 8 7 1 5 3 3 5 0 1 3 5 5 3 2 5
   Count each 5 above that has a 3 next after it.
   Tell how many 5's you count.

4. heavier   lead   cork   is   than
   If the words above were rearranged to make a good sentence, with what letter would the FIRST word of the sentence begin? (Make the letter like a printed capital.)

5. A lamp is to light as _____ is to a breeze.
   A. a fan
   B. bright
   C. a sailboat
   D. a window
   E. blow

6. Which one of the seven words below would come FIRST in a dictionary?
   A. Mary
   B. Obey
   C. House
   D. Porch
   E. Elephant
   F. Newly
   G. Fairy

7. The son of my father's sister is my
   A. nephew
   B. uncle
   C. cousin
   D. stepbrother
   E. grandson

8. 5 4 5 6 5 4 5 6 5 6
   One number is wrong in the above series.
   What should that number be?

9. Which one of the five things below is MOST like these three: a ship, a bicycle, and a truck?
   A. A sail
   B. A wheel
   C. A train
   D. The ocean
   E. A tire

10. If Henry is taller than Tom and Henry is shorter than George, then George is _____ Tom.
    A. taller than   B. shorter than
    C. just as tall as   D. cannot say which

11. What is the MOST important reason that we use telephones?
    A. To call the fire department   B. To save time in communication
    C. To chat with our neighbors   D. To hear the bell ring
    E. They give jobs to operators

12. A government in which there are graft and bribery is said to be
    A. anarchistic   B. corrupt   C. autocratic
    D. inefficient   E. disorganized

13. A road is to an automobile as _____ is to an airplane.
    A. flying   B. a propeller   C. speed
    D. the air   E. wings

14. letter Print first year the the word of
    Do what this mixed-up sentence tells you to do.

15. 5 10 15 20 25 31 35 40 45 50
    One number is wrong in the above series.
    What should that number be?

16. Which word means the OPPOSITE of guilty?
    A. Tarnished   B. Brave   C. Unselfish
    D. Cordial   E. Innocent

17. Peace is to war as _____ is to confusion.
    A. explosion   B. order   C. armistice
    D. riot   E. police

18. In an artificial language, bad water = Mullo Nero, bad air = Batti Nero. The word that means *bad* begins with what letter?

19. A man who strives and hopes to achieve success is said to be
    A. ambitious   B. lazy   C. contented
    D. faithful   E. loyal

20. Which one of the five things below is MOST like these three: towel, shirt, and handkerchief?
    A. laundry   B. store   C. bath   D. sail   E. shoe

21. A library is to books as a _____ is to money.
    A. store   B. school   C. bank
    D. knowledge   E. gold

22. If George is taller than Frank and Frank is just as tall as James, then James is _____ George. 22._____
    A. taller than   B. shorter than
    C. just as tall as   D. cannot say which

23. Sentence   Letter   Paragraph   Word   Chapter 23._____
    If the above words were arranged in order, with what letter would the MIDDLE word begin?

24. always   father   A   younger   his   than   boy   is 24._____
    If the above words were rearranged to make a good sentence, with what letter would the SECOND word of the sentence begin? (Make the letter like a printed capital.)

25. If an act conforms to recognized principles or standards, it is said to be 25._____
    A. legislative   B. wicked   C. legitimate
    D. harmonious   E. wrong

KEY (CORRECT ANSWERS)

1.	A	11.	B
2.	A	12.	B
3.	4	13.	D
4.	L	14.	Y
5.	A	15.	360
6.	E	16.	E
7.	C	17.	B
8.	4	18.	N
9.	C	19.	A
10.	A	20.	D

21.	C
22.	B
23.	S
24.	B
25.	C

TEST 3

DIRECTIONS: Each question or incomplete statement is followed by several suggested answers or completions. Select the one that BEST answers the question or completes the statement. *PRINT THE LETTER OF THE CORRECT ANSWER IN THE SPACE AT THE RIGHT.*

1. In an artificial language, rose = Raab, red rose = Raab Lupo. The word that means *red* begins with what letter?

2. If a man has walked north from his home 11 blocks and then walked south 6 blocks, how many blocks is he from home?

3. A vase is to flowers as _____ is to milk
   A. drink   B. a cow   C. white   D. a pitcher   E. cream

4. sum three Write one the five and of
   Do what this mixed-up sentence tells you to do.

5. There is a saying, *Every rose has its thorn.*
   This means:
   A. All rosebushes have thorns.
   B. There is no joy without some sorrow.
   C. Some rose petals are sharp.
   D. All flowers come from bushes.

6. Which tells BEST what a wheel is?
   A. Something that turns
   B. It goes around
   C. A circular rim and hub connected by spokes
   D. A round thing to put on an automobile
   E. A bicycle always has two of them

7. Brick is to a wall as _____ is to a table.
   A. a chair   B. red   C. eat
   D. wood   E. a kitchen

8. sentence the letter Write fifth this in
   Do what this mixed-up sentence tells you to do.

9. Which one of the words below would come LAST in the dictionary?
   A. Emerge   B. Eject   C. Edible
   D. Estate   E. Enter   F. Eternal
   G. Easily   H. Emulate

10. There is a saying, *People who live in glass houses should not throw stones.*
    This means:
    A. Those who have faults should not criticize others.
    B. People should not live in glass houses.
    C. The stones thrown are likely to break the glass in the houses.
    D. People who live in glass houses need all the stones they have.

11. Lunch   Dress   Undress   Supper   Breakfast
    If the above words were arranged in order, with what letter would the MIDDLE word begin?

12. In an artificial language, little dogs = Puri Kamo, little cats = Gatti Kamo, little dogs and cats = Puri Erno Gatti Kamo.
    The word that means *and* begins with what letter?

13. A coin or bill made by dishonest people to deceive the public and pass for real money is said to be
    A. a duplicate   B. counterfeit   C. an imitation
    D. stage money   E. a slug

14. There is a saying, *As you make your bed, so must you lie on it.*
    This means:
    A. You should learn to make your own bed.
    B. You must bear the consequences of your own acts.
    C. You must lie down as soon as your bed is made up.
    D. Sleep is necessary to have good health.

15. Which one of the words below would come LAST in the dictionary?
    A. Harmony   B. Graft   C. Leader
    D. Gallop   E. Lively   F. Know
    G. Habit

16. Which tells BEST what an automobile is?
    A. A horseless carriage   B. A thing with tires
    C. Something to travel in   D. A vehicle propelled by an engine
    E. An engine mounted on wheels

17. Steam is to water as water is to
    A. hot   B. ice   C. an engine
    D. a solid   E. gas

18. Which statement tells BEST just what a hallway is?
    A. A small room
    B. A place to hang your hat and coat
    C. It is long and narrow
    D. A passage giving entrance to a building
    E. Where to say goodbye

19. Which one of the five words below is MOST like these three: small, back, and hard?
    A. Thick   B. Coal   C. Very   D. Soot   E. Color

20. Write the letter that precedes the letter that comes before Q in the alphabet.

21. 1 2 4 8 16 36 64
    One number is wrong in the above series.
    What should that number be?

    21._____

22. A son is to a daughter as an uncle is to a(n)
    A. mother   B. aunt   C. relation
    D. woman   E. sister

    22._____

23. If I have a large box with 5 small boxes in it and 2 very small boxes in each of the small boxes, how many boxes are there in all?

    23._____

24. 3 4 6 7 9 10 12 14
    One number is wrong in the above series.
    What should that number be?

    24._____

25. There is a saying, *An ounce of practice is worth a pound of preaching.*
    This means:
    A. Don't preach   B. Deeds count more than words.
    C. Preaching takes practice

    25._____

KEY (CORRECT ANSWERS)

1.	L	11.	L
2.	5	12.	E
3.	D	13.	B
4.	9	14.	B
5.	B	15.	E
6.	C	16.	D
7.	D	17.	B
8.	E	18.	D
9.	F	19.	A
10.	A	20.	O

21.	32
22.	B
23.	16
24.	13
25.	B

EXAMINATION SECTION
TEST 1

DIRECTIONS: Each question or incomplete statement is followed by several suggested answers or completions. Select the one that BEST answers the question or completes the statement. *PRINT THE LETTER OF THE CORRECT ANSWER IN THE SPACE AT THE RIGHT.*

1. Add: 37.10
       .006
    300.105
     16.02
  7341.
     72.50

1.____

2. Add: 25 7/8
     31 3/4
     72 1/8
     96 1/2
     89 3/8

2.____

3. Multiply: .18902
             .018

3.____

4. Divide: .063)6048

4.____

5. To OSCILLATE means to
  A. quiver   B. freeze
  C. swing back and forth   D. hate
  E. rebound

5.____

6. *A New York broker who studied in Scotland during his younger years took a keen interest in the game of golf as it was played there. When he returned to the United States back in the seventies, he introduced the game over here by reproducing one of England's most famous courses.*
According to the above paragraph, which one of the following statements is TRUE?
  A. Golf originated in the United States.
  B. The first golf course was built in England seventy years ago.
  C. Golf was introduced in the United States in the seventies.
  D. Golf was formerly played only by students.

6.____

7. CAT is to FELINE as COW is to
  A. quadruped   B. pedigreed   C. canine
  D. bovine   E. equine

7.____

2 (#1)

8. BILL is to PAPER as COIN is to 8.____
   A. money   B. heavy   C. shiny   D. metal   E. round

9. WATER is to FLUID as IRON is to 9.____
   A. metal   B. rusty   C. solid   D. rails   E. mines

10. OVER is to UNDER as TRESTLE is to 10.____
    A. tunnel   B. bridge   C. trains
    D. skeleton   E. river

11. VAGUE means MOST NEARLY 11.____
    A. style   B. definite   C. not clear
    D. silly   E. tired

12. To AGGRAVATE is to 12.____
    A. indulge   B. counsel   C. inflate
    D. help   E. make worse

13. PRECISION means MOST NEARLY 13.____
    A. cutting   B. exactness   C. risky
    D. measurement   E. training

14. A TERSE statement is 14.____
    A. long   B. condensed   C. rude
    D. wild   E. exact

15. A car will go 3/8 of a given distance in one hour. 15.____
    What part will it cover in 5/8 of an hour?

16. An incubator was set with 120 eggs. 16.____
    If 18 eggs failed to hatch, what percent hatched?

17. At $2.00 a case, what fraction of a case can be bought for 7/8 of a dollar? 17.____

18. A earns $3.50 a day. B earns ¼ more a day than A does. 18.____
    How many days will it take B to earn the same amount that A earns in 10 days?

19. What is the postage on a package weighing 12 lbs., if the rate is 8 cents 19.____
    for the first pound and 4 cents for each additional pound?

20. *Money order may be cashed without gain or profit by any post office having* 20.____
    surplus money order funds.
    What one word in the above sentence is synonymous to *excess*?

21. The jury AKWITED the prisoner. 21.____
    The word in capitals is misspelled. Write it correctly at the right.

22. Dogs are SUGAYSHUS animals. 22.____
    The word in capitals is misspelled. Write it correctly at the right.

23. The parade caused a TRAFIK jam. 23.____
    The word in capitals is misspelled. Write it correctly at the right.

24. The soldiers were ready to drop with FATEEG. 24.____
    The word in capitals is misspelled. Write it correctly at the right.

25. To TOLERATE is to 25.____
    A. prohibit   B. spoil   C. endure
    D. liberate   E. rejoice

KEY (CORRECT ANSWERS)

1. 7766.731
2. 315 5/8
3. .00340236
4. 9.6
5. C

6. C
7. D
8. D
9. C
10. A

11. C
12. E
13. B
14. B
15. 15/64

16. 85%
17. 7/16
18. 8
19. 52¢
20. surplus

21. acquitted
22. sagacious
23. traffic
24. fatigue
25. C

TEST 2

DIRECTIONS: Each question or incomplete statement is followed by several suggested answers or completions. Select the one that BEST answers the question or completes the statement. *PRINT THE LETTER OF THE CORRECT ANSWER IN THE SPACE AT THE RIGHT.*

1. To CONCUR means to
   A. gather
   B. repeat
   C. assent
   D. cause
   E. put together

2. *The world never knows its great men until it buries them* means MOST NEARLY
   A. worry kills more men than work
   B. when a thing is lost, its worth is known
   C. every shoe fits not every foot
   D. no man really lives who is buried in conceit

3. *The Congress of the United States provided for the cooperation of the federal government with the states in the construction of rural roads all over the country and was a powerful force in the development of highways.*
   Judging from the above paragraph, which one of the following statements is TRUE?
   A. Each state builds its highways and rural post roads unaided.
   B. Congress builds all highways in the United States.
   C. The state receive federal cooperation in the building of all roads.
   D. The federal government assists in the building of post roads.

4. LAKE is to LAND as ISLAND is to
   A. separated
   B. land
   C. lonely
   D. water
   E. large

5. NOVELIST is to FICTION as HISTORIAN is to
   A. war
   B. fact
   C. books
   D. school
   E. primitive

6. Four men agreed to dig a ditch in 20 days. After 10 days, only one-fourth of the ditch was completed.
   How many more men must be engaged to finish on time?

7. *Let a man be true to his intentions and his efforts to fulfill them, and the point is gained, whether he succeed or not.*
   The above statement states that
   A. a man cannot succeed unless he makes an effort to be true to his intentions
   B. he may be satisfied with himself if he makes an effort to be true to his intentions
   C. every point is gained whether a man succeeds or fails
   D. no special effort is necessary for success
   E. a certain amount of accomplishment always attends conscientious effort

2 (#2)

8. MASS is to the WHOLE as ATOM is to
   A. physics   B. weight   C. solids   D. part   E. theory

9. DIME is to CENT a DOLLAR is to
   A. silver   B. dime   C. nickel   D. paper   E. coin

10. WISE is to FOOLISH as KNOWLEDGE is to
    A. simple   B. ignorance   C. books
    D. learned   E. intolerance

11. REPUBLIC is to PRESIDENT as MONARCHY is to
    A. communists   B. ruler   C. constitution
    D. elections   E. emperor

12. The distance from A to C is 423 miles. Tourists left A at 7 A.M. and traveled 225 miles at 45 miles an hour, then stopped 30 minutes for lunch. The remainder of the trip was made at 36 miles an hour.
    At what time did they arrive at C?

13. The TRANSHENT population is quite large.
    The word in capitals is misspelled. Write it correctly at the right.

14. The LYOOTENANT wore a new uniform.
    The word in capitals is misspelled. Write it correctly at the right.

15. He stepped on the AKELURAYTER.
    The word in capitals is misspelled. Write it correctly at the right.

16. Paper is easily PUNGKTYOORD.
    The word in capitals is misspelled. Write it correctly at the right.

17. Even in hot weather, the water supply is ADEKWAYT.
    The word in capitals is misspelled. Write it correctly at the right.

18. PLAUSIBLE explanations are
    A. ample   B. untrue   C. courageous
    D. apparently right   E. impossible

19. Which one of the following words may be applied to OPTION but not to PURCHASE or SALE?
    A. Legal   B. Document   C. Permanent
    D. Abstract   E. Temporary   F. Concession

20. ATTENTUATE means to
    A. wire   B. flatter   C. heed
    D. lessen   E. be present   F. extend

21. GIVING is to LENDING as TAKING is to   21._____
    A. alms   B. prison   C. thieves
    D. stealing   E. kindness   F. borrowing

22. A and B together earned $180.00 on piece work. B worked only 2/3 as fast   22._____
    as A, but he worked 6 days more and received $90.00.
    How many days did A work?

23. CHEAP is to ABUNDANT as COSTLY is to   23._____
    A. plenty   B. inexpensive   C. high priced
    D. scarce   E. frugal

24. *Two-thirds of all American fires are home fires, and the preponderant cause*   24._____
    is carelessness. This source of economic waste and human suffering can be
    checked only as we exercise greater care to eliminate such fire hazards as the
    accumulation of inflammable rubbish, careless smoking habits, overheated
    stoves, etc. Remember this, that even though you have no fire loss, you share
    in the loss of every fire in the country.
    According to the above paragraph, which one of the following statements is
    TRUE?
    A. There are fewer fires in homes than in industrial plants.
    B. Fires are no loss when they are covered by insurance.
    C. This economic waste can be overcome only as we exercise greater care.
    D. Waste is the preponderant cause of home fires.
    E. Carelessness in the accumulation of rubbish causes fires.

25. If a stock of 500 rungs is divided into two parts, one of which contains 2/3 as   25._____
    many as the other, how many rugs are there in the smaller part?

4 (#2)

KEY (CORRECT ANSWERS)

1.	C		11.	E
2.	B		12.	6:00 P.M
3.	D		13.	transient
4.	D		14.	lieutenant
5.	B		15.	accelerator
6.	8		16.	accumulated
7.	E		17.	adequate
8.	D		18.	D
9.	B		19.	E
10.	B		20.	D

21. F
22. 12
23. D
24. C
25. 200

TEST 3

DIRECTIONS: Each question or incomplete statement is followed by several suggested answers or completions. Select the one that BEST answers the question or completes the statement. *PRINT THE LETTER OF THE CORRECT ANSWER IN THE SPACE AT THE RIGHT.*

1. John travels a mile in 1/3 of an hour. Ben travels a mile in 3/10 of an hour. How many minutes does Ben finish before John, each traveling 12 miles?   1.____

2. KITTEN is to CAT as COLT is to   2.____
    A. young   B. pasture   C. horse
    D. donkey   E. cattle

3. WOLF is to HOWL as DOG is to   3.____
    A. bite   B. pet   C. bark
    D. pedigree   E. whine

4. DYNAMYT is used for blasting.   4.____
    The word in capitals is misspelled. Write it correctly at the right.

5. The champion's OPOHNENT won the boxing match.   5.____
    The word in capitals is misspelled. Write it correctly at the right.

6. The hungry man's appetite was APEEZD.   6.____
    The word in capitals is misspelled. Write it correctly at the right.

7. WHEN is to WHERE as TIME is to   7.____
    A. hour   B. place   C. clock   D. here   E. work

8. ATLANTIC is to OCEAN as BRAZIL is to   8.____
    A. South America   B. country   C. river
    D. large   E. small

9. REGIMENT is to ARMY as SHIP is to   9.____
    A. marines   B. wars   C. navy
    D. submarine   E. commerce

10. *Substitute or temporary clerks shall be paid at the rate of $9.76 an hour for each hour or part hour after 6:00 P.M.*   10.____
    What one word in the above quotation is synonymous to a fixed value?

11. *The United States leads the world in the amount of sugar consumed per capita, more than a hundred pounds annually for every person in the nation. The rest of the world is just as fond of sugar but not so able to buy it.*   11.____
    Judging from the above paragraph, which one of the following statements is TRUE?

A. The United States leads in sugar production.
B. Europeans pay more for sugar.
C. Each person in the United States consumes a pound of sugar each week.
D. The per capita consumption of sugar in the United States is the largest in the world.
E. Americans are not so able to buy sugar as the rest of the world.
F. More sugar is consumed in the United States than in the rest of the world.

12. HABITUAL means MOST NEARLY
    A. healthy   B. customary   C. clothing
    D. harness   E. deadly

13. A COMPETENT man is one who is
    A. capable   B. clever   C. idle
    D. ambitious   E. punctual

14. To ADHERE is to
    A. hate   B. tape   C. degrade
    D. cling to   E. listen

15. To CALCULATE is to
    A. number   B. compute   C. whitewash
    D. tell tales   E. think

16. Which one of the following terms may be applied to MOTORCYCLE and AIRPLANE but not to BICYCLE?
    A. High speed   B. Padded seats   C. Metal
    D. Rubber tires   E. Two wheels

17. *He can who believes he can.*
    The above quotation means MOST NEARLY
    A. to believe a thing impossible is the way to make it go
    B. we are able when we feel so
    C. the man who believes is the man who achieves
    D. we walk by faith, not by sight
    E. nothing is impossible to him who tries

18. *How many acquaintances, but few friends.*
    The above quotation means MOST NEARLY
    A. be courteous to all, but intimate with few
    B. a true friend is forever a friend
    C. friends in distress make trouble less
    D. the only way to have a friend is to be one
    E. make friends of all you meet

19. *A man of many trades begs his bread on Sunday.*
    The above quotation means MOST NEARLY
    A. with too many irons in the fire some will burn
    B. doing everything is doing nothing
    C. one cannot do many things profitably at the same time
    D. an intense hour will do more than two dreamy years
    E. A man without a trade will beg his bread

20. *Caution is the parent of safety.*
    The above quotation means MOST NEARLY
    A. all things belong to the prudent
    B. better a mistake avoided than two corrected
    C. look before you leap
    D. better go around than jump and fall short

KEY (CORRECT ANSWERS)

1.	24 min.	11.	D
2.	C	12.	B
3.	C	13.	A
4.	dynamite	14.	D
5.	opponent	15.	B
6.	appeased	16.	A
7.	B	17.	C
8.	B	18.	A
9.	C	19.	C
10.	rate	20.	D

VERBAL ABILITIES TEST
DIRECTIONS AND SAMPLE QUESTIONS

Study the sample questions carefully. Each question has four suggested answers. Decide which one is the best answer. Find the question number on the Sample Answer Sheet. Show your answer to the question by printing the letter of the correct answer in the space at the right. If you have to erase a mark, be sure to erase it completely. Mark only one answer for each question. Do NOT mark space E for any question.

SAMPLE VERBAL QUESTIONS

I. *Previous* means MOST NEARLY   I.____
    A. abandoned   B. former   C. timely   D. younger

II. (Reading) "Just as the procedure of a collection department must be clear cut and definite, the steps being taken with the sureness of a skilled chess player, so the various paragraphs of a collection letter must show clear organization, giving evidence of a mind that, from the beginning, has had a specific end in view."   II.____
The quotation BEST supports the statement that a collection letter should always
    A. show a spirit of sportsmanship   B. be divided into several paragraphs
    C. be brief, but courteous   D. be carefully planned

III. Decide which sentence is preferable with respect to grammar and usage suitable for a formal letter or report.   III.____
    A. They do not ordinarily present these kind of reports in detail like this.
    B. A report of this kind is not hardly ever given in such detail as this one.
    C. This report is more detailed than what such reports ordinarily are.
    D. A report of this kind is not ordinarily presented in as much detail as this one is.

IV. Find the correct spelling of the word and print the letter of the correct answer in the space at the right. If no suggested spelling is correct, print the letter D.   IV.____
    A. athalete   B. athelete   C. athlete   D. none of these

V. SPEEDOMETER is related to POINTER as WATCH is related to   V.____
    A. case   B. hands   C. dial   D. numerals

EXAMINATION SECTION

TEST 1

DIRECTIONS: Each question or incomplete statement is followed by several suggested answers or completions. Select the one that BEST answers the question or completes the statement. *PRINT THE LETTER OF THE CORRECT ANSWER IN THE SPACE AT THE RIGHT.*

1. *Flexible* means MOST NEARLY
   A. breakable   B. flammable   C. pliable   D. weak

2. *Option* means MOST NEARLY
   A. use   B. choice   C. value   D. blame

3. To *verify* means MOST NEARLY to
   A. examine   B. explain   C. confirm   D. guarantee

4. *Indolent* means MOST NEARLY
   A. moderate   B. happiness   C. selfish   D. lazy

5. *Respiration* means MOST NEARLY
   A. recovery   B. breathing   C. pulsation   D. sweating

6. PLUMBER is related to WRENCH as PAINTER related to
   A. brush   B. pipe   C. shop   D. hammer

7. LETTER is related to MESSAGE as PACKAGE is related to
   A. sender   B. merchandise
   C. insurance   D. business

8. FOOD is related to HUNGER as SLEEP is related to
   A. night   B. dream   C. weariness   D. rest

9. KEY is related to TYPEWRITER as DIAL is related to
   A. sun   B. number   C. circle   D. telephone

GRAMMAR

10. A. I think that they will promote whoever has the best record.
    B. The firm would have liked to have promoted all employees with good records.
    C. Such of them that have the best records have excellent prospects of promotion.
    D. I feel sure they will give the promotion to whomever has the best record.

11. A. The receptionist must answer courteously the questions of all them callers.
    B. The receptionist must answer courteously the questions what are asked by the callers.
    C. There would have been no trouble if the receptionist had have always answered courteously.
    D. The receptionist should answer courteously the questions of all callers.

11._____

SPELLING

12. A. collapsible   B. colapseble
    C. collapseble   D. none of the above

12._____

13. A. ambigeuous   B. ambigeous
    C. ambiguous   D. none of the above

13._____

14. A. predesessor   B. predecesar
    C. predecesser   D. none of the above

14._____

15. A. sanctioned   B. sancktioned
    C. sanctionned   D. none of the above

15._____

READING

16. "The secretarial profession is a very old one and has increased in importance with the passage of time. In modern times, the vast expansion of business and industry has greatly increased the need and opportunities for secretaries, and for the first time in history their number has become large."
    The above quotation BEST supports the statement that the secretarial profession
    A. is older than business and industry
    B. did not exist in ancient times
    C. has greatly increased in size
    D. demands higher training than it did formerly

16._____

17. "Civilization started to move ahead more rapidly when man freed himself of the shackles that restricted his search for the truth."
    The above quotation BEST supports the statement that the progress of civilization
    A. came as a result of man's dislike for obstacles
    B. did not begin until restrictions on learning were removed
    C. has been aided by man's efforts to find
    D. the truth is based on continually increasing efforts

17._____

18. *Vigilant* means MOST NEARLY
    A. sensible   B. watchful   C. suspicious   D. restless

18._____

19. *Incidental* means MOST NEARLY
    A. independent   B. needless   C. infrequent   D. casual

19._____

20. *Conciliatory* means MOST NEARLY
    A. pacific   B. contentious   C. obligatory   D. offensive

21. *Altercation* means MOST NEARLY
    A. defeat
    B. concurrence
    C. controversy
    D. vexation

22. *Irresolute* means MOST NEARLY
    A. wavering
    B. insubordinate
    C. impudent
    D. unobservant

23. DARKNESS is related to SUNLIGHT as STILLNESS is related to
    A. quiet   B. moonlight   C. sound   D. dark

24. DESIGNED is related to INTENTION as ACCIDENTAL is related to
    A. purpose   B. caution   C. damage   D. chance

25. ERROR is related to PRACTICE as SOUND is related to
    A. deafness   B. noise   C. muffler   D. horn

26. RESEARCH is related to FINDINGS as TRAINING is related to
    A. skill
    B. tests
    C. supervision
    D. teaching

27. A. If properly addressed, the letter will reach my mother and I.
    B. The letter had been addressed to myself and my mother.
    C. I believe the letter was addressed to either my mother or I.
    D. My mother's name, as well as mine, was on the letter.

28. A. The supervisor reprimanded the typist, whom she believed had made careless errors.
    B. The typist would have corrected the errors had she of known that the supervisor would see the report.
    C. The errors in the typed report were so numerous that they could hardly be overlooked.
    D. Many errors were found in the report which she typed and could not disregard them.

29. A. miniature
    B. minneature
    C. mineature
    D. none of the above

30. A. extemporaneous
    B. extempuraneus
    C. extemporaneous
    D. none of the above

31. A. problemmatical
    B. problematical
    C. problematicle
    D. none of the above

32. A. descendant
    B. decendant
    C. desendant
    D. none of the above

33. "The likelihood of America's exhausting her natural resources seems to be growing less. All kinds of waste are being reworked and new uses are constantly being found for almost everything. We are getting more use out of our goods and are making many new byproducts out of what was formerly thrown away."
The above quotation BEST supports the statement that we seem to be in less danger of exhausting our resources because
    A. economy is found to lie in the use of substitutes
    B. more service is obtained from a given amount of material
    C. we are allowing time for nature to restore them
    D. supply and demand are better controlled

34. "Memos should be clear, concise, and brief. Omit all unnecessary words. The parts of speech most often used in memos are nouns, verbs, adjectives, and adverbs. If possible, do without pronouns, prepositions, articles, and copulative verbs. Use simple sentences, rather than complex or compound ones.
The above quotation BEST supports the statement that in writing memos one should always use
    A. common and simple words
    B. only nouns, verbs, adjectives, and adverbs
    C. incomplete sentences
    D. only the word essential to the meaning

35. To *counteract* means MOST NEARLY to
    A. undermine   B. censure   C. preserve   D. neutralize

36. *Deferred* means MOST NEARLY
    A. reversed   B. delayed
    C. considered   D. forbidden

37. *Feasible* means MOST NEARLY
    A. capable   B. justifiable   C. practicable   D. beneficial

38. To *encounter* means MOST NEARLY to
    A. meet   B. recall   C. overcome   D. retreat

39. *Innate* means MOST NEARLY
    A. eternal   B. well-developed
    C. native   D. prospective

40. STUDENT is to TEACHER as DISCIPLE is related to
    A. follower   B. master   C. principal   D. pupil

41. LECTURE is related to AUDITORIUM as EXPERIMENT is related to
    A. scientist   B. chemistry   C. laboratory   D. discovery

42. BODY is related to FOOD as ENGINE is related to
    A. wheels   B. fuel   C. motion   D. smoke

43. SCHOOL is related to EDUCATION as THEATER is related to
    A. management   B. stage
    C. recreation   D. preparation

44. A. Most all these statements have been supported by persons who are reliable and can be depended upon.
    B. The persons which have guaranteed these statements are reliable.
    C. Reliable persons guarantee the facts with regards to the truth of these statements.
    D. These statements can be depended on, for their truth has been guaranteed by reliable persons.

45. A. The success of the book pleased both his publisher and he.
    B. Both his publisher and he was pleased with the success of the book.
    C. Neither he or his publisher was disappointed with the success of the book.
    D. His publisher was as pleased as he with the success of the book.

46. A. extercate   B. extracate
    C. extricate   D. none of the above

47. A. hereditory   B. hereditary
    C. hereditairy   D. none of the above

48. A. auspiceous   B. auspiseous
    C. auspicious   D. none of the above

49. A. sequance   B. sequence
    C. sequense   D. none of the above

50. "The prevention of accidents makes it necessary not only that safety devices be used to guard exposed machinery but also that mechanics be instructed in safety rules which they must follow for their own protection, and that the lighting in the plant be adequate."
    The above quotation BEST supports the statement that industrial accidents
    A. may be due to ignorance
    B. are always avoidable
    C. usually result from inadequate machinery
    D. cannot be entirely overcome

51. "The English language is peculiarly rich in synonyms, and there is scarcely a language spoken among men that has not some representative in English speech. The spirit of the Anglo-Saxon race has subjugate these various elements to one idiom, making not a patchwork, but a composite language."
    The above quotation BEST supports the statement that the English language
    A. has few idiomatic expressions
    B. is difficult to translate
    C. is used universally
    D. has absorbed words from other languages

52. To *acquiesce* means MOST NEARLY to
    A. assent B. acquire C. complete D. participate

53. *Unanimity* means MOST NEARLY
    A. emphasis
    B. namelessness
    C. harmony
    D. impartiality

54. *Precedent* means MOST NEARLY
    A. example B. theory C. law D. conformity

55. *Versatile* means MOST NEARLY
    A. broad-minded
    B. well-known
    C. up-to-date
    D. many-sided

56. *Authentic* means MOST NEARLY
    A. detailed B. reliable C. valuable D. practical

57. BIOGRAPHy is related to FACT as NOVEL is related to
    A. fiction B. literature C. narration D. book

58. COPY is related to CARBON PAPER as MOTION PICTURE is related to
    A. theater B. film C. duplicate D. television

59. EFFICIENCY is related to REWARD as CARELESSNESS is related to
    A. improvement
    B. disobedience
    C. reprimand
    D. repetition

60. ABUNDANT is related to CHEAP as SCARCE is related to
    A. ample
    B. costly
    C. inexpensive
    D. unobtainable

61. A. Brown's & Company employees have recently received increases in salary.
    B. Brown & Company recently increased the salaries of all its employees.
    C. Recently, Brown & Company has increased their employees' salaries.
    D. Brown & Company have recently increased the salaries of all its employees.

62. A. In reviewing the typists' work reports, the job analyst found records of unusual typing speeds.
    B. It says in the job analyst's report that some employees type with great speed.
    C. The job analyst found that, in reviewing the typists' work reports, that some unusual typing speeds had been made.
    D. In the reports of typists' speeds, the job analyst found some records that are kind of unusual.

63. A. obliterate
    B. oblitterat
    C. obliterate
    D. none of the above

64. A. diagnosis B. diagnosis
    C. diagnosis D. none of the above
    64.____

65. A. contenance B. countenance
    C. knowledge D. none of the above
    65.____

66. A. conceivably B. concieveably
    C. conceiveably D. none of the above
    66.____

67. "Through advertising, manufacturers exercise a high degree of control over consumers' desires. However, the manufacturer assumes enormous risks in attempting to predict what consumers will want and in producing goods in quantity and distributing them in advance of final selection by the consumers."
    The above quotation BEST supports the statement that manufacturers
    A. can eliminate the risk of overproduction by advertising
    B. distribute goods directly to the consumers
    C. must depend upon the final consumers for the success of their undertakings
    D. can predict with great accuracy the success of any product they put on the market
    67.____

68. "In the relations of man to nature, the procuring of food and shelter is fundamental. With the migration of man to various climates, ever new adjustments to the food supply and to the climate became necessary."
    The above quotation BEST supports the statement that the means by which man supplies his material needs are
    A. accidental   B. varied   C. limited   D. inadequate
    68.____

69. *Strident* means MOST NEARLY
    A. swaggering   B. domineering
    C. angry   D. harsh
    69.____

70. To *confine* means MOST NEARLY to
    A. hide   B. restrict   C. eliminate   D. punish
    70.____

71. To *accentuate* means MOST NEARLY to
    A. modify   B. hasten   C. sustain   D. intensify
    71.____

72. *Banal* means MOST NEARLY
    A. commonplace   B. forceful
    C. tranquil   D. indifferent
    72.____

73. *Incorrigible* means MOST NEARLY
    A. intolerable   B. retarded
    C. irreformable   D. brazen
    73.____

74. POLICEMAN is related to ORDER as DOCTOR is related to
    A. physician   B. hospital   C. sickness   D. health
    74.____

75. ARTIST is related to EASEL as WEAVER is related to
    A. loom   B. cloth   C. threads   D. spinner

76. CROWD is related to PERSONS as FLEET is related to
    A. expedition   B. officers   C. navy   D. ships

77. CALENDAR is related to DATE as MAP is related to
    A. geography   B. trip   C. mileage   D. vacation

78. A. Since the report lacked the needed information, it was of no use to him.
    B. This report was useless to him because there were no needed information in it.
    C. Since the report did not contain the needed information, it was not real useful to him.
    D. Being that the report lacked the needed information, he could not use it.

79. A. The company had hardly declared the dividend till the notices were prepared for mailing.
    B. They had no sooner declared the dividend when they sent the notices to the stockholders.
    C. No sooner had the dividend been declared than the notices were prepared for mailing.
    D. Scarcely had the dividend been declared than the notices were sent out.

80. A. compitition   B. competition
    C. competetion   D. none of the above

81. A. occassion   B. ocassion
    C. occasion   D. none of the above

82. A. knowlege   B. knowledge
    C. knolledge D. none of the above

83. A. deliborate   B. deliberate
    C. deliberate   D. none of the above

84. "What constitutes skill in any line of work is not always easy to determine; economy of time must be carefully distinguished from economy of energy, as the quickest method may require the greatest expenditure of muscular effort, and may not be essential or at all desirable."
    The above quotation BEST supports the statement that
    A. the most efficiently executed task is not always the one done in the shortest time
    B. energy and time cannot both be conserved in performing a single task
    C. a task is well done when it is performed in the shortest time
    D. skill in performing a task should not be acquired at the expense of time

85. "It is difficult to distinguish between bookkeeping and accounting. In attempts to do so, bookkeeping is called the art, and accounting the science, of recording business transactions. Bookkeeping gives the history of the business in a systematic manner; and accounting classifies, analyzes, and interpret the facts thus recorded."
    The above quotation BEST supports the statement that
    A. accounting is less systematic than bookkeeping
    B. accounting and bookkeeping are closely related
    C. bookkeeping and accounting cannot be distinguished from one another
    D. bookkeeping has been superseded by accounting

85._____

KEY (CORRECT ANSWERS)

1.	C	16.	C	31.	B	46.	C	61.	B	76.	D
2.	B	17.	C	32.	A	47.	B	62.	A	77.	C
3.	C	18.	B	33.	B	48.	C	63.	A	78.	A
4.	D	19.	D	34.	D	49.	B	64.	C	79.	C
5.	B	20.	A	35.	D	50.	A	65.	B	80.	B
6.	A	21.	C	36.	B	51.	D	66.	A	81.	B
7.	B	22.	A	37.	C	52.	A	67.	C	82.	C
8.	C	23.	C	38.	A	53.	C	68.	B	83.	B
9.	D	24.	D	39.	C	54.	A	69.	D	84.	A
10.	A	25.	C	40.	B	55.	D	70.	B	85.	B
11.	D	26.	A	41.	C	56.	B	71.	D		
12.	A	27.	D	42.	B	57.	A	72.	A		
13.	C	28.	C	43.	C	58.	B	73.	C		
14.	D	29.	D	44.	D	59.	C	74.	D		
15.	A	30.	A	45.	D	60.	B	75.	A		

TEST 2

DIRECTIONS: Each question or incomplete statement is followed by several suggested answers or completions. Select the one that BEST answers the question or completes the statement. *PRINT THE LETTER OF THE CORRECT ANSWER IN THE SPACE AT THE RIGHT.*

1. *Option* means MOST NEARLY
   A. use
   B. choice
   C. value
   D. blame
   E. mistake

2. *Irresolute* means MOST NEARLY
   A. wavering
   B. insubordinate
   C. impudent
   D. determined
   E. unobservant

3. *Flexible* means MOST NEARLY
   A. breakable
   B. inflammable
   C. pliable
   D. weak
   E. impervious

4. To *counteract* means MOST NEARLY to
   A. undermine
   B. censure
   C. preserve
   D. sustain
   E. neutralize

5. To *verify* means MOST NEARLY to
   A. justify
   B. explain
   C. confirm
   D. guarantee
   E. examine

6. *Indolent* means MOST NEARLY
   A. moderate
   B. relentless
   C. selfish
   D. lazy
   E. hopeless

7. To say that an action is *deferred* means MOST NEARLY that it is
   A. delayed
   B. reversed
   C. considered
   D. forbidden
   E. followed

8. To *encounter* means MOST NEARLY to
   A. meet
   B. recall
   C. overcome
   D. weaken
   E. retreat

9. *Feasible* means MOST NEARLY
   A. capable
   B. practicable
   C. justifiable
   D. beneficial
   E. reliable

10. *Respiration* means MOST NEARLY
    A. dehydration
    B. breathing
    C. pulsation
    D. sweating
    E. recovery

1.____
2.____
3.____
4.____
5.____
6.____
7.____
8.____
9.____
10.____

11. *Vigilant* means MOST NEARLY
    A. sensible   B. ambitious   C. watchful
    D. suspicious   E. restless

12. To say that an action is taken *before the proper time* means MOST NEARLY that it is taken
    A. prematurely   B. furtively   C. temporarily
    D. punctually   E. presently

13. *Innate* means MOST NEARLY
    A. eternal   B. learned   C. native
    D. prospective   E. well-developed

14. *Precedent* means MOST NEARLY
    A. duplicate   B. theory   C. law
    D. conformity   E. example

15. To say that the flow of work into an office is *incessant* means MOST NEARLY that it is
    A. more than can be handled   B. uninterrupted
    C. scanty   D. decreasing in volume
    E. orderly

16. *Unanimity* means MOST NEARLY
    A. emphasis   B. namelessness   C. disagreement
    D. harmony   E. impartiality

17. *Incidental* means MOST NEARLY
    A. independent   B. needless   C. infrequent
    D. necessary   E. casual

18. *Versatile* means MOST NEARLY
    A. broad-minded   B. well-known   C. old-fashioned
    D. many-sided   E. up-to-date

19. *Conciliatory* means MOST NEARLY
    A. pacific   B. contentious   C. disorderly
    D. obligatory   E. offensive

20. *Altercation* means MOST NEARLY
    A. defeat   B. concurrence   C. controversy
    D. consensus   E. vexation

21. "The secretarial profession is a very old one and has increased in importance with the passage of time. In modern times, the vast expansion of business and industry has greatly increased the need and opportunities for secretaries, and for the first time in history their number as become large."

The above quotation BEST supports the statement that the secretarial profession
- A. is older than business and industry
- B. did not exist in ancient times
- C. has greatly increased in size
- D. demands higher training than it did formerly
- E. has always had many members

22. "The modern system of production unites various kinds of workers into a well-organized body in which each has a definite place."
The above quotation BEST supports the statement that the modern system of production
- A. increases production
- B. trains workers
- C. simplifies tasks
- D. combines and places workers
- E. combines the various plants

23. "The prevention of accidents makes it necessary not only that safety devices be used to guard exposed machinery but also that mechanics be instructed in safety rules which they must follow for their own protection, and that the lighting in the plant be adequate.
The above quotation BEST supports the statement that industrial accidents
- A. may be due to ignorance
- B. are always avoidable
- C. usually result from inadequate machinery
- D. cannot be entirely overcome
- E. result in damage to machinery

24. "It is wise to choose a duplicating machine that will do the work required with the greatest efficiency and at the least cost. Users with a large volume of business need speedy machines that cost little to operate and are well made."
The above quotation BEST supports the statement that
- A. most users of duplicating machines prefer low operating cost to efficiency
- B. a well-built machine will outlast a cheap one
- C. a duplicating machine is not efficient unless it is sturdy
- D. a duplicating machine should be both efficient and economical
- E. in duplicating machines speed is more usual than low operating cost

25. "The likelihood of America's exhausting her natural resources seems to be growing less. All kinds of waste are being reworked and new uses are constantly being found for almost everything. We are getting more use out of our goods and are making many new byproducts out of what was formerly thrown away."
The above quotation BEST supports the statement that we seem to be in less danger of exhausting our resources because
- A. economy is found to lie in the use of substitutes
- B. more service is obtained from a given amount of material
- C. more raw materials are being produced
- D. supply and demand are better controlled
- E. we are allowing time for nature to restore them

26. "Probably few people realize, as they drive on a concrete road, that steel is used to keep the surface flat and even, in spite of the weight of busses and trucks. Steel bars, deeply imbedded in the concrete, provide sinews to take the stresses so that they cannot crack the slab or make it wavy."
The above quotation BEST supports the statement that a concrete road
    A. is expensive to build
    B. usually cracks under heavy weights
    C. looks like any other road
    D. is used exclusively for heavy traffic
    E. is reinforced with other material

27. "Through advertising, manufacturers exercise a high degree of control over consumers' desires. However, the manufacturer assumes enormous risks in attempting to predict what consumers will want and in producing goods in quantity and distributing them in advance of final selection by the consumers."
The above quotation BEST supports the statement that manufacturers
    A. can eliminate the risk of overproduction by advertising
    B. completely control buyers' needs and desires
    C. must depend upon the final consumers for the success of their undertakings
    D. distribute goods directly to the consumers
    E. can predict with great accuracy the success of any product they put on the market

28. "Success in shorthand, like success in any other study, depends upon the interest the student takes in it. In writing shorthand, it is not sufficient to know how to write a word correctly; one must also be able to write it quickly."
The above quotation BEST supports the statement that
    A. one must be able to read shorthand as well as to write it
    B. shorthand requires much study
    C. if a student can write correctly, he can also write quickly
    D. proficiency in shorthand requires both speed and accuracy
    E. interest in shorthand makes study unnecessary

29. "The countries in the Western Hemisphere were settled by people who were ready each day for new adventure. The peoples of North and South America have retained, in addition to expectant and forward-looking attitudes, the ability and the willingness that they have often shown in the past to adapt themselves to new conditions.
The above quotation BEST supports the statement that the peoples in the Western Hemisphere
    A. no longer have fresh adventures daily
    B. are capable of making changes as new situations arise
    C. are no more forward-looking than the peoples of other regions
    D. tend to resist regulations
    E. differ considerably among themselves

30. "Civilization started to move ahead more rapidly when man freed himself of the shackles that restricted his search for the truth."
The above quotation BEST supports the statement that the progress of civilization
   A. came as a result of man's dislike for obstacles
   B. did not begin until restrictions on learning were removed
   C. has been aided by man's efforts to find the truth
   D. is based on continually increasing efforts
   E. continues at a constantly increasing rate

30._____

31. "It is difficult to distinguish between bookkeeping and accounting. In attempts to do so, bookkeeping is called the art, and accounting the science, of recording business transactions. Bookkeeping gives the history of the business in a systematic manner, and accounting classifies, analyzes, and interprets the facts thus recorded."
The above quotation BEST supports the statement that
   A. accounting is less systematic than bookkeeping
   B. accounting and bookkeeping are closely related
   C. bookkeeping and accounting cannot be distinguish from one another
   D. bookkeeping has been superseded by accounting
   E. the facts recorded by bookkeeping may be interpreted in many ways

31._____

32. "Some specialists are willing to give their services to the Government entirely free of charge; some feel that a nominal salary, such as will cover traveling expenses, is sufficient for a position that is recognized as being somewhat honorary in nature; many other specialists value their time so highly that they will not devote any of it to public service that does not repay them at a rate commensurate with the fees that they can obtain from a good private clientele."
The above quotation BEST supports the statement that the use of specialists by the Government
   A. is rare because of the high cost of securing such persons
   B. may be influenced by the willingness of specialists to serve
   C. enables them to secure higher salaries in private fields
   D. has become increasingly common during the past few years
   E. always conflicts with private demands for their services

32._____

33. "The leader of an industrial enterprise has two principal functions. He must manufacture and distribute a product at a profit, and he must keep individuals and groups of individuals working effectively together."
The above quotation BEST supports the statement that an industrial leader should be able to
   A. increase the distribution of his plant's product
   B. introduce large-scale production methods
   C. coordinate the activities of his employees
   D. profit by the experience of other leaders
   E. expand the business rapidly

33._____

34. "The coloration of textile fabrics composed of cotton and wool generally requires two processes, as the process used in dyeing wool is seldom capable of fixing the color upon cotton. The usual method is to immerse the fabric in the requisite baths to dye the wool and then to treat the partially dyed material in the manner found suitable for cotton."
The above quotation BEST supports the statement that the dyeing of textile fabrics composed of cotton and wool
    A. is less complicated than the dyeing of wool alone
    B. is more successful when the material contains more cotton than wool
    C. is not satisfactory when solid colors are desired
    D. is restricted to two colors for any one fabric
    E. is usually based upon the methods required for dyeing the different materials

35. "The fact must not be overlooked that only about one-half of the international trade of the world crosses the oceans. The other half is merely exchanges of merchandise between countries lying alongside each other or at least within the same continent."
The above quotation BEST supports the statement that
    A. the most important part of any country's trade is transoceanic
    B. domestic trade is insignificant when compared with foreign trade
    C. the exchange of goods between neighboring countries is not considered international trade
    D. foreign commerce is not necessarily carried on by water
    E. about one-half of the trade of the world is international

36. "In the relations of man to nature, the procuring of food and shelter is fundamental. With the migration of man to various climate, ever new adjustments to the food supply and to the climate became necessary."
The above quotation BEST supports the statement that the means by which man supplies his material needs are
    A. accidental   B. varied   C. limited
    D. uniform   E. inadequate

37. "Every language has its peculiar word associations that have no basis in logic and cannot therefore be reasoned about. These idiomatic expressions are ordinarily acquired only by much reading and conversation although questions about such matters may sometimes be answered by the dictionary. Dictionaries large enough to include quotations from standard authors are especially serviceable in determining questions of idiom."
The above quotation BEST supports the statement that idiomatic expressions
    A. give rise to meaningless arguments because they have no logical basis
    B. are widely used by recognized authors
    C. are explained in most dictionaries
    D. are more common in some languages than in others
    E. are best learned by observation of the language as actually used

38. "Individual differences in mental traits assume importance in fitting workers to jobs because such personal characteristics are persistent and are relatively little influenced by training and experience."
The above quotation BEST supports the statement that training and experience
   A. are limited in their effectiveness in fitting workers to jobs
   B. do not increase a worker's fitness for a job
   C. have no effect upon a person's mental traits
   D. have relatively little effect upon the individual's chances for success
   E. should be based on the mental traits of an individual

38.____

39. "The telegraph networks of the country now constitute wonderfully operated institutions, affording for ordinary use of modern, business an important means of communication. The transmission of message by electricity has reached the goal for which the postal service has long been striving, namely, the elimination of distance as an effective barrier of communication."
The above quotation BEST supports the statement that
   A. a new standard of communication has been attained
   B. in the telegraph service, messages seldom go astray
   C. it is the distance between the parties which creates the need for communication
   D. modern business relies more upon the telegraph than upon the mails
   E. the telegraph is a form of postal service

39.____

40. "The competition of buyers tends to keep prices up, the competition of sellers to send them down. Normally, the pressure of competition among sellers is stronger than that amount by buyers since the seller has his article to sell and must get rid of it, whereas the buyer is not committed to anything."
The above quotation BEST supports the statement that low prices are caused by
   A. buyer competition
   B. competition of buyers with sellers fluctuations in demand
   C. greater competition among sellers than among buyers
   D. more sellers than buyers

40.____

Questions 41-60.

DIRECTIONS: In answering Questions 41 through 60, find the CORRECT spelling of the word. Sometimes there is no correct spelling; if none of the suggested spellings is correct, indicate the letter D in the space at the right.

41. A. compitition   B. competition   41.____
    C. competetion   D. none of the above

42. A. diagnoesis   B. diagnossis   42.____
    C. diagnosis   D. none of the above

43. A. contenance   B. countenance   43.____
    C. countinance   D. none of the above

8 (#2)

44. A. deliborate   B. deliberate   44._____
    C. deliberate   D. none of the above

45. A. knowlege   B. knolledge   45._____
    C. knowledge   D. none of the above

46. A. occassion   B. occasion   46._____
    C. ocassion   D. none of the above

47. A. sanctioned   B. sancktioned   47._____
    C. sanctionned   D. none of the above

48. A. predesessor   B. predecesar   48._____
    C. predecessor   D. none of the above

49. A. problemmatical B. problematical   49._____
    C. problematicle D. none of the above

50. A. descendant   B. decendant   50._____
    C. desendant   D. none of the above

51. A. collapsible   B. collapseable   51._____
    C. collapseble   D. none of the above

52. A. sequance   B. sequence   52._____
    C. sequense   D. none of the above

53. A. obliterate   B. obbliterate   53._____
    C. obliterate   D. none of the above

54. A. ambigeuous   B. ambiguous   54._____
    C. ambiguous   D. none of the above

55. A. minieture   B. minneature   55._____
    C. miniature   D. none of the above

56. A. extemporaneous B. extempuraneus   56._____
    C. extemperaneous D. none of the above

57. A. hereditory   B. hereditary   57._____
    C. hereditairy   D. none of the above

58. A. conceivably   B. concieveably   58._____
    C. conceiveably   D. none of the above

59. A. extercate   B. extracate   59._____
    C. extricate   D. none of the above

60. A. auspiceous B. auspiseous 60._____
    C. auspicious D. none of the above

Questions 61-80.

DIRECTIONS: In answering Questions 61 through 80, select the sentence that is preferable with respect to grammar and usage such as would be suitable in a formal letter or report.

61. A. The receptionist must answer courteously the questions of all them callers. 61._____
    B. The questions of all callers had ought to be answered courteously.
    C. The receptionist must answer courteously the questions what are asked by the callers.
    D. There would have been no trouble if the receptionist had have always answered courteously.
    E. The receptionist should answer courteously the questions of all callers.

62. A. I had to learn a great number of rules, causing me to dislike the course. 62._____
    B. I disliked that study because it required the learning of numerous rules.
    C. I disliked that course very much, caused by the numerous rules I had to memorize.
    D. The cause of my dislike was on account of the numerous rules I had to learn in that course.
    E. The reason I disliked this study was because there were numerous rules that had to be learned.

63. A. If properly addressed, the letter will reach my mother and I. 63._____
    B. The letter had been addressed to myself and mother.
    C. I believe the letter was addressed to either my mother or I.
    D. My mother's name, as well as mine, was on the letter.
    E. If properly addressed, the letter it will reach either my mother or me.

64. A. A knowledge of commercial subjects and a mastery of English are essential if one wishes to be a good secretary. 64._____
    B. Two things necessary to a good secretary are the she should speak good English and too know commercial subjects.
    C. One cannot be a good secretary without she knows commercial subjects and English grammar.
    D. Having had god training in commercial subjects, the rules of English grammar should also be followed.
    E. A secretary seldom or ever succeeds without training in English as well as in commercial subjects.

10 (#2)

65.
- A. He suspicions that the service is not so satisfactory as it should be.
- B. He believes that we should try and find whether the service is satisfactory.
- C. He raises the objection that the way which the service is given is not satisfactory.
- D. He believes that the quality of our services are poor.
- E. He believes that the service that we are giving is unsatisfactory.

65.____

66.
- A. Most all these statements have been supported by persons who are reliable and can be depended upon.
- B. The persons which have guaranteed these statements are reliable.
- C. Reliable persons guarantee the facts with regard to the truth of these statements.
- D. These statements can be depended on, for their truth has been guaranteed by reliable persons.
- E. Persons as reliable as what these are can be depended upon to make accurate statements.

66.____

67.
- A. Brown's & Company's employees have all been given increases in salary.
- B. Brown & Company recently increased the salaries of all its employees.
- C. Recently Brown & Company has increased their employees' salaries.
- D. Brown's & Company employees have recently received increases in salary.
- E. Brown & Company have recently increased the salaries of all its employees.

67.____

68.
- A. The personnel office has charge of employment, dismissals, and employee's welfare.
- B. Employment, together with dismissals and employees' welfare, are handled by the personnel department.
- C. The personnel office takes charge of employment, dismissals, and etc.
- D. The personnel office hires and dismisses employees, and their welfare is also its responsibility.
- E. The personnel office is responsible for the employment, dismissal, and welfare of employees.

68.____

69.
- A. This kind of pen is some better than that kind.
- B. I prefer having these pens than any other.
- C. This kind of pen is the most satisfactory for my use.
- D. In comparison with that kind of pen, this kind is more preferable.
- E. If I were to select between them all, I should pick this pen.

69.____

70.
- A. He could not make use of the report, as it was lacking of the needed information.
- B. This report was useless to him because there were no needed information in it.
- C. Since the report lacked the needed information, it was of no use to him.
- D. Being that the report lacked the needed information, he could not use it.
- E. Since the report did not contain the needed information, it was not real useful to him.

70.____

71. A. The paper we use for this purpose must be light, glossy, and stand hard usage as well. 71.____
    B. Only a light and a glossy, but durable, paper must be used for this purpose.
    C. For this purpose, we want a paper that is light, glossy, but that will stand hard wear.
    D. For this purpose, paper that is light, glossy, and durable is essential.
    E. Light and glossy paper, as well as standing hard usage, is necessary for this purpose.

72. A. The company had hardly declared the dividend till the notices were prepared for mailing. 72.____
    B. They had no sooner declared the dividend when they sent the notices to the stockholders.
    C. No sooner had the dividend been declared than the notices were prepared for mailing.
    D. Scarcely had the dividend been declared than the notices were sent out.
    E. The dividend had not scarcely been declared when the notices were ready for mailing.

73. A. Of all the employees, he spends the most time at the office. 73.____
    B. He spends more time at the office than that of his employees.
    C. His working hours are longer or at least equal to those of the other employees.
    D. He devotes as much, if not more, time to his work than the rest of the employees.
    E. He works the longest of any other employee in the office.

74. A. In the reports of typists' speeds, the job analyst found some records that are kind of unusual. 74.____
    B. It says in the job analyst's report that some employees type with great speed.
    C. The job analyst found that, in reviewing the typists' work Reports, that some unusual typing speeds had been made.
    D. Work reports showing typing speeds include some typists who are unusual.
    E. In reviewing the typists' work reports, the job analyst found records of unusual typing speeds.

75. A. It is quite possible that we shall reemploy anyone whose training fits them to do the work. 75.____
    B. It is probable that we shall reemploy those who have been trained to do the work.
    C. Such of our personnel that have been trained to do the work will be again employed.
    D. We expect to reemploy the ones who have had training enough that they can do the work.
    E. Some of these people have been trained.

76. A. He as well as his publisher were pleased with the success of the book.
    B. The success of the book pleased both his publisher and he.
    C. Both his publisher and he was pleased with the success of the book.
    D. Neither he or his publisher was disappointed with the success of the book.
    E. His publisher was as pleased as he with the success of the book.

77. A. You have got to get rid of some of these people if you expect to have the quality of the work improve
    B. The quality of the work would improve if they would leave fewer people do it.
    C. I believe it would be desirable to have fewer persons during this work.
    D. If you had planned on employing fewer people than this to do the work, this situation would not have arose.
    E. Seeing how you have all those people on that work, it is not surprising that you have a great deal of confusion.

78. A. She made lots of errors in her typed report, and which caused her to be reprimanded.
    B. The supervisor reprimanded the typist, whom she believed had made careless errors.
    C. Many errors were found in the report which she typed and could not disregard them.
    D. The typist would have corrected the errors, had she of known that the supervisor would see the report.
    E. The errors in the typed report were so numerous that they could hardly be overlooked.

79. A. This kind of a worker achieves success through patience.
    B. Success does not often come to men of this type except they who are patient.
    C. Because they are patient, these sort of workers usually achieve success.
    D. This worker has more patience than any man in his office.
    E. This kind of worker achieves success through patience.

80. A. I think that they will promote whoever has the best record.
    B. The firm would have liked to have promoted all employees with good records.
    C. Such of them that have the best records have excellent prospects of promotion.
    D. I feel sure they will give the promotion to whomever has the best record.
    E. Whoever they find to have the best record will, I think, be promoted.

KEY (CORRECT ANSWERS)

1.	B	21.	C	41.	B	61.	E
2.	A	22.	D	42.	C	62.	B
3.	C	23.	A	43.	B	63.	D
4.	E	24.	D	44.	B	64.	A
5.	C	25.	B	45.	C	65.	E
6.	D	26.	E	46.	B	66.	D
7.	A	27.	C	47.	A	67.	B
8.	A	28.	D	48.	D	68.	E
9.	B	29.	B	49.	B	69.	C
10.	B	30.	C	50.	A	70.	C
11.	C	31.	B	51.	A	71.	D
12.	A	32.	B	52.	B	72.	C
13.	C	33.	C	53.	D	73.	A
14.	E	34.	E	54.	C	74.	E
15.	B	35.	D	55.	D	75.	B
16.	D	36.	B	56.	A	76.	E
17.	E	37.	E	57.	B	77.	C
18.	D	38.	A	58.	A	78.	E
19.	A	39.	A	59.	C	79.	E
20.	C	40.	D	60.	C	80.	A

EXAMINATION SECTION
TEST 1

DIRECTIONS: Each question or incomplete statement is followed by several suggested answers or completions. Select the one that BEST answers the question or completes the statement. *PRINT THE LETTER OF THE CORRECT ANSWER IN THE SPACE AT THE RIGHT.*

Questions 1-22.

DIRECTIONS: Read through each group of words. Indicate in the space at the right the letter of the misspelled word.

1. A. miniature   B. recession   1.____
   C. accommodate   D. supress

2. A. mortgage   B. illogical   2.____
   C. fasinate   D. pronounce

3. A. calendar   B. heros   3.____
   C. ecstasy   D. librarian

4. A. initiative   B. extraordinary   4.____
   C. villian   D. exaggerate

5. A. absence   B. sense   5.____
   C. dosn't   D. height

6. A. curiosity   B. ninety   6.____
   C. truely   D. grammar

7. A. amateur   B. definate   7.____
   C. meant   D. changeable

8. A. excellent   B. studioes   8.____
   C. achievement   D. weird

9. A. goverment   B. description   9.____
   C. sergeant   D. desirable

10. A. proceed   B. anxious   10.____
    C. neice   D. precede

11. A. environment   B. omitted   11.____
    C. apparant   D. misconstrue

12. A. comparative   B. hindrance   12.____
    C. benefited   D. unamimous

57

13. A. embarrass   B. recommend   13.____
    C. desciple   D. argument

14. A. sophomore B. suprintendent 14.____
    C. concievable D. disastrous

15. A. agressive B. questionnaire 15.____
    C. occurred   D. rhythm

16. A. peaceable B. conscientious 16.____
    C. redicule   D. deterrent

17. A. mischievous B. writing   17.____
    C. competition D. athletics

18. A. auxiliary B. synonymous   18.____
    C. maneuver   D. repitition

19. A. existence B. optomistic   19.____
    C. acquitted D. tragedy

20. A. hypocrisy B. parrallel   20.____
    C. exhilaration D. prevalent

21. A. convalesence B. infallible 21.____
    C. destitute D. grotesque

22. A. magnanimity B. asassination 22.____
    C. incorrigible D. pestilence

Questions 23-40.

DIRECTIONS: In Questions 23 through 40, one sentence fragment contains an error in punctuation or capitalization. Indicate the letter of the INCORRECT sentence fragment and place it in the space at the right.

23. A. Despite a year's work   23.____
    B. in a well-equipped laboratory
    C. my Uncle failed to complete his research
    D. now he will never graduate.

24. A. Gene, if you are going to sleep   24.____
    B. all afternoon I will enter
    C. that ladies' golf tournament
    D. sponsored by the Chamber of Commerce.

25. A. Seeing the cat slink toward the barn,
     B. the farmer's wife jumped off the
     C. ladder picked up a broom, and began
     D. shouting at the top of her voice.

26. A. Extending over southeast Idaho and
     B. northwest Wyoming, the Tetons
     C. are noted for their height; however the
     D. highest peak is actually under 14,000 feet.

27. A. "Sarah, can you recall the name
     B. of the English queen
     C. who supposedly said, 'We are not
     D. amused?"

28. A. My aunt's graduation present to me
     B. cost, I imagine more than she could
     C. actually afford. It's a
     D. Swiss watch with numerous features.

29. A. On the left are examples of buildings
     B. from the Classical Period; two temples
     C. one of which was dedicated to Zeus; the
     D. Agora, a marketplace; and a large arch.

30. A. Tired of sonic booms, the people who
     B. live near Springfield's Municipal Airport
     C. formed an anti noise organization
     D. with the amusing name of Sound Off.

31. A. "Joe, Mrs. Sweeney said, "your family
     B. arrives Sunday. Since you'll be in
     C. the Labor Day parade, we could ask Mr.
     D. Krohn, who has a big car, to meet them."

32. A. The plumber emerged from the basement and
     B. said, "Mr. Cohen I found the trouble in
     C. your water heater. Could you move those
     D. Schwinn bikes out of my way?"

33. A. The President walked slowly to the
     B. podium, bowed to Edward Everett Hale
     C. the other speaker, and began his formal address:
     D. "Fourscore and seven years ago...."

34. A. Mr. Fontana, I hope, will arrive before
     B. the beginning of the ceremonies; however,
     C. if his plane is delayed, I have a substitute
     D. speaker who can be here at a moments' notice.

25.____
26.____
27.____
28.____
29.____
30.____
31.____
32.____
33.____
34.____

35. A. Gladys wedding dress, a satin creation,
    B. lay crumpled on the floor; her veil,
    C. torn and streaked, lay nearby. "Jilted!"
    D. shrieked Gladys. She was clearly annoyed.

36. A. Although it is poor grammar, the word
    B. hopefully has become television's newest
    C. pet expression; I hope (to use the correct
    D. form) that it will soon pass from favor.

37. A.   Plaza Apartment Hotel
    B.   103 Tower road
    C.   Hampstead, Iowa 52025
    D.   March 13, 2021

38. A. Circulation Department
    B. British History Illustrated
    C. 3000 Walnut Street
    D. Boulder Colorado 80302

39. A. Dear Sirs:
    B.   Last spring I ordered a subscription to your
    C. magazine. I had read and enjoyed the May
    D. issue containing the article titled "kings."

40. A.   I have not however, received a
    B. single issue. Will you check this?
    C.   Sincerely,
    D. Maria Herrera

Questions 41-70.

DIRECTIONS: Questions 41 through 70 represent common grammatical concerns: subject-verb agreement, appropriate use of pronouns, and appropriate use of verbs. Read each sentence and indicate the letter of the grammatically CORRECT answer in the space at the right.

41. THE REIVERS, one of William Faulkner's last works, _____ made into a movie starring Steve McQueen.
    A. has been   B. have been   C. are being   D. were

42. He _____ on the ground, his eyes fastened on an ant slowly pushing a morsel of food toward the ant hill.
    A. layed   B. laid   C. had laid   D. lay

43. Nobody in the tri-cities _____ to admit that a flood could be disastrous.
    A. are willing   B. have been willing
    C. is willing   D. were willing

44. "_____," the senator asked, "have you convinced to run against the incumbent?"
    A. Who   B. Whom   C. Whomever   D. Womsoever

45. Of all the psychology courses that I took, Statistics 101 _____ the most demanding.
    A. was   B. are   C. is   D. were

46. Neither the conductor nor the orchestra members _____ the music to be applauded so enthusiastically.
    A. were expecting
    B. was expecting
    C. is expected
    D. has been expecting

47. The requirements for admission to the Lettermen's Club _____ posted outside the athletic director's office for months.
    A. was   B. was being   C. has been   D. have been

48. Please give me a list of the people _____ to compete in the kayak race.
    A. whom you think have planned
    B. who you think has planned
    C. who you think is planning
    D. who you think are planning

49. I saw Eloise and Abelard earlier today; _____ were riding around in a fancy 1956 MG.
    A. she and him   B. her and him   C. she and he   D. her and he

50. If you _____ the trunk in the attic, I'll unpack it later today.
    A. can sit
    B. are able to sit
    C. can set
    D. have sat

51. _____ all of the flour been used, or may I borrow three cups?
    A. Have   B. Has   C. Is   D. Could

52. In exasperation, the cycle shop's owner suggested that _____ there too long.
    A. us boys were
    B. we boys were
    C. us boys had been
    D. we boys had been

53. Idleness as well as money _____ the root of all evil.
    A. have been
    B. were to have been
    C. is
    D. are

54. Only the string players from the quartet—Gregory, Isaac, _____—remained after the concert to answer questions.
    A. him, and I
    B. he, and I
    C. him, and me
    D. he, and me

55. Of all the antiques that _____ for sale, Gertrude chose to buy a stupid glass thimble.
    A. was
    B. is
    C. would have
    D. were

56. The detective snapped, "Don't confuse me with theories about _____ you believe committed the crime!"
    A. who   B. whom   C. whomever   D. which

57. _____ when we first called, we might have avoided our present predicament.
    A. The plumber's coming
    B. If the plumber would have come
    C. If the plumber had come
    D. If the plumber was to have come

58. We thought the sun _____ in the north until we discovered that our compass was defective.
    A. had rose
    B. had risen
    C. had rised
    D. had raised

59. Each play of Shakespeare's _____ more than _____ share of memorable characters.
    A. contain its
    B. contains; its
    C. contains; it's
    D. contain; their

60. Our English teacher suggested to _____ seniors that either Tolstoy or Dickens _____ the outstanding novelist of the nineteenth century.
    A. we; was considered
    B. we; were considered
    C. us; was considered
    D. us; were considered

61. Sherlock Holmes, together with his great friend and companion Dr. Watson, _____ to aid the woman _____ had stumbled into the room.
    A. has agreed; who
    B. have agreed; whom
    C. has agreed; whom
    D. have agreed; who

62. Several of the deer _____ when they spotted my backpack _____ open in the meadow.
    A. was frightened; laying
    B. were frightened; lying
    C. were frightened; laying
    D. was frightened; lying

63. After the Scholarship Committee announces _____ selection, hysterics often _____.
    A. it's; occur
    B. its; occur
    C. their; occur
    D. their; occurs

64. I _____ the key on the table last night so you and _____ could find it.
    A. layed; her
    B. lay; she
    C. laid; she
    D. laid; her

65. Some of the antelope _____ wandered away from the meadow where the rancher _____ the block of salt.
    A. has; sat
    B. has; set
    C. have; had set
    D. has; sets

66. Macaroni and cheese _____ best to us (that is, to Andy and _____) when Mother adds extra cheddar cheese.
    A. tastes; I
    B. tastes; me
    C. taste; me
    D. taste; I

67. Frank said, "It must have been _____ called the phone company."
    A. she who
    B. she whom
    C. her who
    D. her whom

68. The herd _____ moving restlessly at every bolt of lightning; it was either Ted or _____ who saw the beginning of the stampede.
    A. was; me
    B. were; I
    C. was; I
    D. have been; me

69. The foreman _____ his lateness by saying that his alarm clock _____ until six minutes before eight.
    A. explains; had not rang
    B. explained; has not rung
    C. has explained; rung
    D. explained; hadn't rung

70. Of all the coaches, Ms. Cox is the only one who _____ that Sherry dives more gracefully than _____.
    A. is always saying; I
    B. is always saying; me
    C. are always saying; I
    D. were always saying; me

Questions 71-90.

DIRECTIONS: Choose the word in Questions 71 through 90 that is MOST opposite in meaning to the italicized word.

71. *fact*
    A. statistic
    B. statement
    C. incredible
    D. conjecture

72. *stiff*
    A. fastidious
    B. babble
    C. supple
    D. apprehensive

73. *blunt*
    A. concise   B. tactful   C. artistic   D. humble

74. *foreign*
    A. pertinent   B. comely   C. strange   D. scrupulous

75. *anger*
    A. infer   B. pacify   C. taint   D. revile

76. *frank*
    A. earnest   B. reticent   C. post   D. expensive

77. *secure*
    A. precarious   B. acquire   C. moderate   D. frenzied

78. *petty*
    A. harmonious
    C. forthright
    B. careful
    D. momentous

79. *concede*
    A. dispute
    C. subvert
    B. reciprocate
    D. propagate

80. *benefit*
    A. liquidation
    C. detriment
    B. bazaar
    D. profit

81. *capricious*
    A. preposterous
    C. diabolical
    B. constant
    D. careless

82. *boisterous*
    A. devious   B. valiant   C. girlish   D. taciturn

83. *harmony*
    A. congruence   B. discord   C. chagrin   D. melody

84. *laudable*
    A. auspicious
    C. acclaimed
    B. despicable
    D. doubtful

85. *adherent*
    A. partisan   B. stoic   C. renegade   D. recluse

86. *exuberant*
    A. frail   B. corpulent   C. austere   D. bigot

87. *spurn*
    A. accede   B. flail   C. efface   D. annihilate

88. *spontaneous*
    A. hapless
    C. intentional
    B. corrosive
    D. willful

89. *disparage*
    A. abolish   B. exude   C. incriminate   D. extol

90. *timorous*
    A. succinct   B. chaste   C. audacious   D. insouciant

KEY (CORRECT ANSWERS)

1.	D	21.	A	41.	A	61.	A	81.	B
2.	C	22.	B	42.	D	62.		82.	D
3.	B	23.	C	43.	C	63.	B	83.	B
4.	C	24.	B	44.	B	64.	C	84.	B
5.	C	25.	C	45.	A	65.	C	85.	C
6.	C	26.	C	46.	A	66.	B	86.	C
7.	B	27.	D	47.	D	67.	A	87.	A
8.	B	28.	B	48.	A	68.	C	88.	C
9.	A	29.	B	49.	C	69.	D	89.	D
10.	C	30.	C	50.	C	70.	A	90.	C
11.	C	31.	A	51.	B	71.	D		
12.	D	32.	B	52.	D	72.	C		
13.	C	33.	B	53.	C	73.	B		
14.	C	34.	D	54.	B	74.	A		
15.	A	35.	A	55.	D	75.	B		
16.	C	36.	B	56.	B	76.	B		
17.	A	37.	B	57.	C	77.	A		
18.	D	38.	D	58.	B	78.	D		
19.	B	39.	D	59.	B	79.	A		
20.	B	40.	A	60.	C	80.	C		

EXAMINATION SECTION
TEST 1

DIRECTIONS: Each question or incomplete statement is followed by several suggested answers or completions. Select the one that BEST answers the question or completes the statement. *PRINT THE LETTER OF THE CORRECT ANSWER IN THE SPACE AT THE RIGHT.*

Questions 1-25.

DIRECTIONS: Select the word with the MOST appropriate meaning for the italicized word in each of Questions 1 through 25.

1. The directions were *explicit*.
   A. petulant   B. satiric   C. awkward
   D. unequivocal   E. foreign

2. The teacher explained *mutability*.
   A. change   B. harmony   C. annihilation
   D. ethics   E. candor

3. He was a *secular* man.
   A. holy   B. evil   C. worldly
   D. superior   E. small

4. They submitted a list of their *progeny*.
   A. experiments   B. books   C. holdings
   D. theories   E. offspring

5. She admired his *sententious* replies.
   A. simple   B. pithy   C. coherent
   D. lucid   E. inane

6. He believed in the ancient *dogma*.
   A. priest   B. prophet   C. seer
   D. doctrine   E. ruler

7. They studied a Grecian *archetype*.
   A. model   B. urn   C. epic   D. ode   E. play

8. The *insurrection* was described on the front page.
   A. surgery   B. pageant   C. ceremony
   D. game   E. revolt

9. He was known for his *procrastination*.
   A. justification   B. learning   C. delay
   D. ambition   E. background

10. The doctor analyzed the *toxic* ingredients. 10.____
    A. poisonous   B. anemic   C. trivial
    D. obscure   E. distinct

11. It was a *portentous* occurrence. 11.____
    A. pleasant   B. decisive   C. ominous
    D. monetary   E. hearty

12. His *espousal* of the plan was applauded. 12.____
    A. explanation   B. rejection   C. ridicule
    D. adoption   E. revision

13. Her condition was *lachrymose*. 13.____
    A. improved   B. tearful   C. hopeful
    D. precocious E. tenuous

14. It was a *precarious* situation. 14.____
    A. uncomplicated   B. peaceful   C. precise
    D. uncertain   E. precipitous

15. He was lost in a *reverie*. 15.____
    A. chancery   B. dream   C. forest
    D. cavern   E. tarn

16. The hero was a young *gallant*. 16.____
    A. suitor   B. fool   C. gull
    D. lawyer   E. executive

17. Their practices were *nefarious*. 17.____
    A. unprofitable   B. ignorant   C. multifarious
    D. wicked   E. wishful

18. He insisted upon the *proviso*. 18.____
    A. stipulation   B. pronunciation   C. examination
    D. supply   E. equipment

19. The spirit came from the *nether* regions. 19.____
    A. frozen   B. lower   C. lost
    D. bright   E. mysterious

20. His actions were *malevolent*. 20.____
    A. unassuming   B. silent   C. evil
    D. peaceful   E. constructive

21. He had a *florid* complexion. 21.____
    A. sanguine   B. pallid   C. fair
    D. sickly   E. normal

3 (#1)

22. The lawyer explained the legal *parlance*.
    A. action
    B. maneuver
    C. situation
    D. language
    E. procedure

    22.____

23. They were present at the *interment*.
    A. concert
    B. trial
    C. embarkation
    D. burial
    E. performance

    23.____

24. He made a *moot* point.
    A. definite
    B. sensible
    C. debatable
    D. strong
    E. correct

    24.____

25. They carefully examined the *cryptic* message.
    A. occult
    B. legible
    C. valid
    D. familiar
    E. warning

    25.____

Questions 26-40.

DIRECTIONS: Indicate the number of syllables in each of the following words.

26. vicissitude   26.____
27. blown   27.____
28. maintenance   28.____
29. symbolization   29.____
30. athletics   30.____
31. actually   31.____
32. friend   32.____
33. perseverance   33.____
34. physiology   34.____
35. pronunciation   35.____
36. vacuum   36.____
37. sophomore   37.____
38. opportunity   38.____
39. hungry   39.____
40. temperament   40.____

Questions 41-60.

DIRECTIONS: Indicate the one misspelled work in each of the following Questions 41 through 60 by indicating the letter of the misspelled word in the space at the right.

41. A. holiday B. noticeable C. fourty 41.____
    D. miniature E. yeast

42. A. grievance B. murmur C. occurance 42.____
    D. business E. captain

43. A. succeed B. vegatable C. pleasant 43.____
    D. picnicking E. shepherd

44. A. psychology B. plebian C. exercise 44.____
    D. fiery E. concise

45. A. ninety B. optimistic C. professor 45.____
    D. repitition E. siege

46. A. tarriff B. absence C. grammar 46.____
    D. license E. balloon

47. A. dissipation B. ecstasy C. prarie 47.____
    D. marriage E. consistent

48. A. supersede B. twelfth C. vacillate 48.____
    D. playright E. expense

49. A. fundamental B. government C. accomodate 49.____
    D. cafeteria E. surely

50. A. cemetary B. indispensable C. dormitory 50.____
    D. environment E. divine

51. A. irritible B. permissible C. irresistible 51.____
    D. rhythmical E. source

52. A. interprete B. opinion C. guard 52.____
    D. familiar E. possible

53. A. conscience B. existence C. loneliness 53.____
    D. leisure E. exhileration

54. A. villian B. weird C. seize 54.____
    D. tragedy E. crystal

55. A. develop B. bachelor C. dilemma 55.____
    D. operate E. synonym

56. A. university   B. connoiseur   C. aisle   56.____
     D. transferred   E. division

57. A. zoology   B. conscious   C. aptitude   57.____
     D. restaurant   E. sacriligious

58. A. tendency   B. vital   C. analyze   58.____
     D. consistant   E. proceed

59. A. proceedure   B. surround   C. disastrous   59.____
     D. beginning   E. arrival

60. A. encrease   B. pursuing   C. necessary   50.____
     D. tyranny   E. strength

Questions 61-80.

DIRECTIONS: Indicate the part of speech for each italicized word in the following sentences by selecting the letter of the part of speech from the key above each set of questions.

    A. Noun
    B. Pronoun
    C. Verb
    D. Adjective
    E. Adverb

61. You are entirely *wrong*.   61.____

62. On *Sunday*, we will attend church.   62.____

63. *That* is the main problem.   63.____

64. He was invited to the party, *Saturday*.   64.____

65. I shall introduce a *technical* term.   65.____

66. It was a *novel* turn of events.   66.____

67. He wanted *that* gift for himself.   67.____

68. A few definitions will help *us* to understand.   68.____

69. He let them reach their own *conclusions*.   69.____

70. I must ask *you* to remain silent.   70.____

A. Preposition
B. Conjunction
C. Pronoun
D. Adverb
E. Adjective

71. *This* is a stupid answer. 71._____

72. He solved the mystery *without* the police. 72._____

73. She felt *secure* in his protection. 73._____

74. He believed in the *scientific* method. 74._____

75. Do not destroy their *traditional* beliefs. 75._____

76. They chartered the bus, *but* they did not go. 76._____

77. The young men are *quiet* with fear. 77._____

78. She talked *cheerfully* to the visitors. 78._____

79. The candidate was *certain* of victory. 79._____

80. I hope you will take *that* with you. 80._____

Questions 81-100.

DIRECTIONS: Indicate the use of each italicized word in the following sentences by choosing the letter of the CORRECT usage from the key above each set of questions.

A. Subject of Verb
B. Predicate Nominative or Subjective Complement
C. Predicate Adjective
D. Direct Object of Verb
E. Indirect Object of Verb

81. They made *him* president of the club. 81._____

82. There was nothing *odd* about the situation. 82._____

83. Give them *time* enough for thought. 83._____

84. He supervised the *work* himself. 84._____

85. Will you do *me* a favor? 85._____

86. The salad dressing tasted *good*. 86._____

87. In the crash, the *body* was thrown forward. 87.____

88. On a bench in the park was a single *man*. 88.____

89. There were two *men* who carried the trunk. 89.____

90. I am older than *you*. 90.____

      A. Object of Preposition
      B. Subject of Infinitive
      C. Direct Object of Verb
      D. Indirect Object of Verb
      E. Predicate Nominative or Subjective Complement

91. Let *them* suffer the consequences. 91.____

92. Offer *them* the key to the apartment. 92.____

93. He heard the *bell* ring. 93.____

94. Let *us* try another solution. 94.____

95. No one except *John* had volunteered. 95.____

96. Show *us* one example of your style. 96.____

97. Will you send *her* the flowers? 97.____

98. I want *you* to take her home. 98.____

99. He told his *father* that he would obey. 99.____

100. Do not write on the second *page*. 100.____

Questions 101-115.

DIRECTIONS: Indicate the kind of verbal italicized in the following sentences by choosing the appropriate letter from the key below.

      A. Gerund
      B. Participle
      C. Infinitive

101. The manuscript, *corrected* and typed, was on the desk. 101.____

102. He heard the bullet *ricochet*. 102.____

103. *Finding* the answer is a difficult task. 103.____

104. The animal, *hidden* from view, was trembling. 104.____

105. *Pretending* to be asleep, he listened attentively. 105.____

106. The professor, a *qualified* lecturer, entered the room. 106.____

107. They enjoyed *camping* at the lake. 107.____

108. Let them *come* to me. 108.____

109. He was annoyed by the *buzzing* sound. 109.____

110. It was a *stimulating* performance. 110.____

111. He had an accident while *returning* to the city. 111.____

112. *Encouraged* to study, the class opened the books. 112.____

113. He heard the gun *explode*. 113.____

114. They called him the *forgotten* man. 114.____

115. *Realizing* his mistake, he apologized. 115.____

Questions 116-130.

DIRECTIONS: Indicate the CORRECT punctuation for the following sentences by choosing the letter of the correct punctuation from the key below where brackets appear.

    A. Comma
    B. Semicolon
    C. Colon
    D. Dash
    E. No punctuation

116. He explained [ ] that he could not attend. 116.____

117. The executive [ ] prepared for the interview and entered the room. 117.____

118. She admitted [ ] that the suggestion was wrong. 118.____

119. He did not object [ ] to dealing with him. 119.____

120. The chairman disagreed [ ] the members did not. 120.____

121. You must report to duty on November 10 [ ] 2022. 121.____

122. The father [ ] and two sons went fishing. 122.____

123. Act on the following problems [ ] administration, supervision, and policy.   123.____

124. This is excellent [ ] it has insight.   124.____

125. "I will take the car [ ]" he said.   125.____

126. I will do it [ ] however, you must help me.   126.____

127. When the show ended [ ] he returned home.   127.____

128. Stop [ ] making all of that noise.   128.____

129. Be firm [ ] exercise your authority.   129.____

130. The first example is poor [ ] the second is good.   130.____

Questions 131-150.

DIRECTIONS: Place a *C* in the space at the right if the sentence is correctly punctuated and a *W* in the space at the right if the sentence is incorrectly punctuated.

131. Its later than you think.   131.____

132. While I was eating the toast burned.   132.____

133. The fire started at ten o'clock in the morning.   133.____

134. She asked, "Did you say, 'I will go?"   134.____

135. Richards handling of the question warranted praise.   135.____

136. July 4 is a holiday.   136.____

137. Oh perhaps you are right.   137.____

138. Will you answer the door, John?   138.____

139. While he was bathing the dog came in.   139.____

140. He was a calm gentle person.   140.____

141. He wore a new bow tie.   141.____

142. The shout "Block that kick" echoed upon the field.   142.____

143. Ladies and gentlemen take your seats.   143.____

144. However you must do your work.   144.____

10 (#1)

145. My brothers are: John, Bill, and Charles. 145.____

146. While I was painting the neighbor opened the door. 146.____

147. One should fight for honor: not fame. 147.____

148. "Will you sing" he asked? 148.____

149. He played tennis, and then bowled. 149.____

150. On Monday April 5, we leave for Europe. 150.____

KEY (CORRECT ANSWERS)

1. D	31. 4	61. D	91. C	121. A
2. A	32. 1	62. A	92. D	122. E
3. C	33. 4	63. B	93. C	123. C
4. E	34. 5	64. A	94. C	124. D
5. B	35. 5	65. D	95. A	125. A
6. D	36. 2	66. D	96. C	126. B
7. A	37. 3	67. D	97. C	127. A
8. E	38. 5	68. B	98. C	128. E
9. C	39. 2	69. A	99. C	129. B
10. A	40. 3	70. B	100. A	130. B
11. C	41. C	71. C	101. B	131. W
12. D	42. C	72. A	102. B	132. W
13. B	43. B	73. D	103. A	133. C
14. D	44. B	74. E	104. B	134. W
15. B	45. D	75. E	105. A	135. W
16. A	46. A	76. B	106. B	136. C
17. D	47. C	77. E	107. A	137. W
18. A	48. D	78. D	108. C	138. C
19. B	49. C	79. E	109. B	139. W
20. C	50. A	80. C	110. B	140. W
21. A	51. A	81. D	111. A	141. C
22. D	52. A	82. C	112. B	142. W
23. D	53. E	83. D	113. C	143. W
24. C	54. A	84. D	114. B	144. W
25. A	55. C	85. E	115. A	145. W
26. 3	56. B	86. C	116. E	143. W
27. 1	57. E	87. A	117. E	147. W
28. 3	58. D	88. B	118. E	148. W
29. 5	59. A	89. A	119. E	149. W
30. 3	60. A	90. C	120. B	150. W

SPELLING
EXAMINATION SECTION
TEST 1

DIRECTIONS: Each question or incomplete statement is followed by several suggested answers or completions. Select the one that BEST answers the question or completes the statement. *PRINT THE LETTER OF THE CORRECT ANSWER IN THE SPACE AT THE RIGHT.*

Questions 1-5.

DIRECTIONS: Questions 1 through 5 consist of four words. Indicate the letter of the word that is CORRECTLY spelled.

1. A. harassment B. harrasment 1.____
   C. harasment D. harrassment

2. A. maintainance B. maintenence 2.____
   C. maintainence D. maintenance

3. A. comparable B. comprable 3.____
   C. comparible D. commparable

4. A. suficient B. sufficant 4.____
   C. sufficient D. suficiant

5. A. fairly B. fairley C. farely D. fairlie 5.____

Questions 6-10.

DIRECTIONS: Questions 6 through 10 consist of four words. Indicate the letter of the word that is INCORRECTLY spelled.

6. A. pallor B. ballid C. ballet D. pallid 6.____

7. A. urbane B. surburbane 7.____
   C. interurban D. urban

8. A. facial B. physical C. fiscle D. muscle 8.____

9. A. interceed B. benefited 9.____
   C. analogous D. altogether

10. A. seizure B. irrelevant 10.____
    C. inordinate D. dissapproved

KEY (CORRECT ANSWERS)

1.	A	6.	B
2.	D	7.	B
3.	A	8.	C
4.	C	9.	A
5.	A	10.	D

TEST 2

DIRECTIONS: Each of Questions 1 through 15 consists of two words preceded by the letters A and B. In each question, one of the words may be spelled INCORRECTLY or both words may be spelled CORRECTLY. If one of the words in a question is spelled INCORRECTLY, print in the space at the right the capital letter preceding the INCORRECTLY spelled word. If both words are spelled CORRECTLY, print the letter C.

1. A. easely   B. readily   1.____
2. A. pursue   B. decend   2.____
3. A. measure   B. laboratory   3.____
4. A. exausted   B. traffic   4.____
5. A. discussion   B. unpleasant   5.____
6. A. campaign   B. murmer   6.____
7. A. guarantee   B. sanatary   7.____
8. A. communication   B. safty   8.____
9. A. numerus   B. celebration   9.____
10. A. nourish   B. begining   10.____
11. A. courious   B. witness   11.____
12. A. undoubtedly   B. thoroughly   12.____
13. A. accessible   B. artifical   13.____
14. A. feild   B. arranged   14.____
15. A. admittence   B. hastily   15.____

KEY (CORRECT ANSWERS)

1.	A	6.	B	11.	A
2.	B	7.	B	12.	C
3.	C	8.	B	13.	B
4.	A	9.	A	14.	A
5.	C	10.	B	15.	A

TEST 3

DIRECTIONS: In each of the following sentences, one word is misspelled. Following each sentence is a list of four words taken from the sentence. Indicate the letter of the word which is MISSPELLED in the sentence. *PRINT THE LETTER OF THE CORRECT ANSWER IN THE SPACE AT THE RIGHT.*

1. The placing of any inflammable substance in any building, or the placing of any device or contrivance capable of producing fire, for the purpose of causing a fire is an attempt to burn.
    - A. inflammable
    - B. substance
    - C. device
    - D. contrivence

   1._____

2. The word *break* also means obtaining an entrance into a building by any artifice used for that purpose, or by collussion with any person therein.
    - A. obtaining
    - B. entrance
    - C. artifice
    - D. colussion

   2._____

3. Any person who with intent to provoke a breech of the peace causes a disturbance or is offensive to others may be deemed to have committed disorderly conduct.
    - A. breech
    - B. disturbance
    - C. offensive
    - D. committed

   3._____

4. When the offender inflicts a grevious harm upon the person from whose possession, or in whose presence, property is taken, he is guilty of robbery.
    - A. offender
    - B. grevious
    - C. possession
    - D. presence

   4._____

5. A person who wilfuly encourages or advises another person in attempting to take the latter's life is guilty of a felony.
    - A. wilfuly
    - B. encourages
    - C. advises
    - D. attempting

   5._____

6. He maliciously demurred to an ajournment of the proceedings.
    - A. maliciously
    - B. demurred
    - C. ajournment
    - D. proceedings

   6._____

7. His innocence at that time is irrelevant in view of his more recent villianous demeanor.
    - A. innocence
    - B. irrelevant
    - C. villianous
    - D. demeanor

   7._____

8. The mischievous boys aggrevated the annoyance of their neighbor.
    - A. mischievous
    - B. aggrevated
    - C. annoyance
    - D. neighbor

   8._____

9. While his perseverence was commendable, his judgment was debatable.
   A. perseverence
   B. commendable
   C. judgment
   D. debatable

10. He was hoping the appeal would facilitate his aquittal.
    A. hoping
    B. appeal
    C. facilitate
    D. aquittal

11. It would be preferable for them to persue separate courses.
    A. preferable
    B. persue
    C. separate
    D. courses

12. The litigant was complimented on his persistance and achievement.
    A. litigant
    B. complimented
    C. persistance
    D. achievement

13. Ocassionally there are discrepancies in the descriptions of miscellaneous items.
    A. ocassionally
    B. discrepancies
    C. descriptions
    D. miscellaneous

14. The councilmanic seargent-at-arms enforced the prohibition.
    A. councilmanic
    B. seargeant-at-arms
    C. enforced
    D. prohibition

15. The teacher had an ingenious device for maintaining attendance.
    A. ingenious
    B. device
    C. maintaining
    D. attendance

16. A worrysome situation has developed as a result of the assessment that absenteeism is increasing despite our conscientious efforts.
    A. worrysome
    B. assessment
    C. absenteeism
    D. conscientious

17. I concurred with the credit manager that it was practicable to charge purchases on a biennial basis, and the company agreed to adhear to this policy.
    A. concurred
    B. practicable
    C. biennial
    D. adhear

18. The pastor was chagrined and embarassed by the irreverent conduct of one of his parishioners.
    A. chagrined
    B. embarassed
    C. irreverent
    D. parishioners

19. His inate seriousness was belied by his flippant demeanor.
    A. inate
    B. belied
    C. flippant
    D. demeanor

20. It was exceedingly regrettable that the excessive number of challenges in the court delayed the start of the trial.
    A. exceedingly
    B. regrettable
    C. excessive
    D. challanges

    20._____

KEY (CORRECT ANSWERS)

1.	D	11.	B
2.	D	12.	C
3.	A	13.	A
4.	B	14.	B
5.	A	15.	C
6.	C	16.	A
7.	C	17.	D
8.	B	18.	B
9.	A	19.	A
10.	D	20.	D

TEST 4

Questions 1-11.

DIRECTIONS: Each question consists of three words in each question, one of the words may be spelled incorrectly or all three may be spelled correctly. For each question if one of the words is spelled INCORRECTLY, write the letter of the incorrect word in the space at the right. If all three words are spelled CORRECTLY, write the letter D in the space at the right.

SAMPLE I: (A) guide   (B) departmint   (C) stranger
SAMPLE II: (A) comply   (B) valuable   (C) window

In Sample I, departmint is incorrect. It should be spelled department.
Therefore, B is the answer.
In Sample II, all three words are spelled correctly. Therefore, D is the answer.

1.	A. argument	B. reciept	C. complain	1.____
2.	A. sufficient	B. postpone	C. visible	2.____
3.	A. expirience	B. dissatisly	C. alternate	3.____
4.	A. occurred	B. noticable	C. appendix	4.____
5.	A. anxious	B. guarantee	C. calendar	5.____
6.	A. sincerely	B. affectionately	C. truly	6.____
7.	A. excellant	B. verify	C. important	7.____
8.	A. error	B. quality	C. enviroment	8.____
9.	A. exercise	B. advance	C. pressure	9.____
10.	A. citizen	B. expence	C. memory	10.____
11.	A. flexable	B. focus	C. forward	11.____

Questions 12-15.

DIRECTIONS: Each of Questions 12 through 15 consists of a group of four words. Examine each group carefully; then in the space at the right, indicate
A. if only one word in the group is spelled correctly
B. if two words in the group are spelled correctly
C. if three words in the group are spelled correctly
D. if all four words in the group are spelled correctly

12. Wendsday, particular, similar, hunderd   12.____

13. realize, judgment, opportunities, consistent   13.____

14. equel, principle, assistense, committee   14.____

15. simultaneous, privilege, advise, ocassionaly   15.____

KEY (CORRECT ANSWERS)

1. B	6. D	11. A
2. D	7. A	12. B
3. A	8. C	13. D
4. B	9. D	14. A
5. C	10. B	15. C

TEST 5

DIRECTIONS: Each of Questions 1 through 15 consists of two words preceded by the letters A and B. In each item, one of the words may be spelled INCORRECTLY or both words may be spelled CORRECTLY. If one of the words in a question is spelled INCORRECTLY, print in the space at the right the letter preceding the INCORRECTLY spelled word. If bot words are spelled CORRECTLY, print the letter C.

1. A. justified   B. offering   1.____
2. A. predjudice   B. license   2.____
3. A. label   B. pamphlet   3.____
4. A. bulletin   B. physical   4.____
5. A. assure   B. exceed   5.____
6. A. advantagous   B. evident   6.____
7. A. benefit   B. occured   7.____
8. A. acquire   B. graditude   8.____
9. A. amenable   B. boundry   9.____
10. A. deceive   B. voluntary   10.____
11. A. imunity   B. conciliate   11.____
12. A. acknoledge   B. presume   12.____
13. A. substitute   B. prespiration   13.____
14. A. reputable   B. announce   14.____
15. A. luncheon   B. wretched   15.____

KEY (CORRECT ANSWERS)

1.	C	6.	A	11.	A
2.	A	7.	B	12.	A
3.	C	8.	B	13.	B
4.	C	9.	B	14.	A
5.	C	10.	C	15.	C

TEST 6

DIRECTIONS: Questions 1 through 15 contain lists of words, one of which is misspelled. Indicate the MISSPELLED word in each group. *PRINT THE LETTER OF THE CORRECT ANSWER IN THE SPACE AT THE RIGHT.*

1. A. felony B. lacerate 1.____
   C. cancellation D. seperate

2. A. batallion B. beneficial 2.____
   C. miscellaneous D. secretary

3. A. camouflage B. changeable 3.____
   C. embarrass D. inoculate

4. A. beneficial B. disasterous 4.____
   C. incredible D. miniature

5. A. auxilliary B. hypocrisy 5.____
   C. phlegm D. vengeance

6. A. aisle B. cemetary 6.____
   C. courtesy D. extraordinary

7. A. crystallize B. innoculate 7.____
   C. eminent D. symmetrical

8. A. judgment B. maintainance 8.____
   C. bouillon D. eery

9. A. isosceles B. ukulele 9.____
   C. mayonaise D. iridescent

10. A. remembrance B. occurence 10.____
    C. correspondence D. countenance

11. A. corpuscles B. mischievous 11.____
    C. batchelor D. bulletin

12. A. terrace B. banister 12.____
    C. concrete D. masonery

13. A. balluster B. gutter 13.____
    C. latch D. bridging

14. A. personnell B. navel 14.____
    C. therefor D. emigrant

15. A. committee   B. submiting   15._____
     C. amendment   D. electorate

KEY (CORRECT ANSWERS)

1. D	6. B	11. C
2. A	7. B	12. D
3. C	8. B	13. A
4. B	9. C	14. A
5. A	10. B	15. B

TEST 7

Questions 1-5.

DIRECTIONS: Questions 1 through 5 consist of groups of four words. Select answer
A if only one word is spelled correctly in a group
B if TWO words are spelled correctly in a group
C if THREE words are spelled correctly in a group
D if all FOUR words are spelled correctly in a group.

1. counterfeit, embarass, panicky, supercede   1._____

2. benefited, personnel, questionnaire, unparalelled   2._____

3. bankruptcy, describable, proceed, vacuum   3._____

4. handicapped, mispell, offerred, pilgrimmage   4._____

5. corduroy, interfere, privilege, separator   5._____

Questions 6-10.

DIRECTIONS: Questions 6 through 10 consist of four pairs of words each. Some of the words are spelled correctly; others are spelled incorrectly. For each question, indicate in the space at the right the letter preceding that pair of words in which BOTH words are spelled CORRECTLY.

6. A. hygienic, inviegle   B. omniscience, pittance   6._____
    C. plagarize, nullify   D. seargent, perilous

7. A. auxilary, existence   B. pronounciation, accordance   7._____
    C. ignominy, indegence   D. suable, baccalaureate

8. A. discreet, inaudible   B. hypocrisy, currupt   8._____
    C. liquidate, maintainance   D. transparancy, onerous

9. A. facility; stimulent   B. frugel, sanitary   9._____
    C. monetary, prefatory   D. punctileous, credentials

10. A. bankruptsy, perceptible   B. disuade, resilient   10._____
    C. exhilerate, expectancy   D. panegyric, disparate

Questions 11-15.

DIRECTIONS: Each question or incomplete statement is followed by several suggested answers or completions. Select the one that BEST answers the question or completes the statement. PRINT THE LETTER OF THE CORRECT ANSWER IN THE SPACE AT THE RIGHT.

2 (#7)

11. The silent *e* must be retained when the suffix *–able* is added to the word 11._____
    A. argue B. love C. move D. notice

12. The CORRECTLY spelled word in the choices below is 12._____
    A. kindergarden B. zylophone
    C. hemorrhage D. mayonaise

13. Of the following words, the one spelled CORRECTLY is 13._____
    A. begger B. cemetary
    C. embarassed D. coyote

14.
    A. dandilion B. wiry C. sieze D. rythmic 14._____

15. A. beligerent B. anihilation
    C. facetious D. adversery

KEY (CORRECT ANSWERS)

1. B	6. B	11. D
2. C	7. D	12. C
3. D	8. A	13. D
4. A	9. C	14. B
5. D	10. D	15. C

TEST 8

DIRECTIONS: In each of the following sentences, one word is misspelled. Following each sentence is a list of four words taken from the sentence. Indicate the letter of the word which is MISSPELLED. *PRINT THE LETTER OF THE CORRECT ANSWER IN THE SPACE AT THE RIGHT.*

1. If the administrator attempts to withold information, there is a good likelihood that there will be serious repercussions.
    A. administrator
    B. withold
    C. likelihood
    D. repercussions

    1.____

2. He condescended to apologize, but we felt that a beligerent person should not occupy an influential position.
    A. condescended
    B. apologize
    C. beligerent
    D. influential

    2.____

3. Despite the sporadic delinquent payments of his indebtedness, Mr. Johnson has been an exemplery customer.
    A. sporadic
    B. delinquent
    C. indebtedness
    D. exemplery

    3.____

4. He was appreciative of the support he consistantly acquired, but he felt that he had waited an inordinate length of time for it.
    A. appreciative
    B. consistantly
    C. acquired
    D. inordinate

    4.____

5. Undeniably they benefited from the establishment of a receivership, but the question of statutary limitations remained unresolved.
    A. undeniably
    B. benefited
    C. receivership
    D. statutary

    5.____

6. Mr. Smith profered his hand as an indication that he considered it a viable contract, but Mr. Nelson alluded to the fact that his colleagues had not been consulted.
    A. profered
    B. viable
    C. alluded
    D. colleagues

    6.____

7. The treatments were beneficial according to the optomotrists, and the consensus was that minimal improvement could be expected.
    A. beneficial
    B. optomotrists
    C. consensus
    D. minimal

    7.____

8. Her frivolous manner was unbecoming because the air of solemnity at the cemetery was pervasive.
    A. frivolous
    B. solemnity
    C. cemetery
    D. pervasive

    8.____

92

9. The clandestine meetings were designed to make the two adversaries more amicable, but they served only to intensify their emnity.
   A. clandestine
   B. adversaries
   C. amicable
   D. emnity

9.____

10. Do you think that his innovative ideas and financial acumen will help stabalize the fluctuations of the stock market?
    A. innovative
    B. acumen
    C. stabalize
    D. fluctuations

10.____

11. In order to keep a perpetual inventory, you will have to keep an uninterrupted surveillance of all the miscellanious stock.
    A. perpetual
    B. uninterrupted
    C. surveillance
    D. miscellanious

11.____

12. She used the art of pursuasion on the children because she found that caustic remarks had no perceptible effect on their behavior.
    A. pursuasion
    B. caustic
    C. perceptible
    D. effect

12.____

13. His sacreligious outbursts offended his constituents, and he was summarily removed from office by the City Council.
    A. sacreligious
    B. constituents
    C. summarily
    D. Council

13.____

14. They exhorted the contestants to greater efforts, but the exhorbitant costs in terms of energy expended resulted in a feeling of lethargy.
    A. exhorted
    B. contestants
    C. exhorbitant
    D. lethargy

14.____

15. Since he was knowledgable about illicit drugs, he was served with a subpoena to appear for the prosecution.
    A. knowledgable
    B. illicit
    C. subpoena
    D. prosecution

15.____

16. In spite of his lucid statements, they denigrated his report and decided it should be succintly paraphrased.
    A. lucid
    B. denigrated
    C. succintly
    D. paraphrased

16.____

17. The discussion was not germane to the contraversy, but the indicted man's insistence on further talk was allowed.
    A. germane
    B. contraversy
    C. indicted
    D. insistence

17.____

18. The legislators were enervated by the distances they had traveled during the election year to fullfil their speaking engagements.
    A. legislators
    B. enervated
    C. traveled
    D. fullfil

18.____

19. The plaintiffs' attornies charge the defendant in the case with felonious assault.
    A. plaintiffs'
    B. attornies
    C. defendant
    D. felonious

    19._____

20. It is symptomatic of the times that we try to placate all, but a proposal for new forms of disciplinery action was promulgated by the staff.
    A. symptomatic
    B. placate
    C. disciplinery
    D. promulgated

    20._____

KEY (CORRECT ANSWERS)

1.	B	11.	D
2.	C	12.	A
3.	D	13.	A
4.	B	14.	C
5.	D	15.	A
6.	A	16.	C
7.	B	17.	B
8.	A	18.	D
9.	D	19.	B
10.	C	20.	C

TEST 9

DIRECTIONS: Each of Questions 1 through 15 consists of a single word which is spelled either correctly or incorrectly. If the word is spelled CORRECTLY, you are to print the letter C (Correct) in the space at the right. If the word is spelled INCORRECTL, you are to print the letter W (Wrong).

1. pospone 1._____
2. diffrent 2._____
3. height 3._____
4. carefully 4._____
5. ability 5._____
6. temper 6._____
7. deslike 7._____
8. seldem 8._____
9. alcohol 9._____
10. expense 10._____
11. vegatable 11._____
12. dispensary 12._____
13. specemin 13._____
14. allowance 14._____
15. exersise 15._____

KEY (CORRECT ANSWERS)

1.	W	6.	C	11.	W
2.	W	7.	W	12.	C
3.	C	8.	W	13.	W
4.	C	9.	C	14.	C
5.	C	10.	C	15.	W

TEST 10

DIRECTIONS: Each of Questions 1 through 10 consists of four words, one of which may be spelled incorrectly or all four words may be spelled correctly. If one of the words in a question is spelled incorrectly, print in the space at the right the capital letter preceding the word which is spelled INCORRECTLY. If all four words are spelled CORRECTLY, print the letter E.

1. A. dismissal B. collateral 1.____
   C. leisure D. proffession

2. A. subsidary B. outrageous 2.____
   C. liaison D. assessed

3. A. already B. changeable 3.____
   C. mischevous D. cylinder

4. A. supersede B. deceit 4.____
   C. dissension D. imminent

5. A. arguing B. contagious 5.____
   C. comparitive D. accessible

6. A. indelible B. existance 6.____
   C. presumptuous D. mileage

7. A. extention B. aggregate 7.____
   C. sustenance D. gratuitous

8. A. interrogate B. exaggeration 8.____
   C. vacillate D. moreover

9. A. parallel B. derogatory 9.____
   C. admissible D. appellate

10. A. safety B. cumalative 10.____
    C. disappear D. usable

KEY (CORRECT ANSWERS)

1. D   6. B
2. A   7. A
3. C   8. E
4. E   9. C
5. C   10. B

TEST 11

DIRECTIONS: Each of questions 1 through 10 consists of four words, one of which may be spelled incorrectly or all four words may be spelled correctly. If one of the words in a question is spelled INCORRECTLY, print in the space at the right the capital letter preceding the word which is spelled incorrectly. If all four words are spelled CORRECTLY, print the letter E.

1. A. vehicular B. gesticulate 1._____
   C. manageable D. fullfil

2. A. inovation B. onerous 2._____
   C. chastise D. irresistible

3. A. familiarize B. dissolution 3._____
   C. oscillate D. superflous

4. A. census B. defender 4._____
   C. adherence D. inconceivable

5. A. voluminous B. liberalize 5._____
   C. bankrupcy D. conversion

6. A. justifiable B. executor 6._____
   C. perpatrate D. dispelled

7. A. boycott B. abeyence 7._____
   C. enterprise D. circular

8. A. spontaineous B. dubious 8._____
   C. analyze D. premonition

9. A. intelligible B. apparently 9._____
   C. genuine D. crucial

10. A. plentiful B. ascertain 10._____
    C. carreer D. preliminary

KEY (CORRECT ANSWERS)

1.	D	6.	C
2.	A	7.	B
3.	D	8.	A
4.	E	9.	E
5.	C	10.	C

TEST 12

DIRECTIONS: Each of questions 1 through 25 consists of four words, one of which may be spelled incorrectly or all four words may be spelled correctly. If one of the words in a question is spelled INCORRECTLY, print in the space at the right the capital letter preceding the word which is spelled incorrectly. If all four words are spelled CORRECTLY, print the letter E.

1. A. temporary B. existance 1.____
   C. complimentary D. altogether

2. A. privilege B. changeable 2.____
   C. jeopardize D. commitment

3. A. grievous B. alloted 3.____
   C. outrageous D. mortgage

4. A. tempermental B. accommodating 4.____
   C. bookkeeping D. panicky

5. A. auxiliary B. indispensable 5.____
   C. ecstasy D. fiery

6. A. dissappear B. buoyant 6.____
   C. imminent D. parallel

7. A. loosly B. medicine 7.____
   C. schedule D. defendant

8. A. endeavor B. persuade 8.____
   C. retroactive D. desparate

9. A. usage B. servicable 9.____
   C. disadvantageous D. remittance

10. A. beneficary B. receipt 10.____
    C. excitable D. implement

11. A. accompanying B. intangible 11.____
    C. offerred D. movable

12. A. controlling B. seize 12.____
    C. repetitious D. miscellaneous

13. A. installation B. accommodation 13.____
    C. consistant D. illuminate

14. A. incidentaly B. privilege 14.____
    C. apparent D. chargeable

15. A. prevalent B. serial C. briefly D. disatisfied   15.____
16. A. reciprocal B. concurrence C. persistence D. withold   16.____
17. A. deferred B. suing C. fulfilled D. pursuant   17.____
18. A. questionable B. omission C. acknowledgment D. insistent   18.____
19. A. guarantee B. committment C. mitigate D. publicly   19.____
20. A. prerogative B. apprise C. extrordinary D. continual   20.____
21. A. arrogant B. handicapped C. judicious D. perennial   21.____
22. A. permissable B. deceive C. innumerable D. retrieve   22.____
23. A. notable B. allegiance C. reimburse D. illegal   23.____
24. A. wholly B. disbursement C. hindrance D. conciliatory   24.____
25. A. guidance B. condemn C. publically D. coercion   25.____

KEY (CORRECT ANSWERS)

1.	B	11.	C
2.	E	12.	E
3.	B	13.	C
4.	A	14.	A
5.	E	15.	D
6.	A	16.	D
7.	A	17.	E
8.	D	18.	A
9.	B	19.	B
10.	A	20.	C

21. E
22. A
23. E
24. E
25. C

READING COMPREHENSION
UNDERSTANDING AND INTERPRETING
WRITTEN MATERIAL

COMMENTARY

The ability to read and understand written materials—texts, publications, newspapers, orders, directions, expositions—is a skill basic to a functioning democracy and to an efficient business or viable government.

That is why almost all examinations—for beginning, middle, and senior levels—test reading comprehension, directly or indirectly.

The reading test measures how well you understand what you read. This is how it is done: You read a short paragraph and five statements. From the five statements, you choose the one statement, or answer, that is BEST supported by, or best matches, what is said in the paragraph.

SAMPLE QUESTIONS

DIRECTIONS: Each question has five suggested answers, lettered A, B, C, D, and E. Decide which one is the BEST answer. *PRINT THE LETTER OF THE CORRECT ANSWER IN THE SPACE AT THE RIGHT.*

1. The prevention of accidents makes it necessary not only that safety devices be used to guard exposed machinery but also that mechanics be instructed in safety rules which they must follow for their own protection and that the light in the plant be adequate.
   The paragraph BEST supports the statement that industrial accidents
   A. are always avoidable
   B. may be due to ignorance
   C. usually result from inadequate machinery
   D. cannot be entirely overcome
   E. result in damage to machinery

1.____

2

ANALYSIS

Remember what you have to do:
- First - Read the paragraph
- Second - Decide what the paragraph means
- Third - Read the five suggested answers.
- Fourth - Select the one answer which BEST matches what the paragraph says or is BEST supported by something in the paragraph. (Sometimes you may have to read the paragraph again in order to be sure which suggested answer is best.

This paragraph is talking about three steps that should be taken to prevent industrial accidents
1. Use safety devices on machines
2. Instruct mechanics in safety rules
3. provide adequate lighting

SELECTION

With this in mind, let's look at each suggested answer. Each one starts with "Industrial accidents…"

SUGGESTED ANSWER A
Industrial accidents (A) are always avoidable.
(The paragraph talks about how to avoid accidents, but does not say that accidents are always avoidable.)

SUGGESTED ANSWER B
Industrial accidents (B) may be due to ignorance.
(One of the steps given in the paragraph to prevent accidents is to instruct mechanics on safety rules. This suggests that lack of knowledge or ignorance of safety rules causes accidents. This suggested answer sounds like a good possibility for being the right answer.)

SUGGESTED ANSWER C
Industrial accidents (C) usually result from inadequate machinery.
(The paragraph does suggest that exposed machines cause accidents, but it doesn't say that it is the usual cause of accidents. The word usually makes this a wrong answer.)

SUGGESTED ANSWER D
Industrial accidents (D) cannot be entirely overcome.
(You may know from your own experience that this is a true statement. But that is not what the paragraph is talking about. Therefore, it is NOT the correct answer.)

SUGGESTED ANSWER E
Industrial accidents (E) result in damage to machinery.
(This is a statement that may or may not be true, but in any case it is NOT covered by the paragraph.)

Looking back, you see that the one suggested answer of the five given that BEST matches what the paragraph says is: Industrial accidents (B) may be due to ignorance.

The CORRECT answer then is B.

Be sure to read ALL the possible answers before you make your choice. You may think that none of the five answers is really good, but choose the BEST one of the five.

---

2. Probably few people realize, as they drive on a concrete road, that steel is used to keep the surface flat in spite of the weight of the busses and trucks. Steel bars, deeply embedded in the concrete, provide sinews to take the stresses so that the stresses cannot crack the slab or make it wavy.
The paragraph BEST supports the statement that a concrete road
   A. is expensive to build
   B. usually cracks under heavy weights
   C. looks like any other road
   D. is used only for heavy traffic
   E. is reinforced with other material

2.____

ANALYSIS

This paragraph is commenting on the fact that
   1. few people realize, as they drive on a concrete road, that steel is deeply embedded
   2. steel keeps the surface flat
   3. steel bars enable the road to take the stresses without cracking or becoming wavy

SELECTION

Now read and think about the possible answers:
   A. A concrete road is expensive to build. (Maybe so but that is not what the paragraph is about.)
   B. A concrete road usually cracks under heavy weights. (The paragraph talks about using steel bars to prevent heavy weights from cracking concrete roads. It says nothing about how usual it is for the roads to crack. The word usually makes this suggested answer wrong.)
   C. A concrete road looks like any other road. (This may or may not be true. The important thing to note is that it has nothing to do with what the paragraph is about.)
   D. A concrete road is used only for heavy traffic. (This answer at least has something to do with the paragraph—concrete roads are used with heavy traffic—but it does not say "used only.")
   E. A concrete road is reinforced with other material. (This choice seems to be the correct one on two counts: First, the paragraph does suggest that concrete roads are made

stronger by embedding steel bars in them. This is another way of saying "concrete roads are reinforced with steel bars." Second, by the process of elimination, the other four choices are ruled out as correct answers simply because they do not apply.)

You can be sure that not all the reading questions will be so easy as these.

HINTS FOR ANSWERING READING QUESTIONS

1. Read the paragraph carefully. Then read each suggested answer carefully. Read every word, because often one word can make the difference between a right and a wrong answer.

2. Choose that answer which is supported in the paragraph itself. Do not choose an answer which is a correct statement unless it is based on information in the paragraph.

3. Even though a suggested answer has many of the words used in the paragraph, it may still be wrong.

4. Look out for words—such as *always*, *never*, *entirely*, or *only*—which tend to make a suggested answer wrong.

5. Answer first those questions which you can answer most easily. Then work on the other questions.

6. If you can't figure out the answer to the question, guess.

READING COMPREHENSION
UNDERSTANDING WRITTEN MATERIALS
COMMENTARY

The ability to read and understand written materials—texts, publications, newspapers, orders, directions, expositions—is a skill basic to a functioning democracy and to an efficient business or viable government.

That is why almost all examinations—for beginning, middle, and senior levels—test reading comprehension, directly or indirectly.

The reading test measures how well you understand what you read. This is how it is done: You read a passage followed by several statements. From these statements, you choose the one statement, or answer, that is BEST supported by, or BEST matches, what is said in the paragraph. PRINT THE LETTER OF THE CORRECT ANSWER IN THE SPACE AT THE RIGHT.

SAMPLE QUESTION

DIRECTIONS: Answer Question 1 ONLY according to the information given in the following passage.

1. A cashier has to make many arithmetic calculations in connection with his work. Skill in arithmetic comes readily with practice; no special talent is needed.
On the basis of the above statement, it is MOST accurate to state that
    A. the most important part of a cashier's job is to make calculations
    B. few cashiers have the special ability needed to handle arithmetic problems easily
    C. without special talent, cashiers cannot learn to do the calculations they are required to do in their work
    D. a cashier can, with practice, learn to handle the computations he is required to make

1._____

The CORRECT answer is D.

EXAMINATION SECTION
TEST 1

DIRECTIONS: Questions 1 through 5 are to be answered on the basis of the following reading passage. *PRINT THE LETTER OF THE CORRECT ANSWER IN THE SPACE AT THE RIGHT.*

The size of each collection route will be determined by the amount of waste per stop, distance between stops, speed of loading, speed of truck, traffic conditions during loading time, etc.

Basically, the route should consist of a proper amount of work for a crew for the daily work period. The crew should service all properties eligible for this service in their area. Routes should, whenever practical, be compact, with a logical progression through the area. Unnecessary travel should be avoided. Traffic conditions on the route should be thoroughly studied to prevent lost time in loading, to reduce hazards to employees, and to minimize tying up of regular traffic movements by collection forces. Natural and physical barriers and arterial streets should be used as route boundaries wherever possible to avoid lost time in travel.

Routes within a district should be laid out so that the crews start at the point farthest from the disposal area and, as the day progresses, move toward that area, thus reducing the length of the haul. When possible, the work of the crews in a district should be parallel as they progress throughout the day, with routes finishing up within a short distance of each other. This enables the supervisor to be present when crews are completing their work and enables him to shift crews to trouble spots to complete the day's work.

1. Based on the above passage, an advantage of having collection routes end near one another is that
   A. routes can be made more compact
   B. unnecessary travel is avoided, saving manpower
   C. the length of the haul is reduced
   D. the supervisor can exercise better manpower control

1.____

2. Of the factors mentioned above which affect the size of a collection route, the two over which the sanitation forces have LEAST control are
   A. amount of waste; traffic conditions
   B. speed of loading; amount of waste
   C. speed of truck; distance between stops
   D. traffic conditions; speed of truck

2.____

3. According to the above passage, the size of a collection route is probably good if
   A. it is a fair day's work for a normal crew
   B. it is not necessary for the trucks to travel too fast
   C. the amount of waste collected can be handled properly
   D. the distance between stops is approximately equal

3.____

4. Based on the above passage, it is reasonable to assume that a sanitation officer laying out collection routes should NOT try to have
   A. an arterial street as a route boundary
   B. any routes near the disposal area
   C. the routes overlap a little
   D. the routes run in the same direction

5. The term "logical progression," as used in the second paragraph of the passage refers MOST NEARLY to
   A. collecting from street after street in order
   B. numbering streets one after the other
   C. rotating crew assignments
   D. using logic as a basis for assigned crews

KEY (CORRECT ANSWERS)

1. D
2. A
3. A
4. C
5. A

TEST 2

DIRECTIONS: Questions 1 through 3 are to be answered on the basis of the following reading passage. *PRINT THE LETTER OF THE CORRECT ANSWER IN THE SPACE AT THE RIGHT.*

In an open discussion designed to arrive at solutions to community problems, the person leading the discussion group should give the members a chance to make their suggestions before he makes his. He must not be afraid of silence; if he talks just to keep things going, he will find he can't stop, and good discussion will not develop. In other words, the more he talks, the more the group will depend on him. If he finds, however, that no one seems ready to begin the discussion, his best "opening" is to ask for definitions of terms which form the basis of the discussion. By pulling out as many definitions or interpretations as possible, he can get the group started "thinking out load," which is essential to good discussion.

1. According to the above passage, good group discussion is MOST likely to result if the person leading the discussion group
    A. keeps the discussion going by speaking whenever the group stops speaking
    B. encourages the group to depend on him by speaking more than any other group member
    C. makes his own suggestions before the group has a chance to make theirs
    D. encourages discussion by asking the group to interpret the terms to be discussed

1._____

2. According to the above passage, "thinking out loud" by the discussion group is
    A. *good* practice, because "thinking out loud" is important to good discussion
    B. *poor* practice, because group members should think out their ideas before discussing them
    C. *good* practice, because it will encourage the person leading the discussion to speak more
    D. *poor* practice, because it causes the group to fear silence during discussion

2._____

3. According to the above passage, the one of the following which is LEAST desirable at an open discussion is having
    A. silent periods during which none of the group members speaks
    B. differences of opinion among the group members concerning the definition of terms
    C. a discussion leader who uses "openings" to get the discussion started
    D. a discussion leader who provides all suggestions and definitions for the group

3._____

KEY (CORRECT ANSWERS)

1. D
2. A
3. D

TEST 3

DIRECTIONS: Questions 1 through 4 are to be answered on the basis of the following reading passage. *PRINT THE LETTER OF THE CORRECT ANSWER IN THE SPACE AT THE RIGHT.*

The insects you will control are just a minute fraction of the millions which inhabit the world. Man does well to hold his own in the face of the constant pressures that insects continue to exert upon him. Not only are the total numbers tremendous, but the number of individual kinds, or species, certainly exceeds 800,000—number greater than that of all other animals combined. Many of these are beneficial but some are especially competitive with man. Not only are insects numerous, but they are among the most adaptable of all animals. In their many forms, they are fitted for almost any specific way of life. Their adaptability, combined with their tremendous rate of reproduction, gives insects an unequaled potential for survival!

The food of insects includes almost anything that can be eaten by any other animal as well as many things which cannot even be digested by any other animals. Most insects do not harm the products of man or carry diseases harmful to him; however, many do carry diseases and others feed on his food and manufactured goods. Some are adapted to living only in open areas while others are able to live in extremely confined spaces. All of these factor combined make the insects a group of animals having many members which are a nuisance to man and thus of great importance.

The control of insects requires an understanding of their way of life. Thus, it is necessary to understand the anatomy of the insect, its method of growth, the time it takes for the insect to grow from egg to adult, its habits, the stage of its life history in which it causes damage, its food, and its common living places. In order to obtain the best control, it is especially important to be able to identify correctly the specific insect involved because, without this knowledge, it is impossible to prescribe a proper treatment.

1. Which one of the following is a CORRECT statement about the insect population of the world, according to the above passage? The
    A. total number of insects is less than the total number of all other animals combined
    B. number of species of insects is greater than the number of species of all other animals combined
    C. total number of harmful insects is less than the number of species of those which are harmful
    D. number of species of harmless insects is less than the number of species of those which are harmful

1.____

2. Insects will be controlled MOST efficiently if you
    A. understand why the insects are so numerous
    B. know what insects you are dealing with
    C. see if the insects compete with man
    D. are able to identify the food which the insects digest

2.____

3. According to the above passage, insects are of importance to a scientist PRIMARILY because they
   A. can be annoying, destructive, and harmful to man
   B. are able to thrive in very small spaces
   C. cause damage during their growth stages
   D. are so adaptable that they can adjust to any environment

4. According to the above passage, insects can eat
   A. everything that any other living thing can eat
   B. man's food and thing which he makes
   C. anything which other animals can't digest
   D. only food and food products

KEY (CORRECT ANSWERS)

1. B
2. B
3. A
4. B

TEST 4

DIRECTIONS: Questions 1 through 3 are to be answered on the basis of the following reading passage. *PRINT THE LETTER OF THE CORRECT ANSWER IN THE SPACE AT THE RIGHT.*

Telephone service in a government agency should be adequate and complete with respect to information given or action taken. It must be remembered that telephone contacts should receive special consideration since the caller cannot see the operator. People like to feel that they are receiving personal attention and that their requests or criticisms are receiving individual rather than routine consideration. All this contributes to what has come to be known as *tone of service*. The aim is to use standards which are clearly very good or superior. The factors to be considered in determining what makes good tone of service are speech, courtesy, understanding, and explanations. A caller's impression of tone of service will affect the general public attitude toward the agency and city services in general.

1. The above passage states that people who telephone a government agency like to feel that they are
    A. creating a positive image of themselves
    B. being given routine consideration
    C. receiving individual attention
    D. setting standards for telephone service

    1.____

2. Which one of the following is NOT mentioned in the above passage as a factor in determining good tone of service?
    A. Courtesy   B. Education   C. Speech   D. Understanding

    2.____

3. The above passage implies that failure to properly handle telephone calls is MOST likely to result in
    A. a poor impression of city agencies by the public
    B. a deterioration of courtesy toward operators
    C. an effort by operators to improve the Tone of Service
    D. special consideration by the public of operator difficulties

    3.____

KEY (CORRECT ANSWERS)

1. C
2. B
3. A

TEST 5

DIRECTIONS: Questions 1 through 5 are to be answered on the basis of the following reading passage. *PRINT THE LETTER OF THE CORRECT ANSWER IN THE SPACE AT THE RIGHT.*

For some office workers it is useful to be familiar with the four main classes of domestic mail; for others, it is essential. Each class has a different rate of postage and some have requirements concerning wrapping, sealing, or special information to be placed on the package.

First-class mail, the class which may not be opened for postal inspection, includes letters, postcards, business reply cards, and other kinds of written matter. There are different rates for some of the kinds of cards which can be sent by first-class mail. The maximum weight for an item sent by first-class mail is 70 pounds. An item which is not letter size should be marked "First Class: on all sides.

Although office workers most often come into contact with first-class mail, they may find it helpful to know something about the other classes. Second-class mail is generally used for mailing newspapers and magazines. Publishers of these articles must meet certain U.S. Postal Service requirements in order to obtain a permit to use second-class mailing rates. Third-class mail, which must weigh less than 1 pound, includes printed materials and merchandise parcels. There are two rate structure for this class, a single-piece rate and a bulk rate. Fourth-class mail, also known as parcel post, includes packages weighing from one to 40 pounds. For more information about these classes of mail and the actual mailing rates, contact our local post office.

1. According to this passage, first-class mail is the only class which   1.____
    A. has a limit on the maximum weight of an item
    B. has different rates for items within the class
    C. may not be opened for postal inspection
    D. should be used by office workers

2. According to this passage, the one of the following items which may CORRECTLY   2.____
    be sent by fourth-class mail is a
    A. magazine weighing one-half pound
    B. package weighing one-half pound
    C. package weighing two pounds
    D. postcard

3. According to this passage, there are different postage rates for   3.____
    A. a newspaper sent by second-class mail and a magazine sent by second-class mail
    B. each of the classes of mail
    C. each pound of fourth-class mail
    D. printed material sent by third-class mail and merchandise parcels sent by third-class mail

4. In order to send a newspaper by second-class mail, a publisher must
   A. have met certain postal requirements and obtained a permit
   B. indicate whether he wants to use the single-piece or the bulk rate
   C. make certain that the newspaper weighs less than one pound
   D. mark the newspaper "Second Class" on the top and bottom of the wrapper

5. Of the following types of information, the one which is NOT mentioned in the passage is the
   A. class of mail to which parcel post belongs
   B. kinds of items which can be sent by each class of mail
   C. maximum weight for an item sent by fourth-class mail
   D. postage rate for each of the four classes of mail

KEY (CORRECT ANSWERS)

1. C
2. C
3. B
4. A
5. D

TEST 6

DIRECTIONS: Questions 1 through 5 are to be answered on the basis of the following reading passage. *PRINT THE LETTER OF THE CORRECT ANSWER IN THE SPACE AT THE RIGHT.*

The thickness of insulation necessary for the most economical results varies with the steam temperature. The standard covering consists of 85 percent magnesia with 10 percent of long-fibre asbestos as a binder. Both magnesia and laminated asbestos-felt and other forms of mineral wool including glass wool are also used for heat insulation. The magnesia and laminated-asbestos coverings may be safely used at temperatures up to 600°F. Pipe insulation is applied in molded sections 3 feet long; the sections are attached to the pipe by means of galvanized iron wire or netting. Flanges and fittings can be insulated by direct application of magnesia cement to the metal without *reinforcement*. Insulation should always be maintained inn good condition because it saves fuel. Routine maintenance of warm-pipe insulation should include prompt repair of damaged surfaces. Steam and hot-water leaks concealed by insulation will be difficult to detect. Underground steam or hot-water pipes are best insulated using a concrete trench with removable cover.

1. The word *reinforcement*, as used above, means MOST NEARLY
   A. resistance
   B. strengthening
   C. regulation
   D. removal

2. According to the above paragraph, magnesia and laminated asbestos coverings may be safely used at temperatures up to
   A. 800°F   B. 720°F   C. 675°F   D. 600°F

3. According to the above paragraph, insulation should *always* be maintained in good condition because it
   A. is laminated
   B. saves fuel
   C. is attached to the pipe
   D. prevents leaks

4. According to the above paragraph, pipe insulation sections are attached to the pipe by means of
   A. binders
   B. mineral wool
   C. netting
   D. staples

5. According to the above paragraph, a leak in a hot-water pipe may be difficult to detect because, when insulation is used, the leak is
   A. underground   B. hidden   C. routine   D. cemented

KEY (CORRECT ANSWERS)

1. B
2. D
3. B
4. C
5. B

TEST 7

DIRECTIONS: Questions 1 through 4 are to be answered on the basis of the following reading passage. *PRINT THE LETTER OF THE CORRECT ANSWER IN THE SPACE AT THE RIGHT.*

    Cylindrical surfaces are the most common form of finished surfaces found on machine parts, although flat surfaces are also very common; hence, many metal-cutting processes are for the purpose of producing either cylindrical or flat surfaces. The machines used for cylindrical or flat shapes may be, and often are, utilized also for forming the various irregular or special shapes required on many machine parts. Because of the prevalence of cylindrical and flat surfaces, the student of manufacturing practice should learn first about the machines and methods employed to produce these surfaces. The cylindrical surfaces may be internal as in holes and cylinders. Any one part may, of course, have cylindrical sections of different diameters and lengths and include flat ends or shoulders and, frequently, there is a threaded part or, possibly, some finished surface that is not circular in cross-section. The prevalence of cylindrical surfaces on machine parts explains why lathes are found in all machine shops. It is important to understand the various uses of the lathes because many of the operations are the same fundamentally as those performed on other types of machine tools.

1. According to the above passage, the MOST common form of finished surfaces found on machine parts is
   A. cylindrical   B. elliptical   C. flat   D. square

2. According to the above passage, any one part of cylindrical surfaces may have
   A. chases   B. shoulders   C. keyways   D. splines

3. According to the above passage, lathes are found in all machine shops because cylindrical surfaces on machine parts are
   A. scarce   B. internal   C. common   D. external

4. As used in the above paragraph, the word *processes* means
   A. operations   B. purposes   C. devices   D. tools

KEY (CORRECT ANSWERS)

1. A
2. B
3. C
4. A

TEST 8

DIRECTIONS: Questions 1 and 2 are to be answered on the basis of the following reading passage. *PRINT THE LETTER OF THE CORRECT ANSWER IN THE SPACE AT THE RIGHT.*

The principle of interchangeability requires manufacture to such specification that component parts of a device may be selected at random and assembled to fit and operate satisfactorily. Interchangeable manufacture, therefore, requires that parts be made to definite limits of error, and to fit gages instead of mating parts. Interchangeability does not necessarily involve a high degree of precision; stove lids, for example, are interchangeable but are not particularly accurate, and carriage bolts and nuts are not precision products but are completely interchangeable. Interchangeability may be employed in unit-production as well as mass-production systems of manufacture.

1. According to the above paragraph, in order for parts to be interchangeable, they must be 1._____
    - A. precision-machined
    - B. selectively-assembled
    - C. mass-produced
    - D. made to fit gages

2. According to the above paragraph, carriage bolts are interchangeable because they are 2._____
    - A. precision-made
    - B. sized to specific tolerances
    - C. individually matched products
    - D. produced in small units

KEY (CORRECT ANSWERS)

1. D
2. B

READING COMPREHENSION
UNDERSTANDING WRITTEN MATERIALS
COMMENTARY

The ability to read and understand written materials—texts, publications, newspapers, orders, directions, expositions—is a skill basic to a functioning democracy and to an efficient business or viable government.

That is why almost all examinations—for beginning, middle, and senior levels—test reading comprehension, directly or indirectly.

The reading test measures how well you understand what you read. This is how it is done: You read a passage followed by several statements. From these statements, you choose the one statement, or answer, that is BEST supported by, or BEST matches, what is said in the paragraph. PRINT THE LETTER OF THE CORRECT ANSWER IN THE SPACE AT THE RIGHT.

SAMPLE QUESTIONS

DIRECTIONS: Answer Questions 1 and 2 ONLY according to the information given in the following passage.

1. When a fingerprint technician inks and takes rolled impressions of a subject's fingers, the degree of downward pressure the technician applies is important. The correct pressure may best be determined through experience and observation. It is quite important, however, that the subject be cautioned to relax and not help the fingerprint technician by also applying pressure, as this prevents the fingerprint technician from gaging the amount needed. A method which is helpful in getting the subject to relax his hand is to instruct him to look at some distant object and not to look at his hands.

1. According to this passage, the technician tries to relax the subject's hands by 1.____
    A. instructing him to let his hands hang loosely
    B. telling him that being fingerprinted is painless
    C. asking him to look at this hand instead of some distant object
    D. asking him to look at something other than his hand

2. The subject is asked NOT to press down on his fingers while being fingerprinted 2.____
    because
    A. the impressions taken become rolled
    B. the subject may apply too little downward pressure and spoil the impressions
    C. the technician cannot tell whether he is applying the right degree of pressure
    D. he doesn't have the experience to apply the exact amount of pressure

CORRECT ANSWERS
1. D
2. C

EXAMINATION SECTION

TEST 1

DIRECTIONS: Questions 1 through 3 are to be answered on the basis of the following reading passage. *PRINT THE LETTER OF THE CORRECT ANSWER IN THE SPACE AT THE RIGHT.*

Thermostats should be tested in hot water for proper opening. A bucket should be filled with sufficient water to cover the thermostat and fitted with a thermometer suspended in the water so that the sensitive bulb portion does not rest directly on the bucket. The water is then heated on a stove. As the temperature of the water passes the 160-165° range, the thermostat should start to open and should be completely opened when the temperature has risen to 185-190°. Lifting the thermostat into the air should cause a pronounced closing action and the unit should be closed entirely within a short time.

1. The thermostat described above is a device which opens and closes with changes in the
   A. position   B. pressure   C. temperature   D. surroundings

   1.____

2. According to the above passage, the closing action of the thermostat should be tested by
   A. working the thermostat back and forth
   B. permitting the water to cool gradually
   C. adding cold water to the bucket
   D. removing the thermostat from the bucket

   2.____

3. The bulb of the thermometer should not rest directly on the bucket because
   A. the bucket gets hotter than the water
   B. the thermometer might be damaged in that position
   C. it is difficult to read the thermometer in that position
   D. the thermometer might interfere with operation of the thermostat

   3.____

KEY (CORRECT ANSWERS)

1. C
2. D
3. A

TEST 2

DIRECTIONS: Questions 1 through 3 are to be answered on the basis of the following reading passage. *PRINT THE LETTER OF THE CORRECT ANSWER IN THE SPACE AT THE RIGHT.*

All idle pumps should be turned daily by hand, and should be run under power at least once a week. Whenever repairs are made on a pump, a record should be kept so that it will be possible to judge the success with which the pump is performing its functions. If a pump fails to deliver liquid, there may be an obstruction in the suction line, the pump's parts may be badly worn, or the packing defective.

1. According to the above passage, pumps 1.____
   A. in use should be turned by hand every day
   B. which are not in use should be run under power every day
   C. which are in daily use should be run under power several times a week
   D. which are not in use should be turned by hand every day

2. According to the above passage, the reason for keeping records of repairs made on pumps is to 2.____
   A. make certain that proper maintenance is being performed
   B. discover who is responsible for improper repairs
   C. rate the performance of the pumps
   D. know when to replace worn parts

3. The one of the following causes of pump failure which is NOT mentioned in the above passage is 3.____
   A. excessive suction lift   B. clogged lines
   C. bad packing   D. worn parts

KEY (CORRECT ANSWERS)

1. A
2. C
3. A

TEST 3

DIRECTIONS: Questions 1 through 5 are to be answered on the basis of the following reading passage. *PRINT THE LETTER OF THE CORRECT ANSWER IN THE SPACE AT THE RIGHT.*

Floors in warehouses, storerooms, and shipping rooms must be strong enough to stay level under heavy loads. Unevenness of floors may cause boxes of materials to topple and fall. Safe floor load capacities and maximum heights to which boxes may be stacked should be posted conspicuously so all can notice it. Where material in boxes, containers, or cartons of the same weight is regularly stored, it is good practice to paint a horizontal line on the wall indicating the maximum height to which the material may be piled. A qualified expert should determine floor load capacity from the building plans, the age and condition of the floor supports, the type of floor, and other related information.

Working aisles are those from which material is placed into and removed from storage. Working aisles are of two types: transportation aisles, running the length of the building, and cross aisles, running across the width of the building. Deciding on the number, width, and location of working aisles is important. While aisles are necessary and determine boundaries of storage areas, they reduce the space actually used for storage.

1. According to the above passage, how should safe floor load capacities be made known to employees? They should be
    A. given out to each employee
    B. given to supervisors only
    C. printed in large red letters
    D. posted so that they are easily seen

2. According to the above passage, floor load capacities should be determined by
    A. warehouse supervisors
    B. the fire department
    C. qualified experts
    D. machine operators

3. According to the above passage, transportation aisles
    A. run the length of the building
    B. run across the width of the building
    C. are wider than cross aisles
    D. are shorter than cross aisles

4. According to the above passage, working aisles tend to
    A. take away space that could be used for storage
    B. add to space that could be used for storage
    C. slow down incoming stock
    D. speed up outgoing stock

5. According to the above passage, unevenness of floors may cause
    A. overall warehouse deterioration
    B. piles of stock to fall
    C. materials to spoil
    D. many worker injuries

KEY (CORRECT ANSWERS)

1. D
2. C
3. A
4. A
5. B

TEST 4

DIRECTIONS: Questions 1 through 3 are to be answered on the basis of the following reading passage. *PRINT THE LETTER OF THE CORRECT ANSWER IN THE SPACE AT THE RIGHT.*

In a retail establishment, any overweight means a distinct loss to the merchant, and even an apparently inconsequential overweight on a single package or sale when multiplied by the total number of transactions, could run into large figures. In addition to the use of reliable scales and weights, and their maintenance in proper condition, there must be proper supervision of the selling force. Such supervision is a difficult matter, particularly on the score of carelessness, as the depositing of extra amounts of material on the scale and failure to remove the same when it overbalances the scale may become a habit. In case of underweight, either in the weighing or by the use of fraudulent scales and weights, the seller soon will hear of it, but there is no reason why the amount weighed out should be in excess of what the customer pays for. Checking sales records against invoices and inventories can supply some indication of the tendency of the sales force to become careless in this field.

1. Of the following, the MOST valid implication of the above passage is that
   A. all overweights which occur in retail stores are in small amounts
   B. even-arm and uneven-arm balances and weights which are unreliable lead more often to underweights than to overweights
   C. overweights due to errors of salesclerks necessarily lead to large losses by a retailer
   D. supervision to prevent overweights is more important to a retailer than remedial measures after their occurrence

1.____

2. Of the following, the MOST valid implication of the above passage is that
   A. depositing of insufficient amounts of commodities on scales and failure to add to them may become a habit with salesclerks
   B. salesclerks should be trained in understanding and maintenance of scale mechanisms
   C. supervision of salesclerks to prevent careless habits in weighing must depend upon personal observation

2.____

3. According to the above passage, the MOST accurate of the following statements is:
   A. For the most part, the ideas expressed in the passage do not apply to wholesale establishments.
   B. Inventories of commodities prepacked in the store are the only ones which can be used in checking losses due to overweight.
   C. Invoices which give the value and weight of merchandise received are useful in checking losses due to overweights.
   D. The principal value of inventories is to indicate losses due to overweights.

3.____

KEY (CORRECT ANSWERS)

1. D
2. C
3. C

TEST 5

DIRECTIONS: Questions 1 through 5 are to be answered on the basis of the following reading passage. *PRINT THE LETTER OF THE CORRECT ANSWER IN THE SPACE AT THE RIGHT.*

TITANIC AIR COMPRESSOR

Valves: The compressors are equipped with Titanic plate valves which are automatic in operation. Valves are so constructed that an entire valve assembly can readily be removed from the head. The valves provide large port areas with short lift and are accurately guided to insure positive seating.

Starting Unloader: Each compressor (or air end) is equipped with a centrifugal governor which is bolted directly to the compressor crank shaft. The governor actuates cylinder relief valves so as to relieve pressure from the cylinders during starting and stopping. The motor is never required to start the compressor tinder load.

Air Strainer: Each cylinder air inlet connection is fitted with a suitable combination air strainer and muffler.

Pistons: Pistons are lightweight castings, ribbed internally to secure strength, and are accurately turned and ground. Each piston is fitted with four (4) rings, two of which are oil control rings. Piston pins are hardened and tempered steel of the full floating type. Bronze bushings are used between piston pin and piston

Connecting Rods: Connecting rods are of solid bronze designed for maximum strength, rigidity, and wear. Crank pins are fitted with renewable steel bushings. Connecting rods are of the one-piece type, there being no bolts, nuts, or cotter pins which can come loose. With this type of construction, wear is reduced to a negligible amount, and adjustment of wrist pin and crank pin bearings is unnecessary.

Main Bearings: Main bearings are of the ball type and are securely held in position by spacers. This type of bearing entirely eliminates the necessity of frequent adjustment or attention. The crank shaft is always in perfect alignment.

Crank Shaft: The crank shaft is a one-piece heat-treated forging of best quality open-hearth steel, of rugged design and of sufficient size to transmit the motor power and any additional stresses which may occur in service. Each crank shaft is counter-balanced (dynamically balanced to reduce vibration to a minimum, and is accurately machined to properly receive the ball-bearing races, crank pin bushing, flexible coupling, and centrifugal governor. Suitable provision is made to insure proper lubrication of all crank shaft bearings and bushings with the minimum amount of attention.

Coupling: Compressor and motor shafts are connected through a Morse Chain Company all-metal enclosed flexible coupling. This coupling consists of two sprockets, one mounted on, and keyed to, each shaft; the sprockets are wrapped by a single Morse Chain, the entire assembly being enclosed in a split aluminum grease-packed cover.

1. The crank pin of the connecting rod is fitted with a renewable bushing made of   1.____
    A. solid bronze   B. steel
    C. a lightweight casting   D. ball bearings

2. When the connecting rod is of the one-piece type,
   A. the wrist pins require frequent adjustment
   B. the crank pins require frequent adjustment
   C. the cotter pins frequently will come loose
   D. wear is reduced to a negligible amount

   2.____

3. The centrifugal governor is bolted directly to the
   A. compressor crank shaft   B. main bearing
   C. piston pin   D. muffler

   3.____

4. The number of oil control rings required for each piston is
   A. one   B. two   C. three   D. four

5. The compressor and motor shafts are connected through a flexible coupling. These couplings are _____ to the shafts.
   A. keyed   B. brazed   C. soldered   D. press-fit

   4.____

KEY (CORRECT ANSWERS)

1. B
2. D
3. A
4. B
5. A

TEST 6

DIRECTIONS: Questions 1 through 6 are to be answered on the basis of the following reading passage. *PRINT THE LETTER OF THE CORRECT ANSWER IN THE SPACE AT THE RIGHT.*

    Perhaps the strongest argument the mass transit backer has is the advantage in efficiency that mass transit has over the automobile in the urban traffic picture. It has been estimated that given comparable location and construction conditions, the subway can carry four times as many passengers per hour and cost half as much to build as urban highways. Yet public apathy regarding the mass transportation movement in the 1960's resulted in the building of more roads. Planned to provide 42,000 miles of highways in the period from 1956-72, including 7,500 miles within cities, the Federal Highway System project is now about two-thirds completed. The Highway Trust Fund supplies 90 percent of the cost of the system, with state and local sources putting up the rest of the money. By contrast, a municipality as had to put up the bulk of the cost of a rapid transit system. Although the system and its Trust Fund have come under attack in the past few years from environmentalists and groups opposed to the continued building of urban freeways—considered to be the most expensive, destructive, and inefficient segments of the system—a move by them to get the Trust Fund transformed into a general transportation fund at the expiration of the present program in 1972 seems to be headed nowhere.

1. Given similar building conditions and locations, a city that builds a subway instead of a highway can expect to receive for each dollar spent _____ as much transport value.
   A. half   B. twice   C. four times   D. eight times

1.____

2. The general attitude of the public in the past ten years toward the mass transportation movement has been
   A. favorable   B. indifferent   C. enthusiastic   D. unfriendly

2.____

3. The number of miles of highways still to be completed in the Federal Highway System project is MOST NEARLY
   A. 2,500   B. 5,000   C. 14,000   D. 28,000

3.____

4. What do certain groups who object to some features of the Federal Highway System program want to do with the Highway Trust Fund after 1972?
   A. Extend it in order to complete the project
   B. Change it so that the money can be used for all types of transportation
   C. End it even if the project is not completed
   D. Change it so that the money will be used only for urban freeways

4.____

5. Which one of the following statements is a VALID conclusion based on the facts in the above passage?
   A. The advantage of greater efficiency is the only argument that supporters of the mass transportation movement can offer.
   B. It was easier for cities to build roads rather than mass transit systems in the last 15 years because of the large financial contribution made by the Federal Government.

5.____

127

C. Mass transit systems cause as much congestion and air pollution in cities as automobiles.
D. In 1972, the Highway Trust Fund becomes a general transportation fund.

6. The MAIN idea or theme of the above passage is that the
   A. cost of the Federal Highway System is shared by the federal, state, and local governments
   B. public is against spending money for building mass transportation facilities in the cities
   C. cities would benefit more from expansion and improvement of their mass transit systems than from the building of more highways
   D. building of mass transportation facilities has been slowed by the Highway Trust Fund

6.____

KEY (CORRECT ANSWERS)

1. D
2. B
3. C
4. B
5. B
6. C

TEST 7

DIRECTIONS: Questions 1 through 5 are to be answered on the basis of the following reading passage. *PRINT THE LETTER OF THE CORRECT ANSWER IN THE SPACE AT THE RIGHT.*

The use of role-playing as a training technique was developed during the past decade by social scientists, particularly psychologists, who have been active in training experiments. Originally, this technique was applied by clinical psychologists who discovered that a patient appears to gain understanding of an emotionally disturbing situation when encouraged to act out roles in that situation. As applied in government and business organizations, the purpose of role-playing is to aid employees to understand certain work problems involving interpersonal relations and to enable observers to evaluate various reactions to them. Thus, for example, on the problem of handling grievances, two individuals from the group might be selected to act out extemporaneously the parts of subordinate and supervisor. When this situation is enacted by various pairs among the class and the techniques and results are discussed, the members of the group are presumed to reach conclusions about the most effective means of handling similar situations. Often the use or role reversal, where participants take parts different from their actual work roles, assists individuals to gain more insight into other people's problems and viewpoints. Although role-playing can be a rewarding training device, the trainer must be aware of his responsibilities. If this technique is to be successful, thorough briefing of both actors and observers as to the situation in question, the participants' roles, and what to look for, is essential.

1. The role-playing technique was FIRST used for the purpose of
   A. measuring the effectiveness of training programs
   B. training supervisors in business organizations
   C. treating emotionally disturbed patients
   D. handling employee grievances

2. When role-playing is used in private business as a training device, the CHIEF aim is to
   A. develop better relations between supervisor and subordinate in the handling of grievances
   B. come up with a solution to a specific problem that has arisen
   C. determine the training needs of the group
   D. increase employee understanding of the human-relation factors in work situations

3. From the above passage, it is MOST reasonable to conclude that when role-playing is used, it is preferable to have the roles acted out by
   A. only one set of actors
   B. no more than two sets of actors
   C. several different sets of actors
   D. the trainer or trainers of the group

4. It can be inferred from the above passage that a limitation of role-playing as a training method is that
   A. many work situations do not lend themselves to role-play
   B. employees are not experienced enough as actors to play the roles realistically
   C. only trainers who have psychological training can use it successfully
   D. participants who are observing and not acting do not benefit from it

5. To obtain *good* results from the use of role-play in training, a trainer should give participants
   A. a minimum of information about the situation so that they can act spontaneously
   B. scripts which illustrate the best method for handling the situation
   C. a complete explanation of the problem and the roles to be acted out
   D. a summary of work problems which involve interpersonal relations

KEY (CORRECT ANSWERS)

1. C
2. D
3. C
4. A
5. C

CLERICAL ABILITIES TEST
EXAMINATION SECTION
TEST 1

DIRECTIONS: Each question or incomplete statement is followed by several suggested answers or completions. Select the one that BEST answers the question or completes the statement. *PRINT THE LETTER OF THE CORRECT ANSWER IN THE SPACE AT THE RIGHT.*

Questions 1-10.

DIRECTIONS: Questions 1 through 10 consist of lines of names, dates, and numbers. For each question, you are to choose the option (A, B, C, or D) in Column II which EXACTLY matches the information in Column I. *PRINT THE LETTER OF THE CORRECT ANSWER IN THE SPACE AT THE RIGHT.*

SAMPLE QUESTION

Column I
Schneider 11/16/75 581932

Column II
A. Schneider 11/16/75 518932
B. Schneider 11/16/75 581932
C. Schnieder 11/16/75 581932
D. Shnieder 11/16/75 518932

The correct answer is B. Only Option B shows the name, date, and number exactly as they are in Column I. Option A has a mistake in the number. Option C has a mistake in the name. Option D has a mistake in the name and in the number. Now answer Questions 1 through 10 in the same manner.

	Column I	Column II	
1.	Johnston 12/26/74 659251	A. Johnson 12/23/74 659251 B. Johston 12/26/74 659251 C. Johnston 12/26/74 695251 D. Johnston 12/26/74 659251	1.____
2.	Allison 1/26/75 9939256	A. Allison 1/26/75 9939256 B. Alisson 1/26/75 9939256 C. Allison 1/26/76 9399256 D. Allison 1/26/75 9993356	2.____
3.	Farrell 2/12/75 361251	A. Farell 2/21/75 361251 B. Farrell 2/12/75 361251 C. Farrell 2/21/75 361251 D. Farrell 2/12/75 361151	3.____

4. Guerrero 4/28/72 105689
    A. Guererro 4/28/72 105689
    B. Guererro 4/28/72 105986
    C. Guererro 4/28/72 105869
    D. Guererro 4/28/72 105689

4._____

5. McDonnell 6/05/73 478215
    A. McDonnell 6/15/73 478215
    B. McDonnell 6/05/73 478215
    C. McDonnell 6/05/73 472815
    D. MacDonell 6/05/73 478215

5._____

6. Shepard 3/31/71 075421
    A. Sheperd 3/31/71 075421
    B. Shepard 3/13/71 075421
    C. Shepard 3/31/71 075421
    D. Shepard 3/13/71 075241

6._____

7. Russell 4/01/69 031429
    A. Russell 4/01/69 031429
    B. Russell 4/10/69 034129
    C. Russell 4/10/69 031429
    D. Russell 4/01/69 034129

7._____

8. Phillips 10/16/68 961042
    A. Philipps 10/16/68 961042
    B. Phillips 10/16/68 960142
    C. Phillips 10/16/68 961042
    D. Philipps 10/16/68 916042

8._____

9. Campbell 11/21/72 624856
    A. Campbell 11/21/72 624856
    B. Campbell 11/21/72 624586
    C. Campbell 11/21/72 624686
    D. Campbel 11/21/72 624856

9._____

10. Patterson 9/18/71 76199176
    A. Patterson 9/18/72 76191976
    B. Patterson 9/18/71 76199176
    C. Patterson 9/18/72 76199176
    D. Patterson 9/18/71 76919176

10._____

Questions 11-15.

DIRECTIONS: Questions 11 through 15 consist of groups of numbers and letters which you are to compare. For each question, you are to choose the option (A, B, C, or D) in Column I which EXACTLY matches the group of numbers and letters given in Column I.

SAMPLE QUESTION

Column I
B92466

Column II
A. B92644
B. B94266
C. A92466
D. B92466

3 (#1)

The correct answer is D. Only Option D in Column II shows the group of numbers and letters EXACTLY as it appears in Column I. Now answer Questions 11 through 15 in the same manner.

<u>Column I</u>
11. 925AC5

<u>Column II</u>
A. 952CA5
B. 925AC5
C. 952AC5
D. 925CA6

11.____

12. Y006925

A. Y060925
B. Y006295
C. Y006529
D. Y006925

12.____

13. J236956

A. J236956
B. J326965
C. J239656
D. J932656

13.____

14. AB6952

A. AB6952
B. AB9625
C. AB9652
D. AB6925

14.____

15. X259361

A. X529361
B. X259631
C. X523961
D. X259361

15.____

Questions 16-25.

DIRECTIONS: Each of questions 16 through 25 consists of three lines of code letters and three lines of numbers. The numbers on each line should correspond with the code letters on the same line in accordance with the table below.

Code Letter	S	V	W	A	Q	M	X	E	G	K
Corresponding Number	0	1	2	3	4	5	5	7	8	9

On some of the lines, an error exists in the coding. Compare the letters and numbers in each question carefully. If you find an error or errors on:
    only one of the lines in the question, mark your answer A;
    any two lines in the question, mark your answer B;
    all three lines in the question, mark your answer C;
    none of the lines in the question, mark your answer D.

SAMPLE QUESTION

WQGKSXG	2489068
XEKVQMA	6591453
KMAESXV	9527061

In the above sample, the first line is correct since each code letter listed has the correct corresponding number. On the second line, an error exists because code letter E should have the number 7 instead of the number 5. On the third line, an error exists because the code letter A should have the number 3 instead of the number 2. Since there are errors in two of the three lines, the correct answer is B. Now answer Questions 16 through 25 in the same manner.

16. SWQEKGA   0247983
     KEAVSXM   9731065
     SSAXGKQ   0036894
16._____

17. QAMKMVS   4259510
     MGGEASX   5897306
     KSWMKWS   9125920
17._____

18. WKXQWVE   2964217
     QKXXQVA   4966413
     AWMXGVS   3253810
18._____

19. GMMKASE   8559307
     AWVSKSW   3210902
     QAVSVGK   4310189
19._____

20. XGKQSMK   6894049
     QSVKEAS   4019730
     GSMXKMV   8057951
20._____

21. AEKMWSG   3195208
     MKQSVQK   5940149
     XGQAEVW   6843712
21._____

22. XGMKAVS   6858310
     SKMAWEQ   0953174
     GVMEQSA   8167403
22._____

23. VQSKAVE   1489317
     WQGKAEM   2489375
     MEGKAWQ   5689324
23._____

24. XMQVSKG   6541098
     QMEKEWS   4579720
     KMEVGKG   9571983
24._____

5 (#1)

25. GKVAMEW   88912572   25.____
     AXMVKAE   3651937
     KWAGMAV   9238531

Questions 26-35.

DIRECTIONS: Each of Questions 26 through 35 consists of a column of figures. For each question, add the column of figures and choose the correct answer from the four choices given.

26.   5,665.43   26.____
    2,356.69
    6,447.24
    7,239.65

    A. 20,698.01   B. 21,709.01
    C. 21,718.01   D. 22,609.01

27. 817,209.55   27.____
    264,354.29
     82,368.76
    849,964.89

    A. 1,893.977.49   B. 1,989,988.39
    C. 2,009,077.39   D. 2,013,897.49

28. 156,366.89   28.____
    249,973.23
    823,229.49
     56,869.45

    A. 1,286,439.06   B. 1,287,521.06
    C. 1,297,539.06   D. 1,296,421.06

29.   23,422.15   29.____
    149,696.24
    238,377.53
     86,289.79
    505,533.63

    A. 989,229.34   B. 999,879.34
    C. 1,003,330.34   D. 1,023,329.34

6 (#1)

30. 2,468,926.70
　　656,842.28
　　　49,723.15
　　832,369.59

　　A. 3,218,062.72　　　　B. 3,808,092.72
　　C. 4,007,861.72　　　　D. 4,818,192.72

30._____

31. 　　524,201.52
　　7,775,678.51
　　8,345,299.63
　　40,628,898.08
　　31,374,670.07

　　A. 88,646,647.81　　　　B. 88,646,747.91
　　C. 88,648,647.91　　　　D. 88,648,747.81

31._____

32. 6,824,829.40
　　682,482.94
　　5,542,015.27
　　775,678.51
　　7,732,507.25

　　A. 21,557,513.37　　　　B. 21,567,513.37
　　C. 22,567,503.37　　　　D. 22,567,513.37

32._____

33. 22,109,405.58
　　6,097,093.43
　　5,050,073.99
　　8,118,050.05
　　4,313,980.82

　　A. 45,688,593.87　　　　B. 45,688,603.87
　　C. 45,689,593.87　　　　D. 45,689,603.87

33._____

34. 79,324,114.19
　　99,848,129.74
　　43,331,653.31
　　41,610,207.14

　　A. 264,114,104.38　　　　B. 264,114,114.38
　　C. 265,114,114.38　　　　D. 265,214,104.38

34._____

35. 33,729,653.94
    5,959,342.58
  26,052,715.47
    4,452,669.52
    7,079,953.59

A. 76,374,334.10
B. 76,375,334.10
C. 77,274,335.10
D. 77,275,335.10

35.____

Questions 36-40.

DIRECTIONS: Each of Questions 36 through 40 consists of a single number in Column I and four options in Column II. For each question, you are to choose the option (A, B, C, or D) in Column II which EXACTLY matches the number in Column I.

SAMPLE QUESTION

<u>Column I</u>   <u>Column II</u>
5965121
    A. 5956121
    B. 5965121
    C. 5966121
    D. 5965211

The correct answer is B. Only Option B shows the number EXACTLY as it appears in Column I. Now answer Questions 36 through 40 in the same manner.

<u>Column I</u>   <u>Column II</u>

36. 9643242
A. 9643242
B. 9462342
C. 9642442
D. 9463242

36.____

37. 3572477
A. 3752477
B. 3725477
C. 3572477
D. 3574277

37.____

38. 5276101
A. 5267101
B. 5726011
C. 5271601
D. 5276101

38.____

39. 4469329
A. 4496329
B. 4469329
C. 4496239
D. 4469239

39.____

40. 2326308   A. 2236308   40._____
               B. 2233608
               C. 2326308
               D. 2323608

KEY (CORRECT ANSWERS)

1.	D	11.	B	21.	A	31.	D
2.	A	12.	D	22.	C	32.	A
3.	B	13.	A	23.	B	33.	B
4.	D	14.	A	24.	D	34.	A
5.	B	15.	D	25.	A	35.	C
6.	C	16.	D	26.	B	36.	A
7.	A	17.	C	27.	D	37.	C
8.	C	18.	A	28.	A	38.	D
9.	A	19.	D	29.	C	39.	B
10.	B	20.	B	30.	C	40.	C

TEST 2

DIRECTIONS: Each question or incomplete statement is followed by several suggested answers or completions. Select the one that BEST answers the question or completes the statement. *PRINT THE LETTER OF THE CORRECT ANSWER IN THE SPACE AT THE RIGHT.*

Questions 1-5.

DIRECTIONS: Each of Questions 1 through 5 consists of a name and a dollar amount. In each question, the name and dollar amount in Column II should be an EXACT copy of the name and dollar amount in Column I. If there is:
    a mistake only in the name, mark your answer A;
    a mistake only in the dollar amount, mark your answer B;
    a mistake in both the name and the dollar amount, mark your answer C;
    no mistake in either the name or the dollar amount, mark your answer D.

SAMPLE QUESTION

Column I	Column II
George Peterson	George Petersson
$125.50	$125.50

Compare the name and dollar amount in Column II with the name and dollar amount in Column I. The name *Petersson* in Column II is spelled *Peterson* in Column I. The amount is the same in both columns. Since there is a mistake only in the name, the answer to the sample question is A. Now answer Questions 1 through 5 in the same manner.

	Column I	Column II	
1.	Susanne Shultz $3440	Susanne Schultz $3440	1.____
2.	Anibal P. Contrucci $2121.61	Anibel P. Contrucci $2112.61	2.____
3.	Eugenio Mendoza $12.45	Eugenio Mendozza $12.45	3.____
4.	Maurice Gluckstadt $4297	Maurice Gluckstadt $4297	4.____
5.	John Pampellonne $4656.94	John Pammpellonne $4566.94	5.____

Questions 6-11.

DIRECTIONS: Each of Questions 6 through 11 consist of a set of names and addresses, which you are to compare. In each question, the name and addresses in Column II should be an EXACT copy of the name and address in Column I. If there is:
> a mistake only in the name, mark your answer A;
> a mistake only in the address, mark your answer B;
> a mistake in both the name and address, mark your answer C;
> no mistake in either the name or address, mark your answer D.

SAMPLE QUESTION

Column I	Column II
Michael Filbert	Michael Filbert
456 Reade Street	645 Reade Street
New York, N.Y. 10013	New York, N.Y. 10013

Since there is a mistake only in the address (the street number should be 456 instead of 645), the answer to the sample question is B. Now answer Questions 6 through 11 in the same manner.

	Column I	Column II	
6.	Hilda Goettelmann 55 Lenox Rd. Brooklyn, N.Y. 11226	Hilda Goettelman 55 Lenox Ave. Brooklyn, N.Y. 11226	6._____
7.	Arthur Sherman 2522 Batchelder St. Brooklyn, N.Y. 11235	Arthur Sharman 2522 Batcheder St. Brooklyn, N.Y. 11253	7._____
8.	Ralph Barnett 300 West 28 Street New York, New York 10001	Ralph Barnett 300 West 28 Street New York, New York 10001	8._____
9.	George Goodwin 135 Palmer Avenue Staten Island, New York 10302	George Godwin 135 Palmer Avenue Staten Island, New York 10302	9._____
10.	Alonso Ramirez 232 West 79 Street New York, N.Y. 10024	Alonso Ramirez 223 West 79 Street New York, N.Y. 10024	10._____
11.	Cynthia Graham 149-34 83 Street Howard Beach, N.Y. 11414	Cynthia Graham 149-35 83 Street Howard Beach, N.Y. 11414	11._____

Questions 12-20.

DIRECTIONS: Questions 12 through 20 are problems in subtraction. For each question do the subtraction and select your answer from the four choices given.

12. 232,921.85
    -179,587.68

    A. 52,433.17   B. 52,434.17
    C. 53,334.17   D. 53,343,17

13. 5,531,876.29
    -3,897,158.36

    A. 1,634,717.93   B. 1,644,718.93
    C. 1,734,717.93   D. 1,7234,718.93

14. 1,482,658.22
    -937,925.76

    A. 544,633.46   B. 544,732.46
    C. 545,632.46   D. 545,732.46

15. 937,828.17
    -259,673.88

    A. 678,154.29   B. 679,154.29
    C. 688,155.39   D. 699,155.39

16. 760,412.38
    -263,465.95

    A. 496,046.43   B. 496,946.43
    C. 496,956.43   D. 497,046.43

17. 3,203,902.26
    -2,933,087.96

    A. 260,814.30   B. 269,824.30
    C. 270,814.30   D. 270,824.30

18. 1,023,468.71
    -934,678.88

    A. 88,780.83   B. 88,789.83
    C. 88,880.83   D. 88,889.83

19. 831,549.47
    -772,814.78

    A. 58,734.69
    B. 58,834.69
    C. 59,735.69
    D. 59,834.69

20. 6,306,181.74
    -3,617,376.99

    A. 2,687,904.99
    B. 2,688,904.99
    C. 2,689,804.99
    D. 2,799,905.99

Questions 21-30.

DIRECTIONS: Each of Questions 21 through 30 consists of three lines of code letters and three lines of numbers. The numbers on each line should correspond with the code letters on the same line in accordance with the table below.

Code Letter	J	U	B	T	Y	D	K	R	L	P
Corresponding Number	0	1	2	3	4	5	5	7	8	9

On some of the lines, an error exists in the coding. Compare the letters and numbers in each question carefully. If you find an error or errors on:
only *one* of the lines in the question, mark your answer A;
any *two* lines in the question, mark your answer B;
all *three* lines in the question, mark your answer C;
none of the lines in the question, mark your answer D.

SAMPLE QUESTION

BJRPYUR   2079417
DTBPYKJ   5328460
YKLDBLT   4685283

In the above sample, the first line is correct since each code letter listed has the correct corresponding number. On the second line, an error exists because code letter P should have the number 9 instead of the number 8. The third line is correct since each code letter listed has the correct corresponding number. Since there is an error in *one* of the three lines, the correct answer is A. Now answer Questions 21 through 30 in the same manner.

21. BYPDTJL   2495308
    PLRDTJU   9815301
    DTJRYLK   5207486

22. RPBYRJK   7934706
    PKTYLBU   9624821
    KDLPJYR   6489047

23.	TPYBUJR	3942107	23.____
	BYRKPTU	2476931	
	DUKPYDL	5169458	
24.	KBYDLPL	6345898	24.____
	BLRKBRU	2876261	
	JTULDYB	0318542	
25.	LDPYDKR	8594567	25.____
	BDKDRJL	2565708	
	BDRPLUJ	2679810	
26.	PLRLBPU	9858291	26.____
	LPYKRDJ	88936750	
	TDKPDTR	3569527	
27.	RKURPBY	7617924	27.____
	RYUKPTJ	7426930	
	RTKPTJD	7369305	
28.	DYKPBJT	5469203	28.____
	KLPJBTL	6890238	
	TKPLBJP	3698209	
29.	BTPRJYL	2397148	29.____
	LDKUTYR	8561347	
	YDBLRPJ	4528190	
30.	ULPBKYT	1892643	30.____
	KPDTRBJ	6953720	
	YLKJPTB	4860932	

KEY (CORRECT ANSWERS)

1.	A	11.	D	21.	B
2.	C	12.	C	22.	C
3.	A	13.	A	23.	D
4.	D	14.	B	24.	B
5.	C	15.	A	25.	A
6.	C	16.	B	26.	C
7.	C	17.	C	27.	A
8.	D	18.	B	28.	D
9.	A	19.	A	29.	B
10.	B	20.	B	30.	D

CLERICAL ABILITIES
EXAMINATION SECTION
TEST 1

DIRECTIONS: Each question or incomplete statement is followed by several suggested answers or completions. Select the one that BEST answers the question or completes the statement. *PRINT THE LETTER OF THE CORRECT ANSWER IN THE SPACE AT THE RIGHT.*

Questions 1-4.

DIRECTIONS: Questions 1 through 4 are to be answered on the basis of the information given below.

The most commonly used filing system and the one that is easiest to learn is alphabetical filing. This involves putting records in an A to Z order, according to the letters of the alphabet. The name of a person is filed by using the following order: first, the surname or last name; second, the first name; third, the middle name or middle initial. For example, *Henry C. Young* is filed under *Y* and thereafter under *Young, Henry C.* The name of a company is filed in the same way. For example, *Long Cabinet Co.* is filed under *L* while *John T. Long Cabinet Co.* is filed under *L* and thereafter under *Long, John T. Cabinet Co.*

1. The one of the following which lists the names of persons in the CORRECT alphabetical order is:
   A. Mary Carrie, Helen Carrol, James Carson, John Carter
   B. James Carson, Mary Carrie, John Carter, Helen Carrol
   C. Helen Carrol, James Carson, John Carter, Mary Carrie
   D. John Carter, Helen Carrol, Mary Carrie, James Carson

1.____

2. The one of the following which lists the names of persons in the CORRECT alphabetical order is:
   A. Jones, John C.; Jones, John A.; Jones, John P.; Jones, John K.
   B. Jones, John P.; Jones, John K.; Jones, John C.; Jones, John A.
   C. Jones, John A.; Jones, John C.; Jones, John K.; Jones, John P.
   D. Jones, John K.; Jones, John C.; Jones, John A.; Jones, John P.

2.____

3. The one of the following which lists the names of the companies in the CORRECT alphabetical order is:
   A. Blane Co., Blake Co., Block Co., Blear Co.
   B. Blake Co., Blane Co., Blear Co., Block Co.
   C. Block Co., Blear Co., Blane Co., Blake Co.
   D. Blear Co., Blake Co., Blane Co., Block Co.

3.____

4. You are to return to the file an index card on *Barry C. Wayne Materials and Supplies Co.*
Of the following, the CORRECT alphabetical group that you should return the index card to is
   A. A to G   B. H to M   C. N to S   D. T to Z

Questions 5-10.

DIRECTIONS: In each of Questions 5 through 10, the names of four people are given. For each question, choose as your answer the one of the four names given which should be filed FIRST according to the usual system of alphabetical filing of names, as described in the following paragraph.

In filing names, you must start with the last name. Names are filed in order of the first letter of the last name, then the second letter, etc. Therefore, BAILY would be filed before BROWN, which would be filed before COLT. A name with fewer letters of the same type comes first, i.e., Smith before Smithe. If the last names are the same, the names are filed alphabetically by the first name. If the first name is an initial, a name with an initial would come before a first name that starts with the same letter as the initial. Therefore, I. BROWN would come before IRA BROWN. Finally, if both last name and first name are the same, the name would be filed alphabetically by the middle name, once again an initial coming before a middle name which starts with the same letter as the initial. If there is no middle name at all, the name would come before those with middle initials or names.

SAMPLE QUESTION:
A. Lester Daniels
B. William Dancer
C. Nathan Danzig
D. Dan Lester

The last names beginning with D are filed before the last name beginning with L. Since DANIELS, DANCER, and DANZIG all begin with the same three letters, you must look at the fourth letter of the last name to determine which name should be filed first. C comes before I or Z in the alphabet, so DANCER is filed before DANIELS or DANZIG. Therefore, the answer to the above sample question is B.

5. A. Scott Biala
    B. Mary Byala
    C. Martin Baylor
    D. Francis Bauer

6. A. Howard J. Black
    B. Howard Black
    C. J. Howard Black
    D. John H. Black

7. A. Theodora Garth Kingston
    B. Theadore Barth Kingston
    C. Thomas Kingston
    D. Thomas T. Kingston

8. A. Paulette Mary Huerta
    B. Paul M. Huerta
    C. Paulette L. Huerta
    D. Peter A. Huerta

9. A. Martha Hunt Morgan
    B. Martin Hunt Morgan
    C. Mary H. Morgan
    D. Martine H. Morgan

10. A. James T. Meerschaum
    B. James M. Mershum
    C. James F. Mearshaum
    D. James N. Meshum

Questions 11-14.

DIRECTIONS: Questions 11 through 14 are to be answered SOLELY on the basis of the following information.

You are required to file various documents in file drawers which are labeled according to the following pattern:

DOCUMENTS

MEMOS		LETTERS	
File	Subject	File	Subject
84PM1	(A-L)	84PC1	(A-L)
84PM2	(M-Z)	84PC2	(M-Z)

REPORTS		INQUIRIES	
File	Subject	File	Subject
84PR1	(A-L)	84PQ1	(A-L)
84PR2	(M-Z)	84PQ2	(M-Z)

11. A letter dealing with a burglary should be filed in the drawer labeled
    A. 84PM1   B. 84PC1   C. 84PR1   D. 84PQ2

12. A report on Statistics should be found in the drawer labeled
    A. 84PM1   B. 84PC2   C. 84PR2   D. 84PQS

13. An inquiry is received about parade permit procedures. It should be filed in the drawer labeled
    A. 84PM2   B. 84PC1   C. 84PR1   D. 84PQ2

14. A police officer has a question about a robbery report you filed. You should pull this file from the drawer labeled
    A. 84PM1   B. 84PM2   C. 84PR1   D. 84PR2

Questions 15-22.

DIRECTIONS: Each of Questions 15 through 22 consists of four or six numbered names. For each question, choose the option (A, B, C, or D) which indicates the order in which the names should be filed in accordance with the following filing instructions:
- File alphabetically according to last name, then first name, then middle initial.
- File according to each successive letter within a name.
- When comparing two names in which the letters in the longer name are identical to the corresponding letters in the shorter name, the shorter name is filed first.
- When the last names are the same, initials are always filed before names beginning with the same letter.

15. I. Ralph Robinson
     II. Alfred Ross
     III. Luis Robles
     IV. James Roberts

   The CORRECT filing sequence for the above names should be
     A. IV, II, I, III   B. I, IV, III, II   C. III, IV, I, II   D. IV, I, III, II

16. I. Irwin Goodwin
     II. Inez Gonzalez
     III. Irene Goodman
     IV. Ira S. Goodwin
     V. Ruth I. Goldstein
     VI. M.B. Goodman

   The CORRECT filing sequence for the above names should be
     A. V, II, I, IV, III, VI   B. V, II, VI, III, IV, I
     C. V, II, III, VI, IV, I   D. V, II, III, VI, I, IV

17. I. George Allan
     II. Gregory Allen
     III. Gary Allen
     IV. George Allen

   The CORRECT filing sequence for the above names should be
     A. IV, III, I, II   B. I, IV, II, III   C. III, IV, I, II   D. I, III, IV, II

18.
    I. Simon Kauffman
    II. Leo Kaufman
    III. Robert Kaufmann
    IV. Paul Kauffmann

    The CORRECT filing sequence for the above names should be
    A. I, IV, II, III   B. II, IV, III, I   C. III, II, IV, I   D. I, II, III, IV

    18.____

19.
    I. Roberta Williams
    II. Robin Wilson
    III. Roberta Wilson
    IV. Robin Williams

    The CORRECT filing sequence for the above names should be
    A. III, II, IV, I   B. I, IV, III, II   C. I, II, III, IV   D. III, I, II, IV

    19.____

20.
    I. Lawrence Shultz
    II. Albert Schultz
    III. Theodore Schwartz
    IV. Thomas Schwarz
    V. Alvin Schultz
    VI. Leonard Shultz

    The CORRECT filing sequence for the above names should be
    A. II, V, III, IV, I, VI
    B. IV, III, V, I, II, VI
    C. II, V, I, VI, III, IV
    D. I, VI, II, V, III, IV

    20.____

21.
    I. McArdle
    II. Mayer
    III. Maletz
    IV. McNiff
    V. Meyer
    VI. MacMahon

    The CORRECT filing sequence for the above names should be
    A. I, IV, VI, III, II, V
    B. II, I, IV, VI, III, V
    C. VI, III, II, I, IV, V
    D. VI, III, II, V, I, IV

    21.____

22.
    I. Jack E. Johnson
    II. R.H. Jackson
    III. Bertha Jackson
    IV. J.T. Johnson
    V. Ann Johns
    VI. John Jacobs

    The CORRECT filing sequence for the above names should be
    A. II, III, VI, V, IV, I
    B. III, II, VI, V, IV, I
    C. VI, II, III, I, V, IV
    D. III, II, VI, IV, V, I

    22.____

Questions 23-30.

DIRECTIONS: The code table below shows 10 letters with matching numbers. For each question, there are three sets of letters. Each set of letters is followed by a set of numbers which may or may not match their correct letter according to the code table. For each question, check all three sets of letters and numbers and mark your answer:
    A. if no pairs are correctly matched
    B. if only one pair is correctly matched
    C. if only two pairs are correctly matched
    D. if all three pairs are correctly matched

CODE TABLE

T	M	V	D	S	P	R	G	B	H
1	2	3	4	5	6	7	8	9	0

SAMPLE QUESTION: TMVDSP – 123456
                                RGBHTM – 789011
                                DSPRGB – 256789

In the sample question above, the first set of numbers correctly match its set of letters. But the second and third pairs contain mistakes. In the second pair, M is correctly matched with number 1. According to the code table, letter M should be correctly matched with number 2. In the third pair, the letter D is incorrectly matched with number 2. According to the code table, letter D should be correctly matched with number 4. Since only one of the pairs is correctly matched, the answer to this sample question is B.

23.   RSBMRM – 759262
       GDSRVH – 845730
       VDBRTM - 349713

24.   TGVSDR – 183247
       SMHRDP – 520647
       TRMHSR - 172057

25.   DSPRGM – 456782
       MVDBHT – 234902
       HPMDBT - 062491

26.   BVPTRD – 936184
       GDPHMB – 807029
       GMRHMV - 827032

27.   MGVRSH – 283750
       TRDMBS – 174295
       SPRMGV - 567283

23.____

24.____

25.____

26.____

27.____

28. SGBSDM – 489542
    MGHPTM – 290612
    MPBMHT - 269301

29. TDPBHM – 146902
    VPBMRS – 369275
    GDMBHM - 842902

30. MVPTBV – 236194
    PDRTMB – 47128
    BGTMSM - 981232

28.____

29.____

30.____

KEY (CORRECT ANSWERS)

1.	A	11.	B	21.	C
2.	C	12.	C	22.	B
3.	B	13.	D	23.	B
4.	D	14.	D	24.	B
5.	D	15.	D	25.	C
6.	B	16.	C	26.	A
7.	B	17.	D	27.	D
8.	B	18.	A	28.	A
9.	A	19.	B	29.	D
10.	C	20.	A	30.	A

TEST 2

DIRECTIONS: Each question or incomplete statement is followed by several suggested answers or completions. Select the one that BEST answers the question or completes the statement. *PRINT THE LETTER OF THE CORRECT ANSWER IN THE SPACE AT THE RIGHT.*

Questions 1-10.

DIRECTIONS: Questions 1 through 10 each consists of two columns, each containing four lines of names, numbers and/or addresses. For each question, compare the lines in Column I with the lines in Column II to see if they match exactly, and mark your answer A, B, C, or D, according to the following instructions:
    A. all four lines match exactly
    B. only three lines match exactly
    C. only two lines match exactly
    D. only one line matches exactly

COLUMN I   COLUMN II

1. I. Earl Hodgson   Earl Hodgson
    II. 1409870   1408970
    III. Shore Ave.   Schore Ave.
    IV. Macon Rd.   Macon Rd.

2. I. 9671485   9671485
    II. 470 Astor Court   470 Astor Court
    III. Halprin, Phillip   Halperin, Phillip
    IV. Frank D. Poliseo   Frank D. Poliseo

3. I. Tandem Associates   Tandom Associates
    II. 144-17 Northern Blvd.   144-17 Northern Blvd.
    III. Alberta Forchi   Albert Forchi
    IV. Kings Park, NY 10751   Kings Point, NY 10751

4. I. Bertha C. McCormack   Bertha C. McCormack
    II. Clayton, MO   Clayton, MO
    III. 976-4242   976-4242
    IV. New City, NY 10951   New City, NY 10951

5. I. George C. Morill   George C. Morrill
    II. Columbia, SC 29201   Columbia, SD 29201
    III. Louis Ingham   Louis Ingham
    IV. 3406 Forest Ave.   3406 Forest Ave.

6. I. 506 S. Elliott Pl.   506 S. Elliott Pl.
    II. Herbert Hall   Hurbert Hall
    III. 4712 Rockaway Pkway   4712 Rockaway Pkway
    IV. 169 E. 7 St.   169 E. 7 St.

7. I. 345 Park Ave.   345 Park Pl.
    II. Colman Oven Corp.   Coleman Oven Corp.
    III. Robert Conte   Robert Conti
    IV. 6179846   6179846

7._____

8. I. Grigori Schierber   Grigori Schierber
    II. Des Moines, Iowa   Des Moines, Iowa
    III. Gouverneur Hospital Gouverneur Hospital
    IV. 91-35 Cresskill Pl.   91-35 Cresskill Pl.

8._____

9. I. Jeffery Janssen   Jeffrey Janssen
    II. 8041071   8041071
    III. 40 Rockefeller Plaza 40 Rockafeller Plaza
    IV. 407 6 St.   406 7 St.

9._____

10. I. 5971996   5871996
    II. 3113 Knickerbocker Ave. 31123 Knickerbocker Ave.
    III. 8434 Boston Post Rd. 8424 Boston Post Rd.
    IV. Penn Station   Penn Station

10._____

Questions 11-14.

DIRECTIONS: Questions 11 through 14 are to be answered by looking at the four groups of names and addresses listed below (I, II, III, and IV), and then finding out the number of groups that have their corresponding numbered lies exactly the same.

	GROUP I	GROUP II
Line 1.	Richmond General Hospital	Richman General Hospital
Line 2.	Geriatric Clinic	Geriatric Clinic
Line 3.	3975 Paerdegat St.	3975 Peardegat St.
Line 4.	Loudonville, New York 11538	Londonville, New York 11538

	GROUP III	GROUP IV
Line 1.	Richmond General Hospital	Richmend General Hospital
Line 2.	Geriatric Clinic	Geriatric Clinic
Line 3.	3795 Paerdegat St.	3975 Paerdegat St.
Line 4.	Loudonville, New York 11358	Loudonville, New York 11538

1. In how many groups is line one exactly the same?
    A. Two   B. Three   C. Four   D. None

11._____

12. In how many groups is line two exactly the same?
    A. Two   B. Three   C. Four   D. None

12._____

13. In how many groups is line three exactly the same?
    A. Two   B. Three   C. Four   D. None

13._____

14. In how many groups is line four exactly the same? 14._____
    A. Two   B. Three   C. Four   D. None

Questions 15-18.

DIRECTIONS: Each of Questions 15 through 18 has two lists of names and addresses. Each list contains three sets of names and addresses. Check each of the three sets in the list on the right to see if they are the same as the corresponding set in the list on the left. Mark your answers:
   A. if none of the sets in the right list are the same as those in the left list
   B. if only one of the sets in the right list is the same as those in the left list
   C. if only two of the sets in the right list are the same as those in the left list
   D. if all three sets in the right list are the same as those in the left list

15. Mary T. Berlinger   Mary T. Berlinger   15._____
    2351 Hampton St.   2351 Hampton St.
    Monsey, N.Y. 20117   Monsey, N.Y. 20117

    Eduardo Benes   Eduardo Benes
    483 Kingston Avenue   473 Kingston Avenue
    Central Islip, N.Y. 11734   Central Islip, N.Y. 11734

    Alan Carrington Fuchs   Alan Carrington Fuchs
    17 Gnarled Hollow Road   17 Gnarled Hollow Road
    Los Angeles, CA 91635   Los Angeles, CA 91685

16. David John Jacobson   David John Jacobson   16._____
    178 34 St. Apt. 4C   178 53 St. Apt. 4C
    New York, N.Y. 00927   New York, N.Y. 00927

    Ann-Marie Calonella   Ann-Marie Calonella
    7243 South Ridge Blvd.   7243 South Ridge Blvd.
    Bakersfield, CA 96714   Bakersfield, CA 96714

    Pauline M. Thompson   Pauline M. Thomson
    872 Linden Ave.   872 Linden Ave.
    Houston, Texas 70321   Houston, Texas 70321

17. Chester LeRoy Masterton   Chester LeRoy Masterson   17._____
    152 Lacy Rd.   152 Lacy Rd.
    Kankakee, Ill. 54532   Kankakee, Ill. 54532

    William Maloney   William Maloney
    S. LaCrosse Pla.   S. LaCross Pla.
    Wausau, Wisconsin 52136   Wausau, Wisconsin 52146

    Cynthia V. Barnes   Cynthia V. Barnes
    16 Pines Rd.   16 Pines Rd.
    Greenpoint, Miss. 20376   Greenpoint,, Miss. 20376

4 (#2)

18. Marcel Jean Frontenac
     8 Burton On The Water
     Calender, Me. 01471

     J. Scott Marsden
     174 S. Tipton St.
     Cleveland, Ohio

     Lawrence T. Haney
     171 McDonough St.
     Decatur, Ga. 31304

Marcel Jean Frontenac
6 Burton On The Water
Calender, Me. 01471

J. Scott Marsden
174 Tipton St.
Cleveland, Ohio

Lawrence T. Haney
171 McDonough St.
Decatur, Ga. 31304

18.____

Questions 19-26.

DIRECTIONS: Each of Questions 19 through 26 has two lists of numbers. Each list contains three sets of numbers. Check each of the three sets in the list on the right to see if they are the same as the corresponding set in the list on the left. Mark your answers:
  A. if none of the sets in the right list are the same as those in the left list
  B. if only one of the sets in the right list is the same as those in the left list
  C. if only two of the sets in the right list are the same as those in the left list
  D. if all three sets in the right list are the same as those in the left lists

19. 7354183476
     4474747744
     5791430231

7354983476
4474747774
57914302311

19.____

20. 7143592185
     8344517699
     9178531263

7143892185
8344518699
9178531263

20.____

21. 2572114731
     8806835476
     8255831246

257214731
8806835476
8255831246

21.____

22. 331476853821
     6976658532996
     3766042113715

331476858621
6976655832996
3766042113745

22.____

23. 8806663315
     74477138449
     211756663666

88066633115
74477138449
211756663666

23.____

155

24. 990006966996   99000696996   24._____
     53022219743   53022219843
     4171171117717   4171171177717

25. 24400222433004   24400222433004   25._____
     5300030055000355   5300030055500355
     20000075532002022   20000075532002022

26. 6111666406600011 16 61116664066001116 26._____
     7111300117001100733 7111300117001100733
     26666446664476518   26666446664476518

Questions 27-30.

DIRECTIONS: Questions 27 through 30 are to be answered by picking the answer which is in the correct numerical order, from the lowest number to the highest number, in each question.

27. A. 44533, 44518, 44516, 44547   27._____
     B. 44516, 44518, 44533, 44547
     C. 44547, 44533, 44518, 44516
     D. 44518, 44516, 44547, 44533

28. A. 95587, 95593, 95601, 95620   28._____
     B. 95601, 95620, 95587, 95593
     C. 95593, 95587, 95601. 95620
     D. 95620, 95601, 95593, 95587

29. A. 232212, 232208, 232232, 232223   29._____
     B. 232208, 232223, 232212, 232232
     C. 232208, 232212, 232223, 232232
     D. 232223, 232232, 232208, 232208

30. A. 113419, 113521, 113462, 113462   30._____
     B. 113588, 113462, 113521, 113419
     C. 113521, 113588, 113419, 113462
     D. 113419, 113462, 113521, 113588

KEY (CORRECT ANSWERS)

1.	C	11.	A	21.	C
2.	B	12.	C	22.	A
3.	D	13.	A	23.	D
4.	A	14.	A	24.	A
5.	C	15.	C	25.	C
6.	B	16.	B	26.	C
7.	D	17.	B	27.	B
8.	A	18.	B	28.	A
9.	D	19.	B	29.	C
10.	C	20.	B	30.	D

MECHANICAL APTITUDE EXAMINATION SECTION
TEST 1

MECHANICAL COMPREHENSION

DIRECTIONS: Questions 1 through 4 test your ability to understand general mechanical devices. Pictures are shown and questions asked about the mechanical devices shown in the picture. Read each question and study the picture. Each question is followed by four choices. For each question, choose the one BEST answer (A, B, C, or D). Then, *PRINT THE LETTER OF THE CORRECT ANSWER IN THE SPACE AT THE RIGHT.*

1.

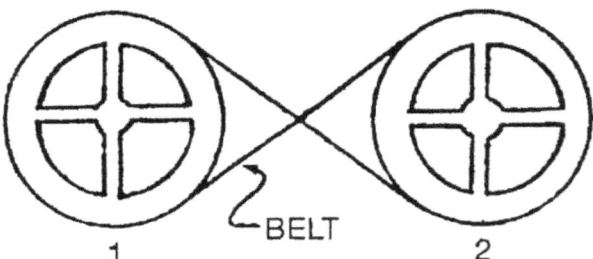

The reason for crossing the belt connecting these wheels is to
   A. make the wheels turn in opposite directions
   B. make wheel 2 turn faster than wheel 1
   C. save wear on the belt
   D. take up slack in the belt

1.____

2.

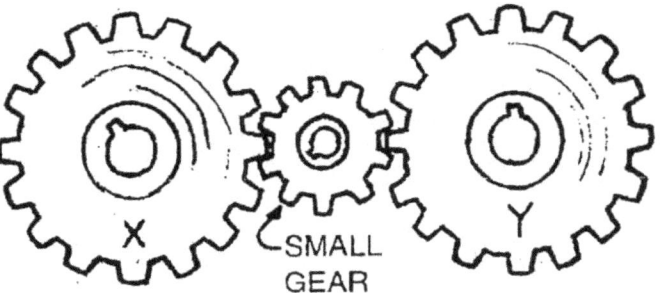

The purpose of the small gear between the two large gears is to
   A. increase the speed of the larger gears
   B. allow the larger gears to turn in different directions
   C. decrease the speed of the larger gears
   D. make the larger gears turn in the same direction

2.____

2 (#1)

3.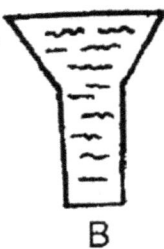

    A   B   C

Each of these three-foot-high water cans have a bottom with an area of one square foot.
The pressure on the bottom of the cans is
   A. least in A   B. least in B   C. least in C   D. the same in all

4.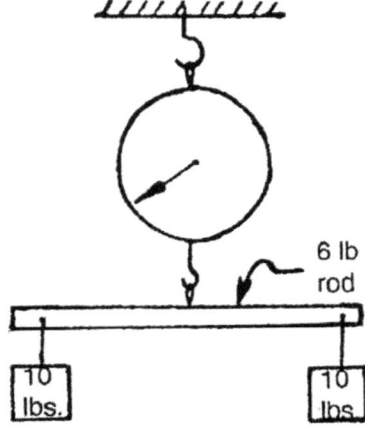

The reading on the scale should be
   A. zero   B. 10 pounds   C. 13 pounds   D. 26 pounds

KEY (CORRECT ANSWERS)

1. A
2. D
3. D
4. D

TEST 2

DIRECTIONS: Questions 1 through 6 test knowledge of tools and how to use them. For each question, decide which one of the four things shown in the boxes labeled A, B, C, or D normally is used with or goes best with the thing in the picture on the left. *PRINT THE LETTER OF THE CORRECT ANSWER IN THE SPACE AT THE RIGHT.*

NOTE: All tools are NOT drawn to the same scale.

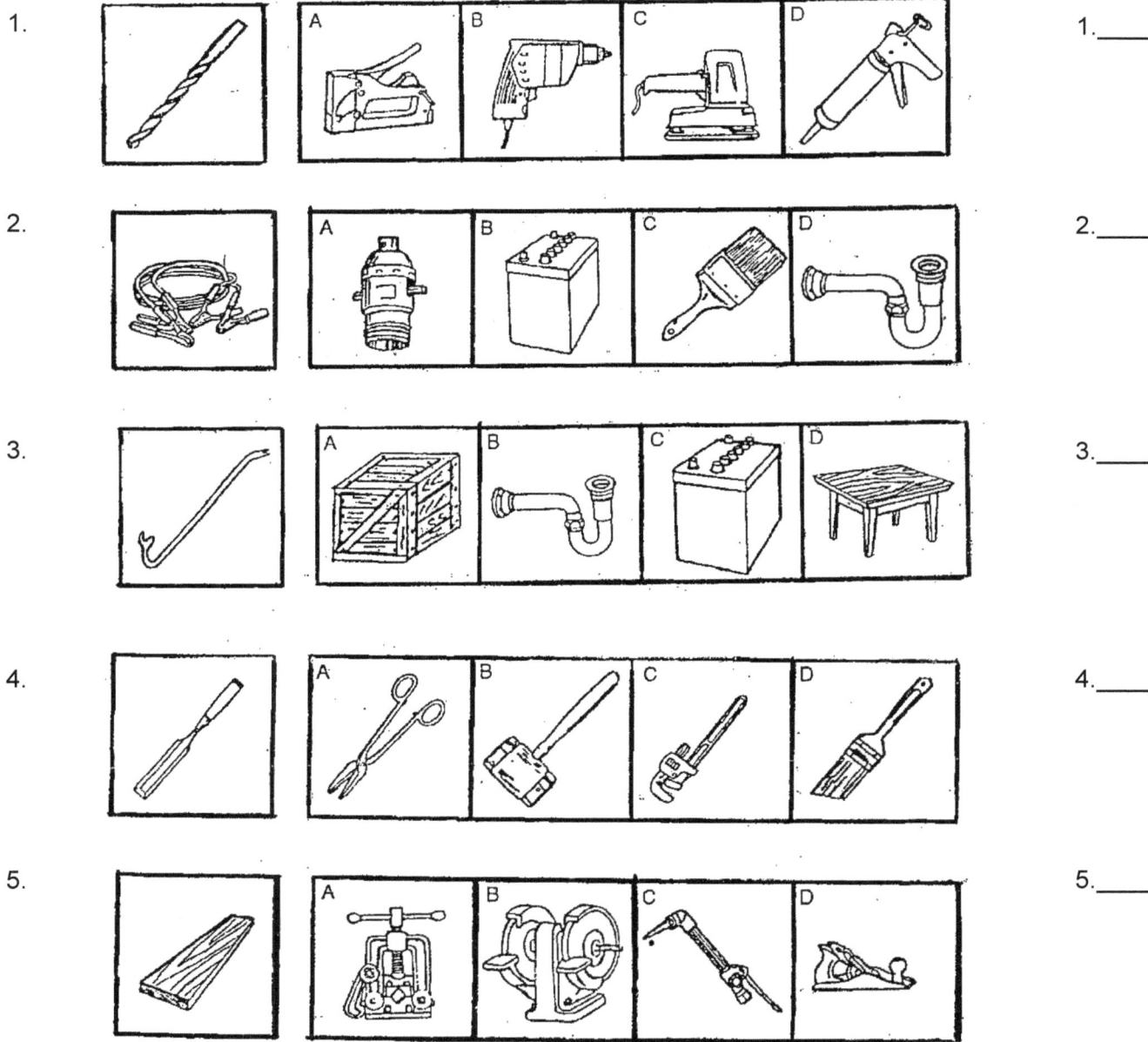

6. 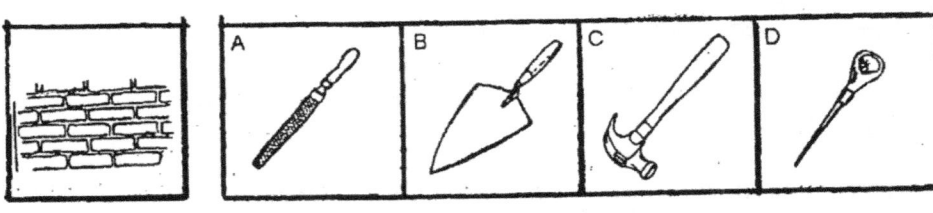   6._____

KEY (CORRECT ANSWERS)

1.	B	4.	B
2.	B	5.	D
3.	A	6.	B

MECHANICAL APTITUDE
EXAMINATION SECTION
TEST 1

DIRECTIONS: Questions 1 through 6 are questions designed to test your ability to distinguish identical forms from unlike forms. In each question, there are five drawings, lettered A, B, C, D, and E. Four of the drawings are alike. You are to find the one drawing that is different from the other four in the question *PRINT THE LETTER OF THE CORRECT ANSWER IN THE SPACE AT THE RIGHT.*

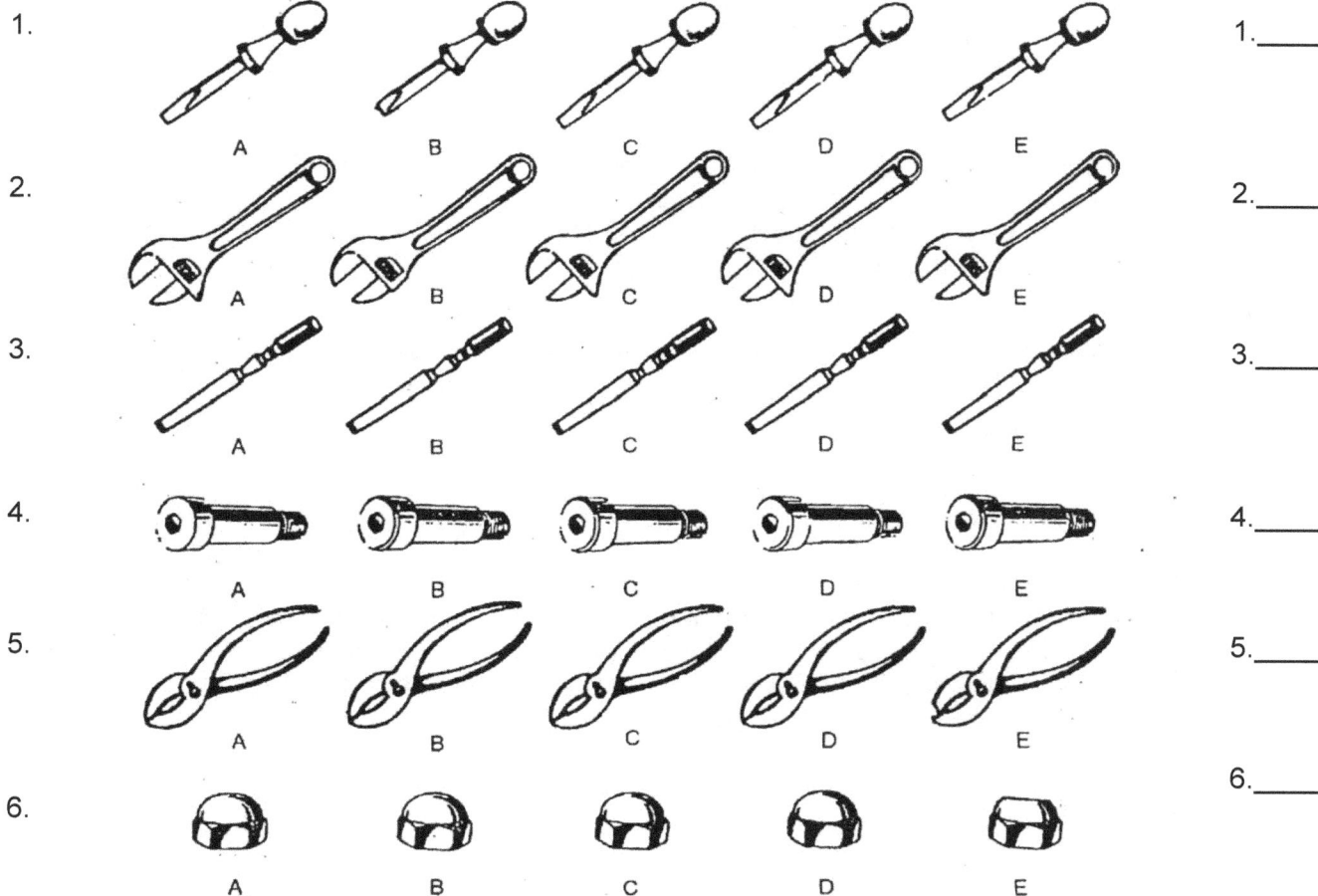

1._____
2._____
3._____
4._____
5._____
6._____

Questions 7-8.

DIRECTIONS: Questions 7 and 8 are questions designed to test your knowledge of pattern matching. Questions 7 and 8 present problems found in making patterns. Each shows, at the left side, two or more separate flat pieces. In each question, select the arrangement lettered A, B, C, or D that shows how these pieces may be turned around or turned over in any way to make them fit together

7.        7.____
                   A   B   C   D

From these pieces, which one of these arrangements can you make?

In Question 7, only the arrangement D can be made from the pieces shown at the left, so space choice D should be printed in the space at the right. (Note that it is necessary to turn the pieces around so that the short sides are at the bottom in the arrangement lettered D. None of the other arrangements show pieces of the given size and shape.)

8.  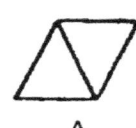  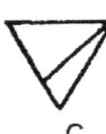    8.____
                   A   B   C   D

Questions 9-10.

DIRECTIONS: Questions 9 and 10 are questions designed to test your ability to identify forms of *Like* and *Unlike* proportions. In each of the questions, select from the drawings of objects labeled A, B, C, and D, the one that would have the TOP, Front, and Right views shown in the drawing at the left. Then, print the letter in the space at the right that has the same letter as your answer.

9. 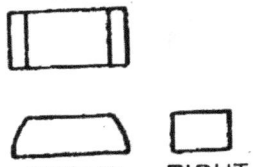   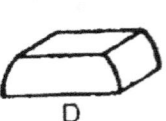   9.____

10. 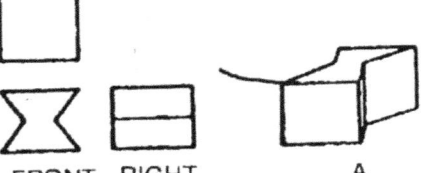  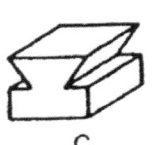 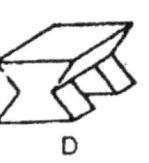   10.____

3 (#1)

Questions 11-14.

Explanation and Commentary:
In each question, ONE rectangle is clearly wrong. For each question, use the measuring gage to check each of the rectangles and to find the WRONG one. Do this by putting the measuring gage rectangle on the question rectangle with the same letter so that the rectangles slightly overlap and the thin lines are parallel, like the one at the right. In this case, the height of the question rectangle exactly matches the height of the measuring gage rectangle, so the question rectangle is the right height.

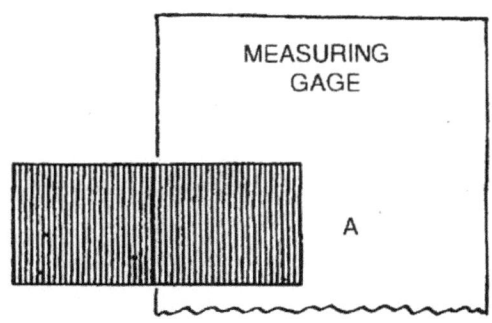

Once in every question when you put a measuring gage rectangle on a question rectangle, you will find that the heights do NOT match and that the question rectangle is clearly wrong, like the one at the right. In this case, you mark in the space at the right the same letter as the wrong rectangle. REMEMBER TO LINE UP THE MEASURING RECTANGLE WITH EACH QUESTION RECTANGLE SO THAT THE THIN LINES ARE EXACTLY PARALLEL.

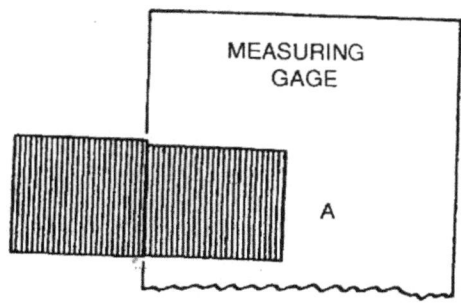

Now cut out the measuring gage on the last page and practice on the questions. The test will be limited, so practice doing them rapidly and accurately.

Questions 11 through 14 test how quickly and accurately you can check the heights of rectangles with a measuring gage. Each question has five rectangles of different heights. The height is the dimension that runs the same way as the thin lines.

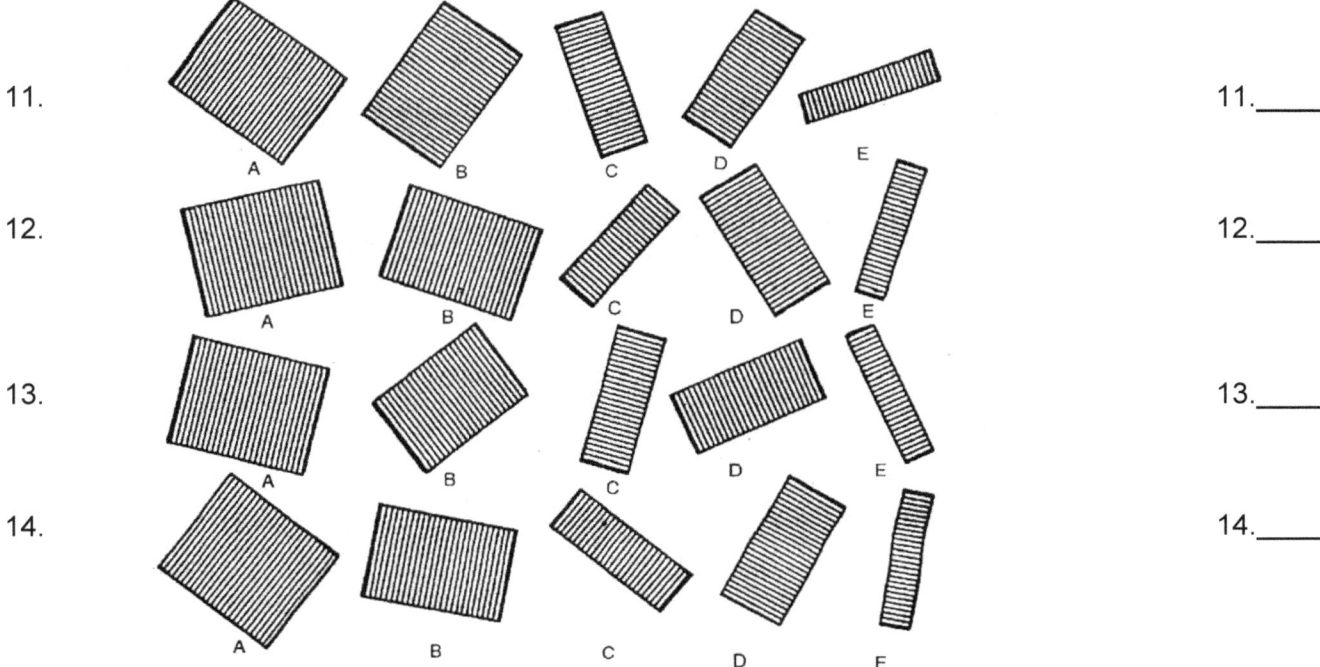

11. 11._____

12. 12._____

13. 13._____

14. 14._____

4 (#1)

MEASURING GAGE

 A

 B

 C

 D

 E

KEY (CORRECT ANSWERS)

1.	B	8.	B
2.	B	9.	D
3.	C	10.	B
4.	A	11.	D
5.	E	12.	C
6.	E	13.	B
7.	D	14.	A

EXAMINATION SECTION
TEST 1

DIRECTIONS: Each question or incomplete statement is accompanied by figures or diagrams with two suggested answers. Select A or B if one of them BEST answers the question or completes the statement. If the two figures have the same value, choose answer C. *PRINT THE LETTER OF THE CORRECT ANSWER IN THE SPACE AT THE RIGHT.*

1. With which windlass can a man raise the heavier weight? 1.____

2. Which of these solid blocks will be the harder to tip over? 2.____

3. Which rock will get hotter in the sun? 3.____

4. Which of these is the more likely picture of a train wreck? 4.____

5. 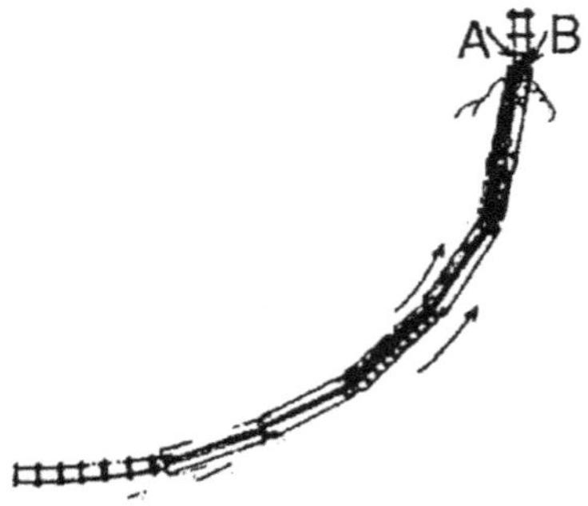 If the track is exactly level, on which rail does more pressure com?   5.____

6. 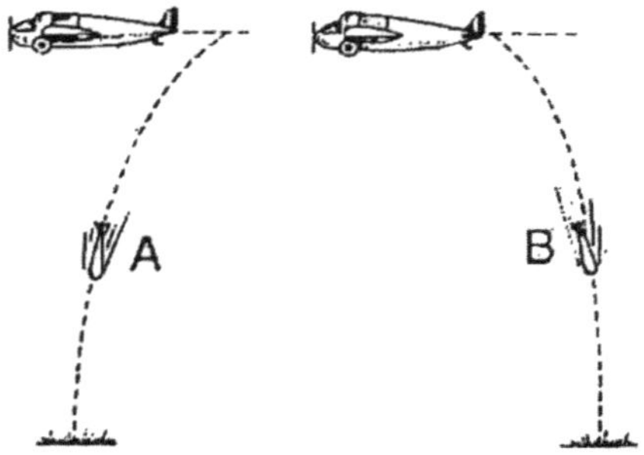 Which picture shows the way a bomb falls from a moving airplane if there is no wind?   6.____

7. 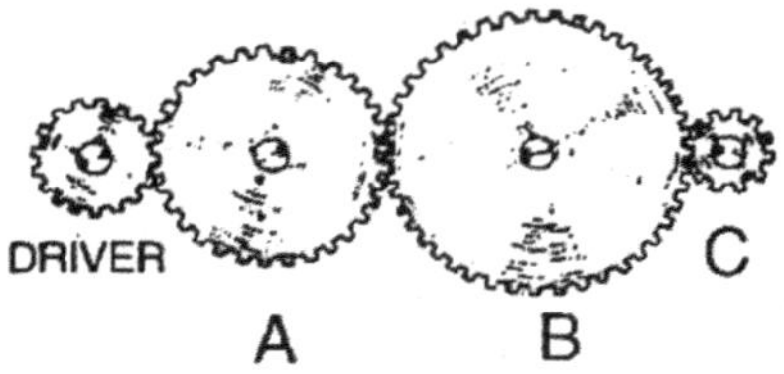 Indicate a gear which turn the same direction as the driver?   7.____

8.  If there are no clouds, on which night will you be able to see more stars?   8.____

3 (#1)

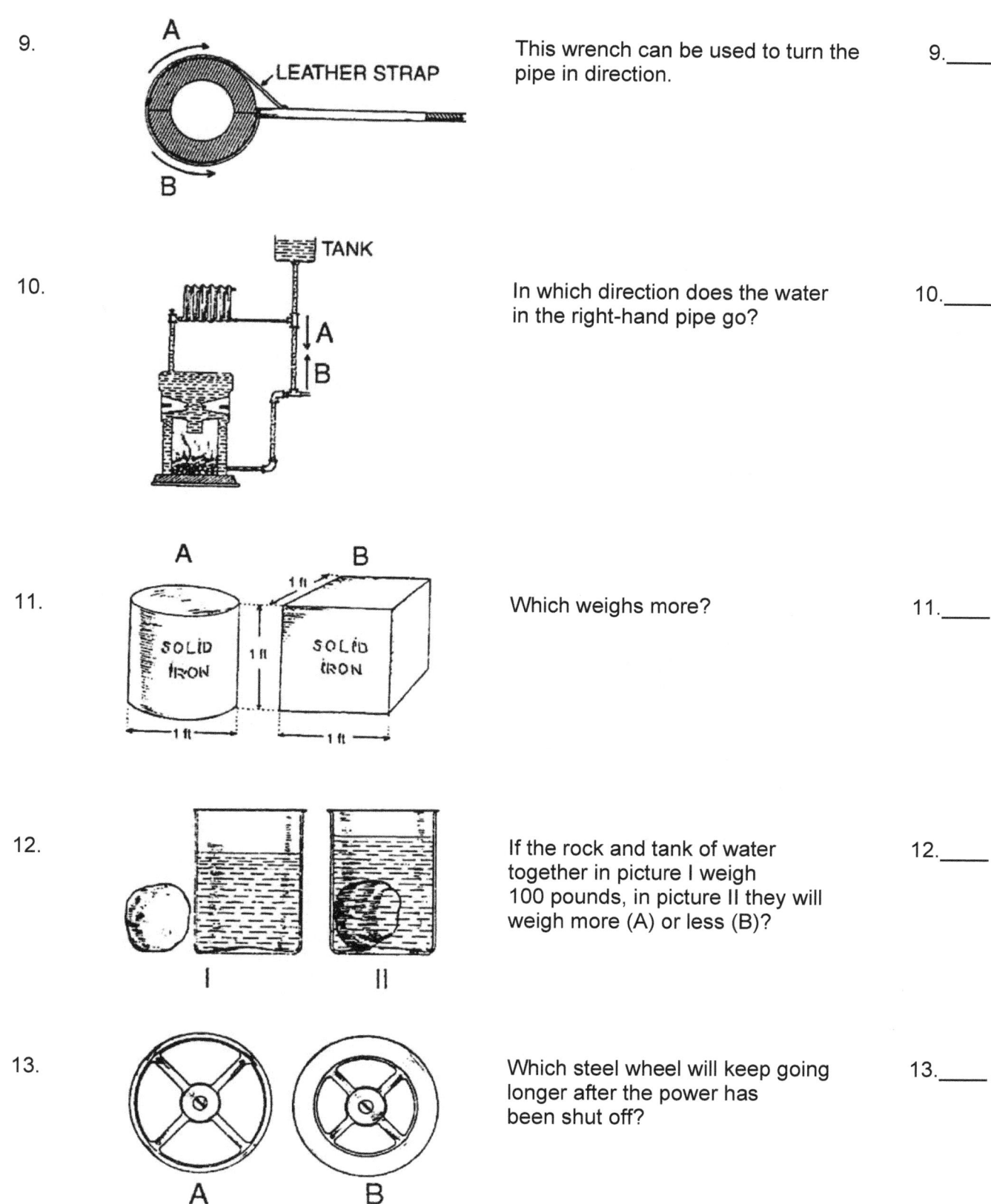

9. This wrench can be used to turn the pipe in direction. 9.____

10. In which direction does the water in the right-hand pipe go? 10.____

11. Which weighs more? 11.____

12. If the rock and tank of water together in picture I weigh 100 pounds, in picture II they will weigh more (A) or less (B)? 12.____

13. Which steel wheel will keep going longer after the power has been shut off? 13.____

14. 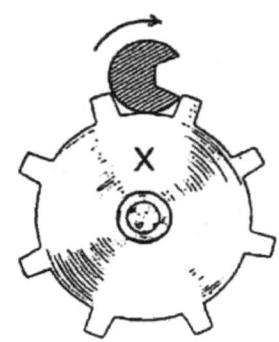 The top of the wheel X will go 14._____
    A. steadily to the right
    B. steadily to the left
    C. by jerks to the left

15. 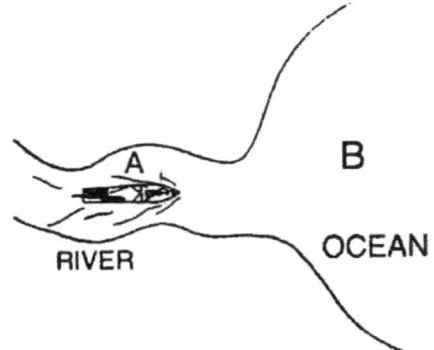 At which point will the boat be lower in the water? 15._____

16. 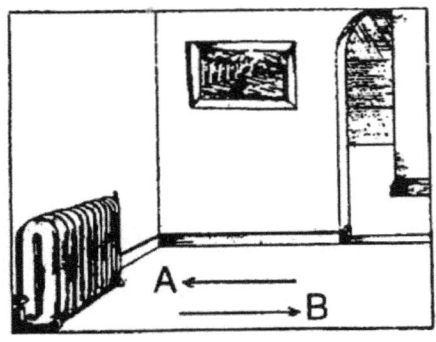 Which arrow shows the way the air will move along the floor when the radiator is turned on? 16._____

17. 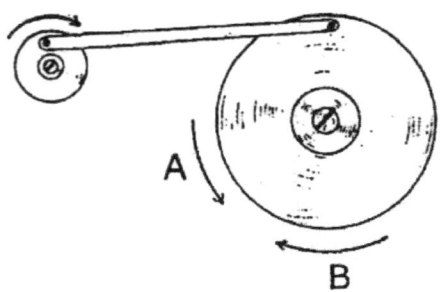 When the little wheel turns around, the big wheel will 17._____
    A. turn in direction A
    B. turn in direction B
    C. move back and forth

5 (#1)

18. [50 WATT BULB / 100 WATT BULB — A, B] Which boy gets more light on the pages of his book?   18.____

19. [Milk bottle A / Cream bottle B] Which weighs more?   19.____

20. [Wire coils A and B] Which of these wires offers more resistance to the passage of an electric current?   20.____

21. [Wheel with points A and B] Which spot on the wheel travels faster?   21.____

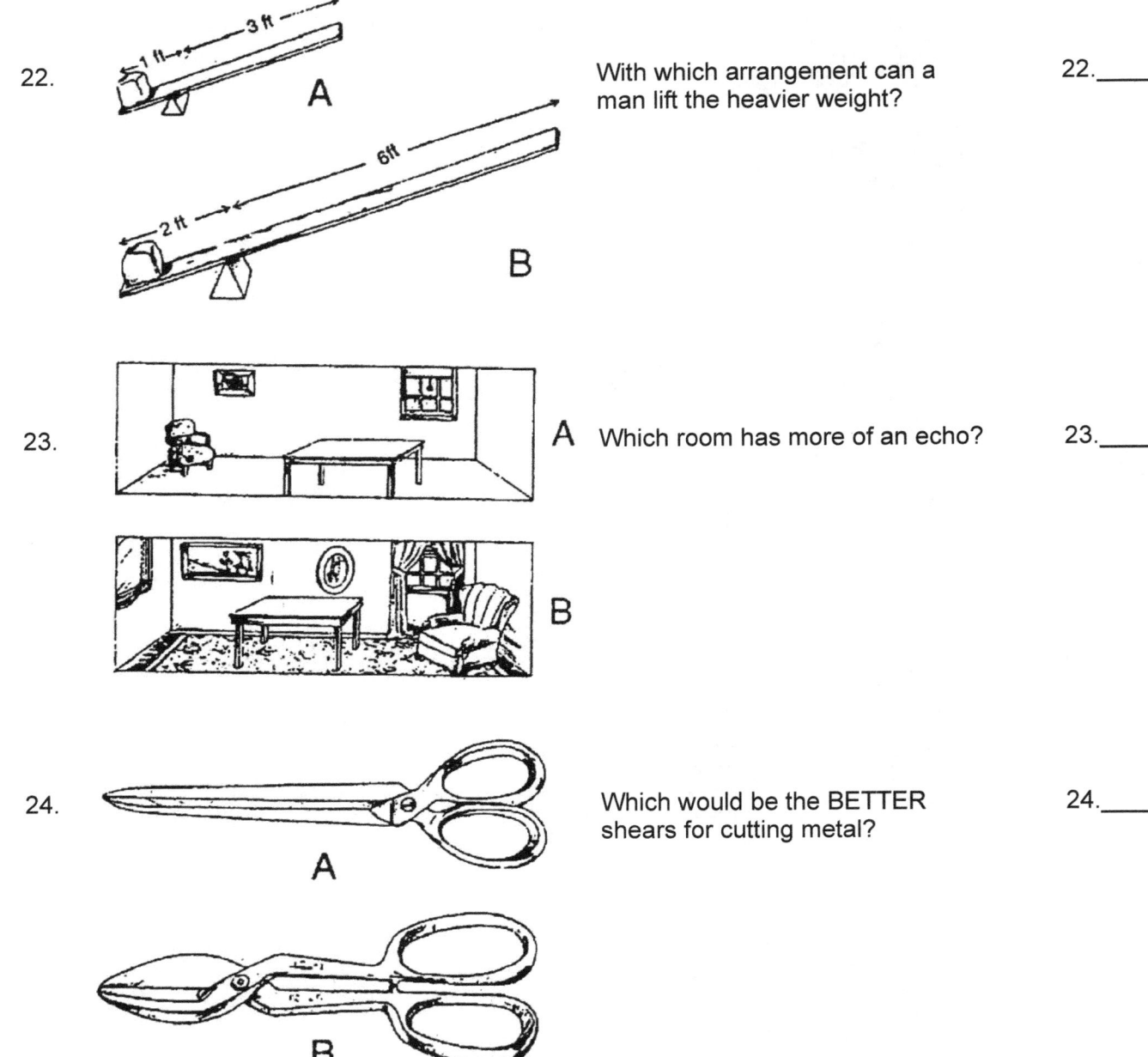

22. With which arrangement can a man lift the heavier weight? 22.____

23. Which room has more of an echo? 23.____

24. Which would be the BETTER shears for cutting metal? 24.____

KEY (CORRECT ANSWERS)

1.	A	11.	B
2.	A	12.	C
3.	A	13.	B
4.	A	14.	C
5.	B	15.	A
6.	A	16.	A
7.	B	17.	C
8.	B	18.	A
9.	A	19.	A
10.	A	20.	A

21. B
22. B
23. A
24. B

ARITHMETIC

EXAMINATION SECTION

TEST 1

DIRECTIONS: Each question or incomplete statement is followed by several suggested answers or completions. Select the one that BEST answers the question or completes the statement. *PRINT THE LETTER OF THE CORRECT ANSWER IN THE SPACE AT THE RIGHT.*

1. The result of a computation using only the numbers 8 and 7 is 15. In this computation, the number 15 is the
   A. product
   B. sum
   C. quotient
   D. difference
   E. average

   1.____

2. Which statement describes how to find the average of a group of scores?
   A. Find the sum of the scores and divide by 2.
   B. Find the sum of the scores and divide by the number of scores.
   C. Arrange the scores from lowest to highest and select the middle one.
   D. Take half the difference between the highest score and the lowest score.
   E. None of the above

   2.____

3. 6428
   974
   86
   7280
   763
   5407

   A. 19,838   B. 20,828   C. 20,838   D. 20,928   E. 20,938

   3.____

4. What is the inverse operation used to check division?
   A. Addition
   B. Subtraction
   C. Multiplication
   D. Division
   E. None of the above

   4.____

5. What is the ratio of 1 inch to 1 yard?
   A. 1   B. 3   C. 12   D. 24   E. 36

   5.____

6. Which of the following is NOT evenly divisible by 8?
   A. 6   B. 8   C. 40   D. 72   4. 104

   6.____

7. Each of the numerals listed below represents a number of feet. Which numeral MOST NEARLY represents the height of an average American man?
   A. .059   B. 0.59   C. 5.90   D. 59.0   E. 590

   7.____

Questions 8-9.

DIRECTIONS: Questions 8 and 9 are to be answered on the basis of the following line.

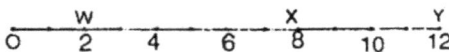

8. The point halfway between W and X would correspond to 8.____
   A. 4   B. 4 ½   C. 5   D. 5 ½   E. 6

9. What number would correspond to point P if it is placed on the number line 9.____
   so that P is between X and Y, and W is between P and X?
   A. 6   B. 7 ½
   C. 9   D. 10
   E. No such point can exist

10. What is the GREATEST common divisor of 24, 40, and 120? 10.____
    A. 2   B. 4   C. 8   D. 10   E. 12

11. Which of these is NOT equal to 4/9? 11.____
    A. 2/3   B. 20/45   C. 8/18   D. 16/36   E. 12/27

12. For which pair of the following operations are the rules for placing the 12.____
    decimal point in the answer the SAME?
    I. Addition   II. Subtraction
    III Multplication   IV. Division
    The CORRECT answer is:
    A. I and II
    B. I and III
    C. II and IV
    D. III and IV
    E. The rules are different for each operation

13. Three of four identical measuring containers  13.____
    are filled as shown at the right. All the
    liquid in the three containers is poured
    into the empty container on the right.
    What fractional part of this container
    will be filled?
    A. 1/10   B. 12/35   C. 7/10   D. 9/10   E. 1

14. 1/2 of 20 is the same as 1/4 of 14.____
    A. 5   B. 10   C. 40   D. 60   E. 80

15. What is the SMALLEST number which can be divided evenly by each of 15.____
    the following numbers: 4, 6, 8?
    A. 48   B. 32   C. 24   D. 16   E. 12

16. (2/3 ÷ 1/2) × $\frac{1}{2}$ =
    A. 1/6   B. 3/8   C. 2/3   D. 3/2   E. 8/3

17. A bank clerk reported that the number of $100 bills in the vault was 10,003. About how much money is this?
    A. $1,000,   B. $10,000   C. $100,000
    D. $1,000,000   E. $10,000,000

18. 3/40 is the same as
    A. .0075   B. .0133   C. .075   D. .1333   E. .75

19. 94/5
    +131 1/4

    A. 22 5/9   B. 22 9/20   C. 23   D. 23 1/20   E. 23 15

20.   36
    52)1872
    To make the answer in the above example four times as large as it is, you could change the number 1872 to
    A. 208   B. 468   C. 936   D. 3944   E. 7488

21. Which of these will produce an even whole number no matter what whole number is put in place of A?
    I.   2 × △ + 1   II. 2 × △ + 2   III. 2 × △ + 3
    The CORRECT answer is:
    A. I only   B. II only   C. III only
    D. I and II only   E. I and III only

22. Which of these shows the CORRECT meaning of 407?
    A. (4 × ten) + (7 × one)
    B. (4 × ten × ten) + (0 × ten) + (7 × one)
    C. (4+0+7) × (one hundred)
    D. (4 × one) + (0 × ten) + (7 × ten × ten)
    E. (4 × one) + (7 × ten)

23. If the scale length of 4 ½ inches represents an actual distance of 72 miles, how many miles does the scale length of 7 inches represent?
    A. 2   B. 56   C. 74 ½   D. 112   E. 504

24. 4 5 6 . 7 2 3 8
    ↑ ↑   ↑ ↑ ↑
    F G   H J K

    In the above numeral, which arrow points to the hundreds place?
    A. F   B. G   C. H   D. J   E. K

25. Which of these is between 5/6 and 7/8?
    A. 2/3   B. 3/4   C. 4/5   D. 6/7   E. 8/9

26. 340.292 ÷ 48.2 =
    A. 706   B. 76   C. 70.6   D. 7.6   E. 7.06

27. Jim started mowing the grass at 1:45 P.M. and finished at 2:15 P.M. How many minutes did Jim take to mow the grass?
    A. 30   B. 70   C. 90   D. 180   E. 240

28. To reduce a fraction to LOWEST terms, what should be done to both numerator and denominator?
    A. Each should be divided by 2.
    B. Each should be multiplied by 2.
    C. Each should be multiplied by the least common multiple.
    D. Each should be divided by the greatest common divisor.
    E. The same number should be subtracted from each.

29. $3 + \sqrt{64} =$
    A. 11   B. 19   C. 24   D. 35   E. $\sqrt{73}$

30. Between 8 A.M. and 3 P.M., the temperature rose 25°. The temperature at 8 A.M. was 10° below zero.
    At 3 P.M., the temperature was _____ zero.
    A. 26° above   B. 15° above   C. 5° above
    D. 5° below   E. 35° below

31. A boy saves 18 dollars in 8 weeks. He continues to save at the same rate. How many weeks will it take him to save 81 dollars?
    A. 13   B. 36   C. 40   D. 71   E. 181 ¼

32. One whole number is divided by another whole number. It is ALWAYS TRUE that the
    A. divisor is smaller than the quotient
    B. remainder is smaller than the divisor
    C. quotient is smaller than the divisor
    D. remainder is smaller than the quotient
    E. dividend is smaller than the remainder

33. Which of these will NEVER change the value of a number?
    I. Multiplying it by 1
    II. Dividing it by 1
    III. Multiplying it by its reciprocal
    The CORRECT answer is:
    A. I only   B. II only   C. III only
    D. I and II only   E. I and III only

34. Which of the following equals 7 × (3+9)?
    A. (7×3) + (7×9)   B. (7×9) + (3×9)
    C. (7×3) + (7×9)   D. 7 × 27
    E. 21 + 9

35.
```
        1
A ___2___ B
        3
C ___4_____ D
```

In the above figure $\frac{\text{length of AB}}{\text{length of CD}} =$

A. 1/2   B. 1/3   C. 2/3   D. 3/2   E. 5/3

36. Which series is NOT in descending order?
    A. 4.04, 4.004, 404   B. 2.1, 1.2, 2.12
    C. .06, .009, .10   D. 13.2, 12/3, 12.03
    E. 736, 631, 367

Questions 37-38.

DIRECTIONS: Questions 37 and 28 are to be answered on the basis of the following graph.

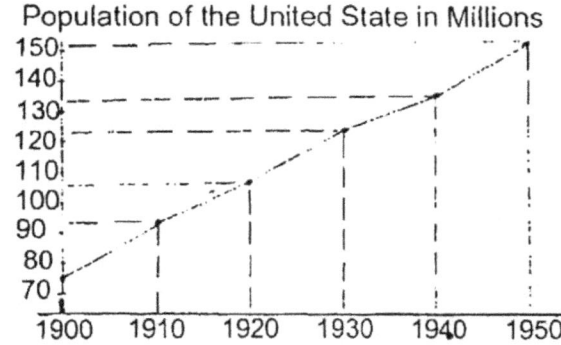

Population of the United State in Millions

37. According to the above graph, the population of the United States in 1935 was about
    A. 127,000   B. 1,270,000   C. 12,700,000
    D. 127,000,000   E. 1,270,000,000

38. What was the AVERAGE increase per year between 1900 and 1950?
    A. 1,500   B. 15,000   C. 150,000
    D. 750,000   E. 1,500,000

39. What is the radio of 2 gallons to 3 quarts?
    A. 8 to 3   B. 3 to 8   C. 3 to 2   D. 2 to 3   E. 1 to 6

40. What percent of the figure at the right is darkened?
    A. 12
    B. 25
    C. 48
    D. 50
    E. 52

41. A cutting edge .004 inch thick is four times as thick as a second cutting edge. How many inches thick is the second cutting edge?
    A. .001   B. .0032   C. .004   D. .016   E. .04

42. 20% in equal to the fraction $\frac{?}{30}$.
    A. 2/3   B. 6   C. 60   D. 150   E. 600

43. In the figure at the right, the two bars whose lengths have the ratio 2 to 2 are
    A. II and III
    B. IV and I
    C. IV and III
    D. I and III
    E. IV and II

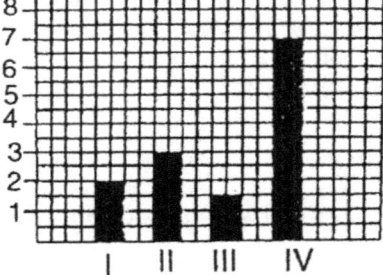

44. The advertisement for a sale reads: *All books reduced more than 20%.* If two books each have the same sale price, which statement MUST be TRUE? The
    A. original prices of both books were the same
    B. original prices of both books were different
    C. percent reduction for both books was the same
    D. sale price of each book is less than 80% of the original price
    E. sale price of each book is more than 80% of the original price.

45. Which of these multiplications will result in an odd number?
    I.   3 0 4 9   II.   7 0 0 2   III.   6 5 4 3   IV.   8 7 6 5
        × 6 4 3 1   × 3 4 8 5   × 3 4 5 6   × 3 4 9 7

    The CORRECT answer is:
    A. I and III only
    B. I and IV only
    C. II and IV only
    D. II, III, and IV only
    E. All of the above

46. A movie opened in a theatre on April 6 and was shown every day through   46.____
    April 27.
    On how many days was it shown?
    A. 20   B. 21   C. 22
    D. 23   E. None of the above

47. A student has an average of 80 for three tests.   47.____
    What must he score on the next test in order to obtain an average of 84?
    A. 80   B. 84   C. 88   D. 91   E. 96

48. Of 28 students in a class, 25 contributed to the Junior Red Cross and   48.____
    16 to the March of Dimes. Every member of the class contributed to AT LEAST
    one of the two organizations.
    The number who contributed to both is
    A. 3   B. 12   C. 14   D. 16   E. 25

49. On an arithmetic test, Bill got 32 as an answer to one problem. In working   49.____
    this problem, Bill's only mistake was multiplying by 4 in the last step when he
    should have divided by 4.
    What is the CORRECT answer to the problem?
    A. 2
    B. 4
    C. 8
    D. 28
    E. It cannot be determined from the information given.

50. Each of two whole numbers is greater than 1. Their product is an odd number.   50.____
    Then, their sum is a(n) _____ their product.
    A. odd number less than   B. even number less than
    C. odd number greater than   D. even number greater than
    E. number equal to

KEY (CORRECT ANSWERS)

1. B	11. A	21. B	31. B	41. A
2. B	12. A	22. B	32. B	42. B
3. E	13. D	23. D	33. D	43. A
4. C	14. C	24. A	34. A	44. D
5. E	15. C	25. D	35. C	45. B
6. A	16. C	26. E	36. C	46. C
7. C	17. D	27. A	37. D	47. E
8. C	18. C	28. D	38. E	48. C
9. E	19. D	29. A	39. A	49. A
10. C	20. E	30. B	40. E	50. B

SOLUTIONS TO PROBLEMS

1. 8 and 7 yield 15 by using sum, since 8 + 7 = 15.

2. To average out a group of numbers, add them and divide by the number of numbers. Ex..
The average of 3, 4, 8 = (3+4+8)/3 = 5.

3. 6428 + 974 + 86 + 7280 + 764 + 5407 = 20,938

4. The inverse of division is multiplication. Ex.: To check that 10 ÷ 2 = 5, we note that (5)(2) = 10.

5. 1 in. to 1 yd. = 1 in. to 36 in. = 1 to 36.

6. 6 is not evenly divisible by 8 since whole number.

7. 5.90 ft. = 5 ft. 10.8 in., which is a reasonable man's height.

8. (2+8) ÷ 2 = 5

9. If P is between X and Y, it corresponds to a point between 8 and 12. It would be impossible for W to be between P and X.

10. The greatest common divisor of 24, 40 and 120 is 8 since 24 ÷ 8, 40 ÷ 8, and 120 ÷ 8 all yield whole numbers. No number larger than 8 will divide evenly into each of 24, 40, and 120.

11. $\frac{2}{3} \neq \frac{4}{9}$ because $(2)(9) \neq (3)(4)$

12. For addition and subtraction, the rules for placing the decimal point in the answer are alike, namely, to line up the decimal point for each number.

13. $\frac{3}{10} + \frac{1}{5} + \frac{8}{20} = \frac{3}{10} + \frac{2}{10} + \frac{4}{10} = \frac{9}{10}$

14. Let x = missing number. Then, $(\frac{1}{2})(20) = \frac{1}{4}x$. $10 = \frac{1}{4}$, so x = 40

15. 24 is the smallest number which can divide evenly by 4, 6, and 8. This is called the least common multiple.

16. $(\frac{2}{3} \div \frac{1}{2}) \times \frac{1}{2} = \frac{4}{3} \times \frac{1}{2} = \frac{4}{6} = \frac{2}{3}$

10 (#1)

17. (10,003)($100) = $1000,300 ≈ $1,000,000

18. $\frac{3}{40} = .075$

19. $9\frac{4}{5} + 13\frac{1}{4} = 9\frac{16}{20} + 13\frac{5}{20} = 22\frac{21}{20} = 23\frac{1}{20}$

20. Using 7488, we get 7488 ÷ 52 = 244, which is 4 times as large as 36.

21. 2x + 2 must be even if x = any whole number. The other choices 2x +1 and 2x + 3 must be odd.

22. 407 = (4 × ten × ten) + (0 × ten) + (7×one).

23. Let x = actual miles. Then, $\frac{4\frac{1}{2}}{72} = \frac{7}{x}$, $4\frac{1}{2}x = 504$, x = 112

24. F points to 4, which is in the hundreds place.

25. lies between and . To check convert to decimals, $\overline{.857142}$ is between $.8\overline{3}$ and .875

26. 340.292 ÷ 48.2 = 7.06

27. From 1:45 PM to 2:15 PM = 30 minutes

28. To completely reduce a fraction, each of numerator and denominator should be divided by the greatest common divisor.

    Ex.: $\frac{18}{30}$ can be reduced to by dividing numerator and denominator by 6. Note: 6 = greatest common divisor of 18 and 30.

29. $3+\sqrt{64} = 3+8 = 11$

30. -10° + 25° = 15° above zero

31. $81 ÷ $18 = 4.5. Then, (4.5)(8) = 36 weeks

32. When dividing one whole number by another whole number, the remainder must be smaller than the divisor.
    Ex.: 39 ÷ 17 = 2 with a remainder of 5, and 5 < 17.

33. Dividing by 1 or multiplying by 1 will never change the value of a number.

34. 7 × (3+9) = 84 = (7×3)+(7×9)

35. $\frac{1}{2}" \div \frac{3}{4}" = (\frac{1}{2})(\frac{4}{3}) = \frac{4}{6} = \frac{2}{3}$

11 (#1)

36. .06, .009, 10 is NOT in descending order. The correct order would be .10, .06, .009.

37. In 1935, the population of the U.S. was about 127,000,000.

38. Average increase = (150,000,000 − 75,000,000) ÷ 50 = 1,500,000.

39. 2 gallons = 8 quarts, so 2 gallons : 3 quarts = 8:3

40. There are 13 darkened boxes out of a total of 25 boxes.

    $\frac{13}{25}$ = 52%

41. Second cutting edge = .004" ÷ 4 = .001 in.

42. 20% = $\frac{1}{5}$ = $\frac{6}{30}$

43. Bar II = 3 units, bar III = 1 ½ units, and 3 to 1 ½ = 2 to 1.

44. If a price is reduced by more than 20%, the sales price MUST be less than 80% of the original price. Ex: Original price = $100, reduced by 22%, sales price = $78 = 78% of original price.

45. Since 9×1 = odd and 5×7 = odd, both (3049)(6431) and (8765)(3497) must result in an odd number.

46. 27 − 6 + 1 + 22 days.

47. Let x = score on 4th test. Then, (80)(3) + x = (84)(4). 240 ÷ x = 336. Solving, x = 96

48. Let x = number who contributed to both, 25 − x = number who contributed only to Junior Red Cross, 16 − x = number who contributed only to March of Dimes. Then, x + 25−x+16 −x = 28, so x =13.

49. Since he multiplied by 4, the next to last number = 8. So, 8 ÷ 4 = 2.

50. Since their product is odd, each number must be odd. Their sum is an even number les than their product.
    Ex: 3 + 5 = 8 < (3)(5) = 15

EXAMINATION SECTION
TEST 1

DIRECTIONS: Each question or incomplete statement is followed by several suggested answers or completions. Select the one that BEST answers the question or completes the statement. *PRINT THE LETTER OF THE CORRECT ANSWER IN THE SPACE AT THE RIGHT.*

1. 2/3 × 12 equals
   A. 4 B. 6 C. 8
   D. 18 E. None of the above

   1.____

2. 83.97
   1.78
   14.36
   9.03
   The sum of the above column is
   A. 99.13 B. 99.24 C. 109.14 D. 109.23 E. 109.24

   2.____

3. The value of x in the equation 5x = 75 is
   A. 13 B. 15 C. 70
   D. 80 E. None of the above

   3.____

4. 65 ÷ .13 equals
   A. .501 B. 5.01 C. 50.1
   D. 501 E. None of the above

   4.____

5. The sum of 6 feet 8 inches and 3 feet 4 inches is
   A. 2 ft. 2 in. B. 9 ft. C. 10 ft.
   D. 10 ft. 12 in. E. None of the above

   5.____

6. 3/4 − 1/2 + 1/8 equals
   A. 3/10 B. 3/8 C. 5/8
   D. 1 3/8 E. None of the above

   6.____

7. 4 5/16 − 2 3/8 equals
   A. 1 15/16 B. 2 1/16 C. 2 ¼
   D. 2 15/16 E. None of the above

   7.____

8. (−12)+(−3) equals
   A. −9 B. +15 C. +9
   D. −15 E. None of the above

   8.____

9. The ratio of the lengths of two lines is 5 to 3. The length of the shorter line is 30 inches. The length of the longer line is _____ inches.
   A. 18 B. 48 C. 50
   D. 140 E. None of the above

   9.____

10. .025 written as a common fraction is
    A. 25/10
    B. 25/100
    C. 25/1000
    D. 25/10,000
    E. None of the above

    10._____

11. In the proportion 5/2 = 9/x the value of x is
    A. 1.8
    B. 3.6
    C. 22.5
    D. 36
    E. None of the above

    11._____

12. 33 1/3 percent of 3 equals
    A. 1
    B. 10
    C. 100/3
    D. 100
    E. None of the above

    12._____

13. $\sqrt{233}$ equals
    A. 15
    B. 20.5
    C. 25
    D. 112.5
    E. None of the above

    13._____

14. On the portion of the scale shown at the right, the reading to which the arrow points is _____ units.
    A. 6 3/16
    B. 6 3/5
    C. 6 3/4
    D. 7 5/8
    E. None of the above

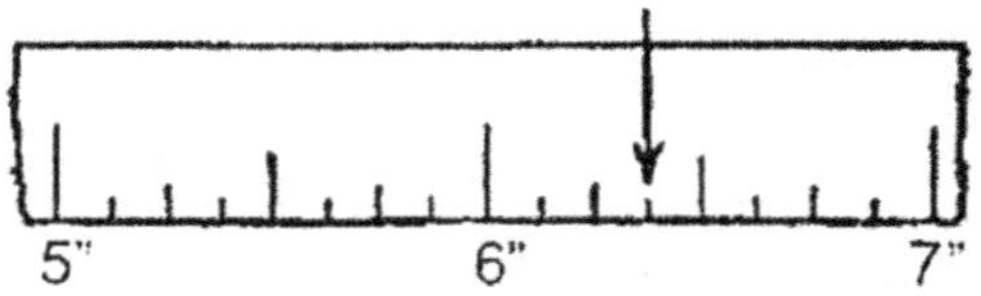

    14._____

15. If 4x/5 − 6 = 10, then x equals
    A. 15 1/5
    B. 5
    C. 4
    D. 3 1/5
    E. None of the above

    15._____

16. The difference between 8 hours 0 minutes 6 seconds and 6 hours 4 minutes 15 seconds is _____ hr. _____ min. _____ seconds.
    A. 0; 54; 51
    B. 1; 54; 51
    C. 2; 4; 9
    D. 2; 54; 45
    E. None of the above

    16._____

17. The scores made by nine pupils on a science test are: 2, 4, 6, 6, 8, 10, 12, 14, 19.
    The MEAN score is
    A. 6
    B. 8
    C. 9
    D. 81
    E. None of the above

    17._____

18. A certain cost formula is represented graphically in the figure at the right. From the graph, when n = 7, the value of C is about
    A. 140
    B. 120
    C. 110
    D. 102
    E. None of the above

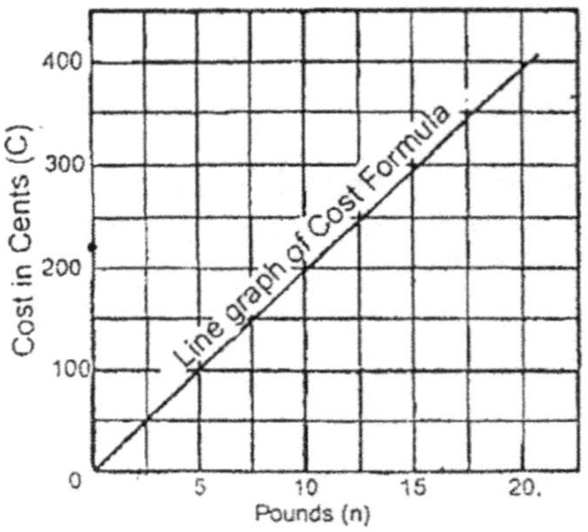

    18._____

19. A simplified form of the expression A = 1/2 bh + 1/2 ah is
    A. A = ½ h(b+a)   B. bh + ah   C. A = abh
    D. $\frac{A}{1/2bh}$ = 1/2 ah   E. None of the above

19.____

20. The ratio of 6 inches to 3 feet is
    A. 6/1   B. 2/1   C. 1/2
    D. 1/18   E. None of the above

20.____

21. The value of s in the equation 3s = 12 – s is
    A. 6   B. 4   C. 3 2/3
    D. 3   E. None of the above

21.____

22. 16 2/3 percent of what number is 30?
    A. 5   B. 18   C. 160
    D. 180   E. None of the above

22.____

23. The line graph shown at the right represents the temperature readings in Albany, New York, at two-hour intervals from 4 A.M. to 10 P.M. on a certain day in February. The APPROXIMATE change in temperature between 7 A.M. and 9 A.M. is _____ degrees.
    A. 3.5
    B. 3.0
    C. 2.5
    D. 2.0
    E. None of the above

23.____

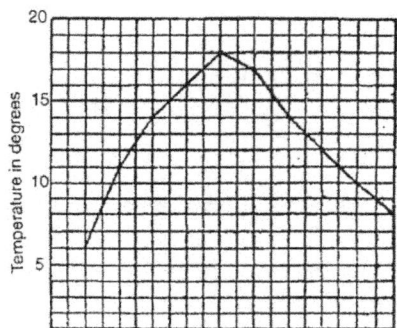

Questions 24-25.

DIRECTIONS: Questions 24 and 25 are to be answered on the basis of the following figure and information.

In the figure below, a square whose side is b is cut from a square whose side is a.

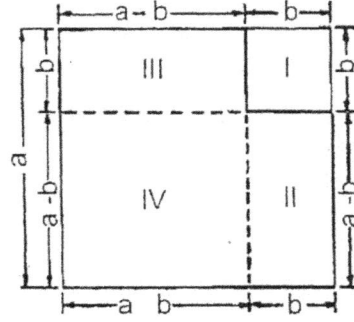

24. The sum of the perimeters of Section I and Section III can be represented by   24._____
    A. b^2 B. $4a - 2b$ C. $2a + 3b$
    D. $a(a-b)$ E. None of the above

25. The sum of the areas of Section II and Section IV can be represented by   25._____
    A. b^2 B. $4a - 2b$ C. $2a + 3b$
    D. $a(a-b)$ E. None of the above

26. The temperature reading (F) on the Fahrenheit scale equals 32 more than   26._____
    9/5 of the Centigrade reading (C).
    This rule when translated into symbols is expressed by
    A. $F = 9/5C + 32$ B. $F = 9/5(C+32)$ C. $F = 9/5 + 32C$
    D. $F + 32 = 9/5C$ E. None of the above

27. In the equation $6x - 114 = .3x$, the value of x is   27._____
    A. 38   B. 20   C. 12 2/3
    D. 2   E. None of the above

28. What percent of 42 is 84?   28._____
    A. 4%   B. 2%   C. 50%
    D. 200%   E. None of the above

29. The CORRECT name of the solid figure at the   29._____
    right is
    A. semicircle
    B. circle
    C. sphere
    D. cone
    E. cylinder

30. Which of these fractions has the LARGEST value?   30._____
    A. 1/2   B. 5/9   C. 7/12
    D. 2/3   E. 3/4

31. The formula for the area of a circle is A =   31._____
    A. π^2 B. $2/3 \pi^2$ C. $2\pi r$
    D. bh E. None of the above

32. The CORRECT name of the figure at the right is   32._____
    A. pentagon
    B. hexagon
    C. rectangle
    D. trapezoid
    E. square

33. The figure at the right is a
    A. rectangle
    B. square
    C. pentagon
    D. trapezoid
    E. parallelogram

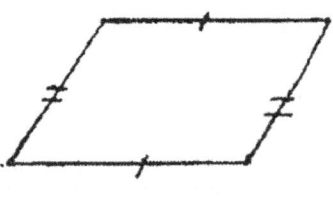

33.____

34. If x = -18, y = 3, and z = -2, then x – y + z equals
    A. 3   B. -3   C. -23   D. -52   E. -56

34.____

35. The number 335,560 rounded off to the nearest thousand is
    A. 335,000   B. 335,500   C. 336,000
    D. 340,000   E. None of the above

35.____

36. In the triangle ABC at the right, the sum of the angles is _____ degrees.
    A. 360
    B. 180
    C. 90
    D. 35
    E. None of the above

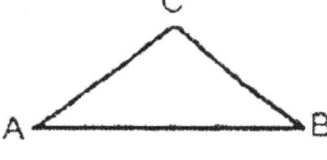

36.____

37. According to the map shown at the right, the APPROXIMATE distance between the southern point of New York City and Albany is _____ miles.
    A. 50
    B. 75
    C. 130
    D. 180
    E. 200

37.____

38. If 6 is added to a certain number n, the result is 1. An equation which expresses this relationship is
    A. n + 6 = 1   B. n – 1 = 6   C. 6 – n = 1
    D. n + 1 = 6   E. None of the above

38.____

39. In the expression $2n^3$, the 3 is called a(n)
    A. coefficient   B. factor   C. exponent
    D. multiplicand   E. None of the above

39.____

40. The number of inches in n feet is represented by
    A. 12n   B. 3n   C. n/3
    D. n/12   E. None of the above

40.____

41. The simple interest on $600 for 3 months at 4 percent per year is represented by 600 × .04x 41.____
   A. 1/4 B. 1/3 C. 3
   D. 4   E. None of the above

42. The circle graph shown at the right indicates how a family's annual budget of $3,000 was planned. 42.____
   Food   40 percent
   Shelter   25 percent
   Clothes   15 percent
   Operating Expenses 10 percent
   Insurance & Savings 10 percent
   The part of the circle representing Shelter is _____ degrees.
   A. 25   B. 45   C. 90
   D. 250 E. None of the above

43. In the parallelogram ABCD shown at the right, each small square represents 4 square inches. The area of the right triangle AED represents _____ square inches. 45.____
   A. 3
   B. 12
   C. 24
   D. 48
   E. None of the above

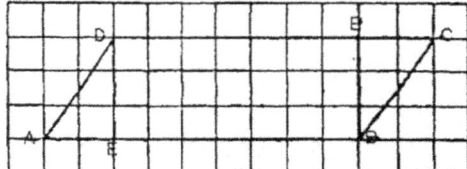

44. A surveyor measured angle x with a transit. (See figure at the right.) Angle x is called 44.____
   A. the angle of depression B from A
   B. an obtuse angle
   C. the supplement of angle
   D. the angle of elevation of B from A
   E. none of the above

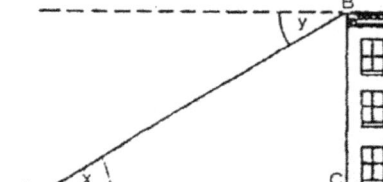

45. In the figure at the right, AOB is a straight line. An equation showing the relationship between u and v is 45.____
   A. u = 1/2v
   B. u = 180 − v
   C. u + v = 90
   D. v = 3u
   E. None of the above

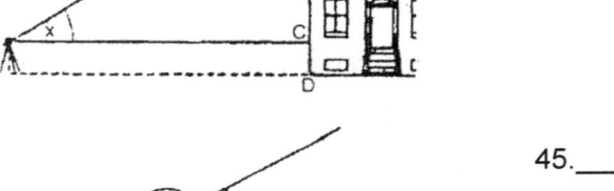

46. If x = 4 when y = 6 and x varies directly as y, then when y = 15, x equals
    A. 20   B. 10   C. 1 3/5
    D. 1 1/3   E. None of the above

47. A discount of 15 percent from a marked price produces a net price which is _____ of the marked price.
    A. .15%   B. .85%   C. 15%   D. 85%   E. 115%

48. When the formula A = P + Prt is solved for t, t equals
    A. A − P − Pr   B. $\frac{A-Pr}{P}$ C. $\frac{A-P}{1+r}$
    D. $\frac{A-P}{Pr}$ E. None of the above

49. The Greek letter π
    A. was assigned the value 3.1416 by the International Court of Law
    B. was given an arbitrary value of 22/7 by a famous mathematician
    C. was discovered to be exactly 3.142
    D. when multiplied by the radius of a circle equals the area
    E. is used as a symbol for the ratio of the circumference of a circle to its diameter

50. If the base and altitude of a triangle are doubled, the area
    A. remains constant   B. is multiplied by 4   C. is doubled
    D. is divided by 4   E. is none of the above

51. Each side of the equilateral triangle in the figure at the right is s inches long. The length of an altitude of the triangle is represented as
    A. s in.
    B. $s\sqrt{2}$
    C. $s\sqrt{3}$
    D. $\frac{s\sqrt{3}}{2}$ in.
    E. None of the above

52. The length of a meter is about _____ inches.
    A. 1   B. 6   C. 12   D. 40   E. 100

53. A point which lies on the straight-line graph of the equation 2x − 3y = 12 is
    A. (3,−2)   B. (2,−3)   C. (−4,0)
    D. (0,6)   E. None of the above

54. If the two parallel lines AB and CD in the figure at the right are cut by a third line, EF, then the FALSE statement is
    A. ∠r + ∠s = ∠s + ∠y
    B. ∠y + ∠w = ∠t + ∠s
    C. ∠u + ∠w = ∠s + ∠x
    D. ∠r + ∠x = ∠t + ∠w
    E. ∠s + ∠u = ∠r + ∠t

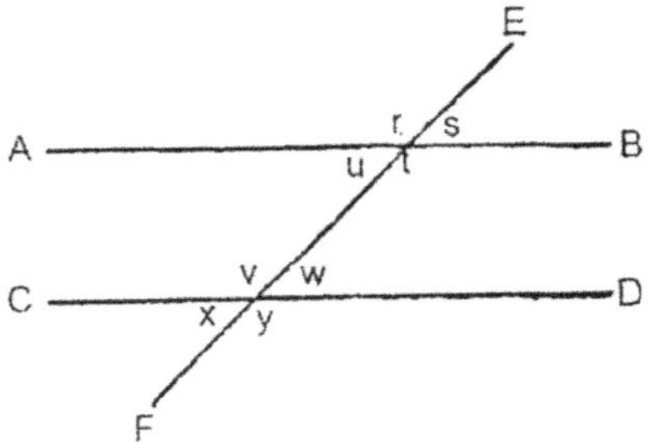

54.____

55. The product of n^4 and n^2 equals
    A. $2n^8$
    B. $2n^6$
    C. n^8
    D. n^2
    E. None of the above

55.____

56. The volume of the rectangular solid shown at the right is
    A. 12 cu. in.
    B. 44 sq. in.
    C. 48 cu. in.
    D. 88 sq. in.
    E. None of the above

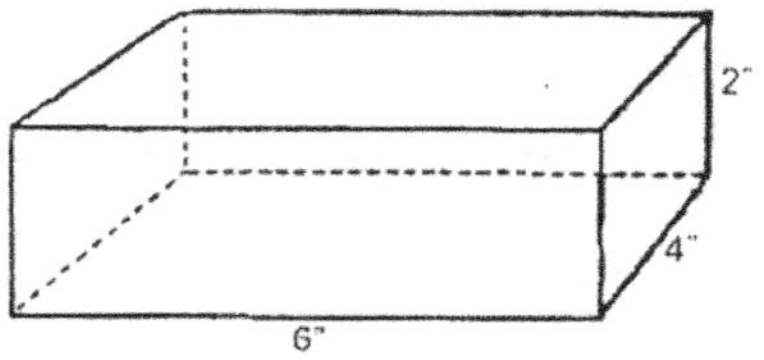

56.____

57. Baseball bats listed at twenty-one dollars per dozen are sold to schools at a discount of 20 percent.
    How much do they cost the schools per dozen?
    A. $4.20
    B. $16.80
    C. $20.80
    D. $25.20
    E. None of the above

57.____

58. Last year a Chicago merchant's total business amounted to $30,000. For the goods sold, he paid $12,000, for rent he paid $2,500, for clerk services $4,742, and for other expenses $1,058.
    His average monthly net profit was
    A. $676.67
    B. $891.67
    C. $2,500.00
    D. $9,700.00
    E. None of the above

58.____

59. If the marked price of an article is $100 and the first discount is 10 percent and the second discount 2 percent, the sale price is
    A. $78.20
    B. $88.00
    C. $88.20
    D. $88.80
    E. None of the above

59.____

60. Mr. Smith agreed to pay an automobile agency a commission of 18 percent of the selling price of his car.
    If the selling price was $1,250, Mr. Smith would receive
    A. $225.00
    B. $1,025.00
    C. $1,227.50
    D. $1,475.00
    E. None of the above

60.____

61. Mr. Browne receives $30.45 per year on an investment of $870.
    At this rate, if his total investment was $1,500, his annual interest would be
    A. $52.50
    B. $62.50
    C. $625.00
    D. $655.45
    E. None of the above

61.____

62. The Ephrata National Bank discounted a 60-day note for $3,500 at 3½ percent per year.
    The proceeds of the note were
    A. $3,377.50 B. $3,479.58 C. $3,520.42
    D. $3,622.50 E. None of the above

    62.____

63. The normal weight of an adult can be found by using the formula w = 5.5(20+d), where w represents the weight in pounds and d the number of inches one's height exceeds 5 feet.
    By this formula, the normal weight of an adult who is 5'6" tall is _____ pounds.
    A. 134 B. 140.25 C. 140.8
    D. 143.0 E. None of the above

    63.____

64. In the figure at the right, triangles ACB and ADE are similar triangles. The length of side DE is _____ feet.
    A. 30
    B. 32
    C. 48
    D. 50
    E. None of the above

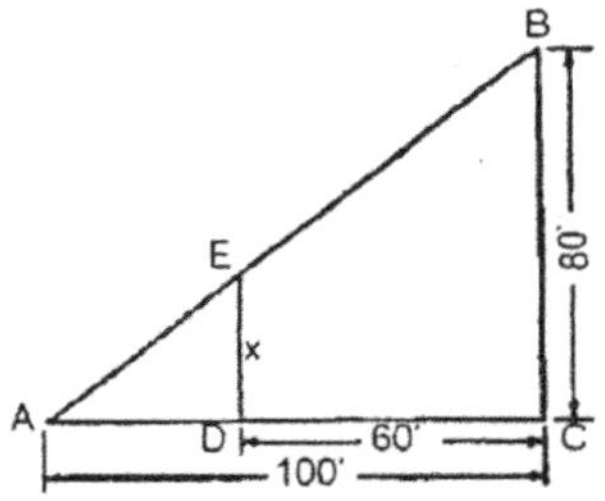

    64.____

65. A square piece of tin shown in the figure at the right is used to make an open box. One-inch squares are cut from each corner of the piece of tin and the sides then turned up, to form a box containing 49 cubic inches.
    The length of a side of the original square piece of tin required to make this box is _____ inches.
    A. 5
    B. 7
    C. 8
    D. 9
    E. None of the above

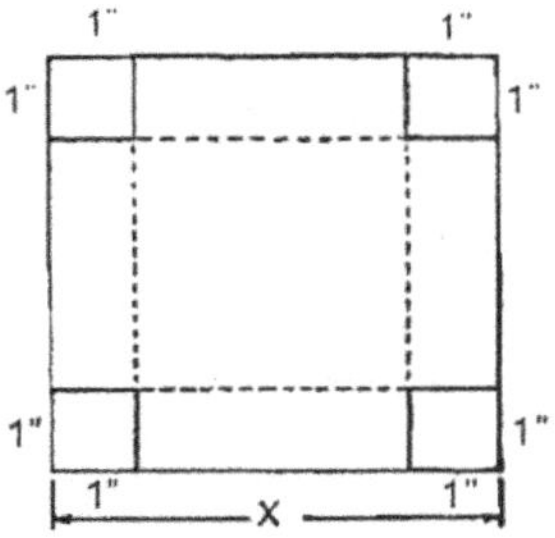

    65.____

KEY (CORRECT ANSWERS)

1. C	11. B	21. D	31. A	41. A	51. D	61. A
2. C	12. A	22. D	32. A	42. C	52. D	62. B
3. B	13. A	23. C	33. E	43. B	53. A	63. D
4. D	14. E	24. E	34. C	44. D	54. E	64. B
5. C	15. E	25. D	35. C	45. B	55. E	65. D
6. B	16. E	26. A	36. B	46. B	56. C	
7. A	17. C	27. B	37. C	47. D	57. B	
8. D	18. A	28. D	38. A	48. D	58. E	
9. C	19. A	29. E	39. C	49. E	59. C	
10. C	20. E	30. E	40. A	50. B	60. B	

SOLUTIONS TO PROBLEMS

1. $2/3 \times 12 = \frac{12}{1} = \frac{24}{3} = 8$

2. Adding, we get 109.14

3. If $5x = 75$, $x = 75/5 = 15$

4. $65.13 \div 13 = 501$

5. 6 ft. 8 in. + 3 ft. 4 in. = 9 ft. 12 in. = 10 ft.

6. $3/4 - 1/2 + 1/8 = 6/8 - 4/8 + 1/8 = 3/8$

7. 4 15/16 − 2 3/8 = 3 21/16 − 2 6/16 = 1 15/16

8. $(-12) + (-3) = -15$

9. Let x = length of longer line. Then, 5:3 = x:30. Solving, x = 50

10. .025 = 25/1000 (Can also be reduced to 1/40)

11. Cross-multiplying, $5x = 18$. Thus, 18/5 = 3.6

12. 33 1/3% of 3 = (1/3)(3) = 1

13. $\sqrt{225} = 15$, since $15^2 = 225$

14. The arrow points to 6 3/8

15. $4x/5 - 6 = 10$. Adding 6, $4x/5 = 16$. Then, $x = 16 \div 4/5 = 20$

16. 8 hrs. 0 min. 6 sec. − 6 hrs. 4 min. 15 sec. can be written as 7 hrs. 59 min. 66 sec. − 6 hrs. 4 min. 15 sec. to get 1 hr. 55 min. 51 sec.

17. Mean = (2+4+6+8+10+12+14+19) ÷ 9 = 9

18. When n = 0, c = 0. When n = 5, c = 100. Thus, c = 20n. Finally, for n = 7, c = (20)(7) = 140

19. $A = 1/2\, bh + 1/2\, h(b+a)$

20. 6 inches : 3 feet = 6 inches : 36 inches = 1/6

21. Add 5 to both sides to get $4s = 12$, so $s = 3$

22. 16 2/3% of x is 30. Then, $1/6\, x = 30$. Then, $1/6\, x = 180$

23. At 7:00 A.M. the temperature was 12.5, while at 9:00 A.M. the temperature was 15. The change was 2.5 degrees.

24. Perimeter of Section I is 4b and the perimeter of Section III is 2b + 2a − 2b = 2a. The sum of the perimeters is 4b + 2a,

25. Area of Section II is b(a−b) = ab − b^2 and the area of Section IV is $(a-b)^2$ = a^2 − 2ab + b^2. The sum of the areas is a^2 − ab = a(a-b).

26. Direct translation of words to symbols yields F = 9/5C + 32

27. Subtract 6x to get -114 = 5.7x. Solving, x = 20

28. (84/42)(100)% = 200%

29. The figure is a cylinder.

30. Converting each choice to a decimal, we get .5, .$\overline{5}$, .58$\overline{3}$, .6, .75. The largest is .75 corresponding to 3/4.

31. For a circle, A = πr^2

32. A five-sided enclosed figure with straight sides is called a pentagon.

33. A quadrilateral with opposite sides parallel is called a parallelogram. Rectangles and squares are parallelograms with 90° angles.

34. x − y + z = 18 − 3 − 2 = 23

35. Since the digit in the hundreds place is 5 or greater, the answer is 336,000.

36. The sum of the angles of any triangle is 180°.

37. The scale difference is about 2 inches, and since 50 miles corresponds to 3/4 inch, the actual distance is about (50)(2÷3/4) = 133 1/3 mi. Closest answer given s 130 mi.

38. 6 added to n means 6 + n. Thus, 6 + n = 1 or n + 6 = 1.

39. 3 is an exponent for 2n^3.

40. 12 inches in 1 foot means 12n inches in n feet.

41. 3 months = 1/4 year

42. 25% of 360 degrees = 90 degrees.

43. Area of △AED = (1/2)(2)(3) = 3 square units = 12 sq. inches.

44. Angle X is the angle of elevation to B from A.

13 (#1)

45. Since u + v = 180, we can also write u = 180 – v

46. 4/x = 6/15 Cross-multiplying, 6x = 60. Solving, x = 10

47. 100% - 15% = 85%

48. A = P + Prt becomes A – P = Prt. Dividing by Pr, we get: t = (A-P)/Pr

49. π = ratio of circumference to diameter of a circle.

50. Let B = base, H = altitude. Original area of triangle = 1/2BH. If new base and altitude are 2B and 2H, new area = ½(2B)(2H) = 2BH, which is 4 times the value of 1/2BH.

51. Let x = altitude. Then, $x^2 + (s/2)^2 = s2$. This becomes $3/4s^2 = x^2$. Solving, x = s √3 /2

52. 1 meter ≈ 39.37 inches ≈ 40 inches.

53. Substituting (3,-2), 2(3) – 3(-2) = 12. The other points do not lie on 2x – 3y = 12.

54. The false statement is ∠2 + ∠u = ∠r + ∠t. It is only true that ∠x = ∠u and∠ r = ∠t).

55. $n^4 • n^2 = n^6$, since exponents are added in multiplication.

56. Volume = (6)(4)(2) = 48 cu. in.

57. ($21)(.80) = $16.80

58. $30,000 - $12,000 - $2,500 - $4,742 - $1,058 = $9,700. The monthly amount is $9,700 ÷ 12 = $808.33

59. ($100)(.90) = $90. Then, ($90)(.98) = $88.20

60. 1,250 – (1,250)(.18) = $1,025

61. $30.45/$870 = 3.5%. Then, 3.5% of $1,500 = $52.50

62. (.035)(60/360) = .00583̄ = discount for 60 days.
The value of the note = (1 - .00583̄)($3500) = $3,479.58.

63. W = 5.5(20+6) = (5.5)(26) = 143

64. x/80 = 40/100. Solving, x = 32. Note that AD:AC = DE:BC

65. When folded, each new side is √49 = 7

EXAMINATION SECTION
TEST 1

DIRECTIONS: Each question or incomplete statement is followed by several suggested answers or completions. Select the one that BEST answers the question or completes the statement. *PRINT THE LETTER OF THE CORRECT ANSWER IN THE SPACE AT THE RIGHT.*

1. Which of the following fractions is the SMALLEST?
   A. 2/3 B. 4/5 C. 5/7 D. 5/11

2. 40% is equivalent to which of the following?
   A. 4/5 B. 4/6 C. 2/5 D. 4/100

3. How many 100's are in 10,000?
   A. 10 B. 100 C. 10,000 D. 100,000

4. $\frac{6}{7} + \frac{11}{12}$ is approximately
   A. 1 B. 2 C. 17 D. 19

5. The time required to heat water to a certain temperature is directly proportional to the volume of water being heated.
   If it takes 12 minutes to heat 1 ½ gallons of water, how many minutes will it take to heat 2 gallons of water?
   A. 12 B. 16 C. 18 D. 24

6. The cost of an item increased by 25%.
   If the original cost was C dollars, identify the expression which gives the new cost of that item.
   A. C + 0.25 B. 1/4 C C. 25C D. 1.25C

7. Given the formula PV = nRT, all of the following are true EXCEPT
   A. T = PV/nR B. P = nRTN C. V = P/nRT D. n = PV/RT

8. If a Fahrenheit (F) temperature reading is 104, find its Celsius (C) equivalent, given that C = i(F-32).
   A. 36 B. 40 C. 72 D. 76

9. If 40% of a graduating class plans to go directly to work after graduation, which of the following must be TRUE?
   A. Less than half of the class plans to go directly to work.
   B. Forty members of the class plan to enter the job market.
   C. Most of the class plans to go directly to work.
   D. Six in ten members of the class are expected not to graduate.

10. Given a multiple-choice test item which has 5 choices, what is the probability of guessing the correct answer if you know nothing about the item content?
    A. 5% B. 10% C. 20% D. 25%

11.

S	T
0	80
5	75
10	65
15	50
20	30
25	5

Which graph BEST represents the data shown in the above table?

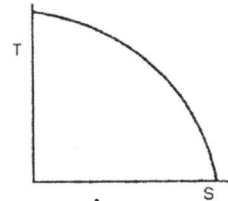
A

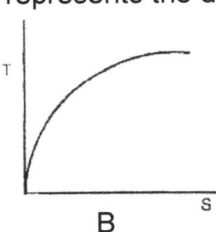
B

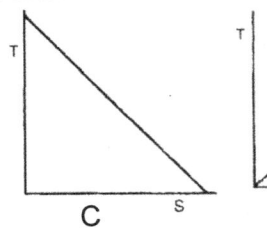
C

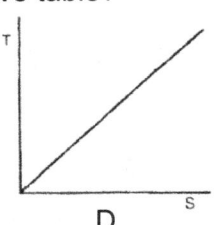
D

12. If 3(x+5y) = 24, find y when x = 3.
    A. 1 B. 3 C. 33/5 D. 7

13. The payroll of a grocery store for its 23 clerks is $395,421. Which expression below shows the average salary of a clerk?
    A. 395,421 × 23
    B. 23 ÷ 395,421
    C. (395,421 × 23
    D. 395,421 ÷ 23

14. If 12.8 pounds of coffee cost $50.80, what is the APPROXIMATE price per pound?
    A. $2.00 B. $3.00 C. $4.00 D. $5.00

15. A road map has a scale where 1 inch corresponds to 150 miles. A distance of 3 3/4 inches on the map corresponds to what actual distance? _____ miles.
    A. 153.75 B. 375 C. 525 D. 562.5

16. How many square feet of plywood are needed to construct the back and 4 adjacent sides of the box shown at the right?
    A. 63
    B. 90
    C. 96
    D. 126

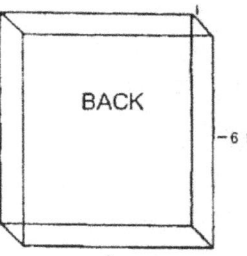

17. One thirty-pound bag of lawn fertilizer costs $20.00 and will cover 600 square feet of lawn. Terry's lawn is a 96 foot by 75 foot rectangle. How much will it cost Terry to buy enough bags of fertilizer for her lawn?
    Which of the following do you NOT need in order to solve this problem? The
    A. product of 96 and 75
    B. fact that one bag weighs 30 pounds
    C. fact that one bag covers 600 square feet
    D. fact that one bag costs $20.00

    17.____

18. On the graph shown at the right, between which hours was the drop in temperature GREATEST?
    A. 11:00 – Noon
    B. Noon – 1:00
    C. 1:00 – 2:00
    D. 2:00 – 3:00

    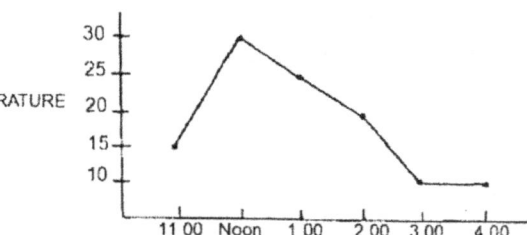

    18.____

19. If on a typical railroad track the distance from the center of one railroad tie to the next is 30 inches, approximately how many ties would be needed for one mile of track?
    A. 180   B. 2,110   C. 6,340   D. 63,360

    19.____

20. Which of the following is MOST likely to be the volume of a wine bottle?
    A. 750 milliliters   B. 7 kilograms
    C. 7 milligrams   D. 7 liters

    20.____

21. What is the reading on the gauge shown at the right?
    A. -7
    B. -3
    C. 1
    D. 3

    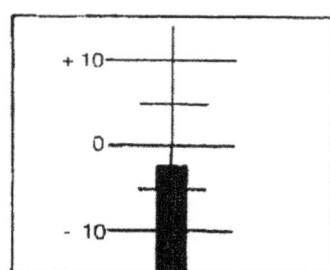

    21.____

22. Which statement below disproves the assertion, *All students in Mrs. Marino's 10th grade geometry class are planning to go to college?*
    A. Albert is in Mrs. Marino's class, but he is not planning to take mathematics next year.
    B. Jorge is not in Mrs. Marino's class, but he is still planning to go to college.
    C. Pierre is in Mrs. Marino's class but says he will not be attending school anymore after this year.
    D. Crystal is in Mrs. Marino's class and plans to attend Yale University when she graduates.

    22.____

23. A store advertisement reads, *Buy not while our prices are low. There will never be a better time to buy.*
    The customer reading this advertisement should assume that
    A. the prices at the store will probably never be lower
    B. right now, this store has the best prices in town
    C. prices are higher at other stores
    D. prices are always lowest at this store

24. *Given any positive integer, there is always a positive number B such that A × B is less than 1.*
    Which statement below supports this generalization?
    A. 8 × 1/16 = 1/2
    B. 8 × 1/2 = 4
    C. 5/2 × 1/10 = 1/4
    D. 1/2 × 1/2 = 1/2

25. Of the following expressions, which is equivalent to 4C + D = 12E?
    A. C = 4(12E-D)
    B. 4 + D = 12E − C
    C. 4C + 12E = -D
    D. $C = \frac{12E-D}{4}$

KEY (CORRECT ANSWERS)

1.	D		11.	A
2.	C		12.	A
3.	B		13.	D
4.	B		14.	C
5.	B		15.	D
6.	D		16.	C
7.	C		17.	B
8.	B		18.	D
9.	A		19.	B
10.	C		20.	A

21.	B
22.	C
23.	A
24.	A
25.	D

SOLUTIONS TO PROBLEMS

1. Converting to decimals, we get $.\overline{6}$, .8, .714 (approx..), $\overline{.45}$. The smallest is $\overline{.45}$ corresponding to 5/11.

2. 40% = 40/100 = 2/5

3. 10,000 ÷ 100 = 100

4. $\frac{6}{7} + \frac{11}{12}$ = (72+77) ÷ 84 = $\frac{149}{84}$ ≈ 1.77 ≈ 2

5. Let x = required minutes. Then, 12/1 ½ = x². This reduces to 1 1/2x = 24. Solving, x = 16.

6. New cost is C + .25C = 1.25C

7. For PV = nRT, V = nRT/P

8. C = 5/9 (104-32) = 5/9(72) = 40

9. Since 40% is less than 50% (or half), we conclude that less than half of the class plans to go to work directly after graduation.

10. The probability of guessing right is 1/5 or 20%

11. Curve A is most accurate since as S increases, we see that T decreases. Note, however, that the relationship is NOT linear. Although S increases in equal amounts, the decrease in T is NOT in equal amounts.

12. 3(3+5y) = 24. This simplifies to 9 + 15y = 24. Solving, y = 1

13. The average salary is $395,421 ÷ 23

14. The price per pound is $50.80 ÷ 12.8 = $3,96875 or approximately $4.

15. Actual distance is (3 3/4)(150) = 562.5 miles.

16. The area of the back = (6)(5) = 30 sq. ft. The combined area of the two vertical sides is (2)(6)(3) = 36 sq. ft. The combined area of the horizontal sides is (2)(5)(3) = 30 sq. ft. Total area = 30 + 36 30 = 96 square feet.

17. Choice B is not relevant to solving the problem since the cost will be [(96)(75)/600][$20] = $240. So, the weight per bag is not needed.

18. For the graph, the largest temperature drop was from 2:00 P.M. to 3:00 P.M. The temperature dropped 20 – 10 = 10 degrees.

19. 1 mile = 5280 feet = 63,360 inches. Then, 63,360 ÷ 30 = 2112 or about 2110 ties are needed.

20. Since 1 liter = 1.06 quarts, 750 milliliters = (750/1000)(1.06) = .795 quarts. This is a reasonable volume for a wine bottle.

21. The reading is -3.

22. Statement C contradicts the given information, since Pierre is in Mrs. Marino's class. Then he should plan to go to college.

23. Since there will never be a better time to buy at this particular store, the customer can assume the current prices will probably never be lower.

24. Statement A illustrates this concept. Note that in general, if n is a positive integer. then $(n)(\frac{1}{n-1}) < 1$

25. _____

TEST 2

DIRECTIONS: Each question or incomplete statement is followed by several suggested answers or completions. Select the one that BEST answers the question or completes the statement. *PRINT THE LETTER OF THE CORRECT ANSWER IN THE SPACE AT THE RIGHT.*

1. Which of the following lists numbers in INCREASING order?
   A. 0.4, 0.04, 0.004
   B. 2.71, 3.15, 2.996
   C. 0.7, 0.77, 0.777
   D. 0.06, 0.5, 0.073

   1.____

2. $\frac{4}{10}+\frac{7}{100}+\frac{5}{1000} =$
   A. 4.75
   B. 0.475
   C. 0.0475
   D. 0.00475

   2.____

3. 700 times what number equals 7?
   A. 10
   B. 0.1
   C. 0.01
   D. 0.001

   3.____

4. 943-251 is approximately
   A. 600
   B. 650
   C. 700
   D. 1200

   4.____

5. The time needed to set up a complicated piece of machinery is inversely proportional to the number of years' experience of the worker.
   If a worker with 10 years' experience needs 6 hours to do the job, how long will it take a worker with 15 years' experience?
   A. 4
   B. 5
   C. 9
   D. 25

   5.____

6. Let W represent the number of waiters and D, the number of diners in a particular restaurant.
   Identify the expression which represents the statement: There are 10 times as many diners as waiters.
   A. 10W = D
   B. 10D = W
   C. 10D + 10W
   D. 10 = D + W

   6.____

7. Which of the following is equivalent to the formula F = XC + Y?
   A. F – C = X + Y
   B. Y = F + XC
   C. $C = \frac{FY}{X}$
   D. $C = \frac{FX}{Y}$

   7.____

8. Given the formula A = BC/D, if A = 12, B = 6, and D = 3, what is the value of C?
   A. 2/3
   B. 6
   C. 18
   D. 24

   8.____

9. 5 is to 7 as X is to 35. X =
   A. 7
   B. 12
   C. 24
   D. 49

   9.____

10. Kramer Middle School has 5 seventh grade mathematics teachers: two of the math teachers are women and three are men.
    If you are assigned a teacher at random, what is the probability of getting a female teacher?
    A. 0.2
    B. 0.4
    C. 0.6
    D. 0.8

    10.____

11. Which statement BEST describes the graph shown at the right?
   Temperature
   A. and time decrease at the same rate
   B. and time increase at the same rate
   C. increases over time
   D. decreases over time

11. _____

12. If $3x + 4 = 22y$, find y when $x = 2$.
   A. 0   B. 3   C. 4 1/2   D. 5

12. _____

13. A car goes 243 miles on 8.7 gallons of gas.
   Which numeric expression should be used to determine the car's miles per gallon?
   A. 243 × 87   B. 8.7 ÷ 243   C. 243 ÷ 8.7   D. 243 − 8.7

13. _____

14. What is the average cost per book if you buy six books at $4.00 each and four books at $5.00 each?
   A. $4.40   B. $4.50   C. $4.60   D. $5.40

14. _____

15. A publisher's sale offers a 15% discount to anyone buying more than 100 workbooks.
   What will be the discount on 200 workbooks selling at $2.25 each?
   A. $15.00   B. $30.00   C. $33.75   D. $67.50

15. _____

16. A road crew erects 125 meters of fencing in one workday.
   How many workdays are required to erect a kilometer of fencing?
   A. 0.8   B. 8   C. 80   D. 800

16. _____

17. Last month Kim made several telephone calls to New York City totaling 45 minutes in all.
   What does Kim need in order to calculate the average duration of her New York City calls?
   The
   A. total number of calls she made to New York City
   B. cost per minute of a call to New York City
   C. total cost of her telephone bill last month
   D. days of the week on which the calls are made

17. _____

18.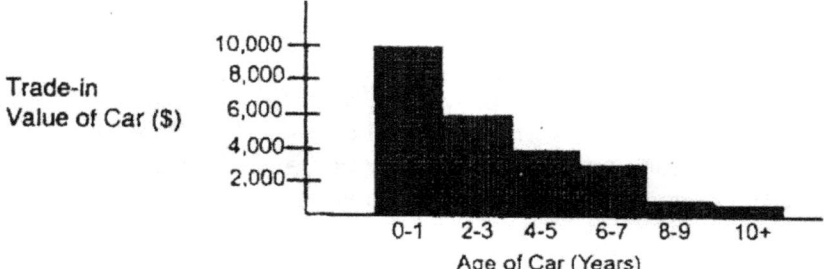

    The above chart relates a car's age to its trade-in value.
    Based on the chart, which of the following is TRUE?
    A. A 4- to 5-year old car has a trade-in value of about $2,000
    B. The trade-in vale of an 8- to 9-year old car is about 1/3 that of a 2- to 3-year old car.
    C. A 6- to 7-year old car has no trade-in value.
    D. A 4- to 5-year old car's trade-in value is about $2,000 less than that of a 2- to 3-year old car.

19. Which of the following expressions could be used to determine how many seconds are in a 24-hour day?
    A. 60 × 60 × 24
    B. 60 × 12 × 24
    C. 60 × 2 × 24
    D. 60 × 24

20. For measuring milk, we could use each of the following EXCEPT
    A. liters
    B. kilograms
    C. millimeters
    D. cubic centimeters

21. What is the reading on the gauge shown at the right?
    A. 51
    B. 60
    C. 62.5
    D. 70

    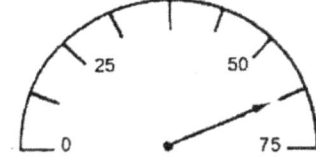

22. Bill is taller than Yvonne. Yvonne is shorter than Sue. Sue is 5' tall.
    Which of the following conclusions must be TRUE?
    A. Bill is taller than Sue.
    B. Yvonne is taller than 5'4".
    C. Sue is taller than Bill.
    D. Yvonne is the shortest.

23. The Bass family traveled 268 miles during the first day of their vacation and another 300 miles on the next day. Maria Bass said they were 568 miles from home.
    Which of the following facts did Maria assume?
    A. They traveled faster on the first day and slower on the second.
    B. If she plotted the vacation route on a map, it would be a straight line.
    C. Their car used more gasoline on the second day.
    D. They traveled faster on the second day than they did on the first day.

24. The word LEFT in a mathematics problem indicate that it is a subtraction problem.
    Which of the following mathematics problems prove this statement FALSE?
    A. I want to put 150 bottles into cartons which hold 8 bottles each. After I completely fill as many cartons as I can, how many bottles will be left?
    B. Sarah has 5 books but gave one to John. How many books did Sarah have left?
    C. Carlos had $4.25 but spent $3.75. How much did he have left?
    D. We had 38 models in stock but after yesterday's sale, only 12 are left. How many did we sell?

25. Let Q represent the number of miles Dave can jog in 15 minutes.
    Identify the expression which represents the number of miles Dave can jog between 3:00 P.M. and 4:45 P.M.
    A. 1 3/4 Q   B. 7Q   C. 15 × 1 3/4xQ   D. Q/7

KEY (CORRECT ANSWERS)

1.	C	11.	D
2.	B	12.	D
3.	C	13.	C
4.	C	14.	A
5.	A	15.	D
6.	A	16.	B
7.	C	17.	A
8.	B	18.	D
9.	C	19.	A
10.	B	20.	C

21. C
22. D
23. B
24. A
25. B

5 (#2)

SOLUTIONS TO PROBLEMS

1. Choice C is in ascending order since .y < .77 < .777

2. Rewrite in decimal form: .4 + .07 + .005 = .475

3. Let x = missing number. Then, 700x = 7. Solving, x = 7/700 = .01

4. 943 – 251 = 692 ≈ 700

5. Let x = hours needed. Then, 10/15 = x/6. Solving, x = 4

6. The number of diners (D) is 10 times as many waiters (10W). So, D = 10W, or 10W = D

7. Given F = XC + Y, subtract Y from each side to get F – Y = XC. Finally, dividing by X, we get (F-Y)/X = C

8. 12 = 6C/3. Then, 12 = 2C, so C = 6

9. 5/7 = x/35. Then, 7x = 175, so x = 25

10. Probability of a female teacher = 2/5 = .4

11. Statement D is best, since as time increases, the temperature decreases.

12. (3)(2) + 4 = 2y. Then, 10 = 2y, so y = 5.

13. Miles per gallon = 243/8.7

14. Total purchase is (6)($4) + (4)($5) = $44. The average cost per book is $44 ÷ 10 = $4.40

15. (220)($2.25) = $450. The discount is (.15)($450) = $67.50

16. The number of workdays is 1000 ÷ 125 = 8

17. Choice A is correct because the average duration of the phone calls = total time ÷ total number of calls.

18. Statement D is correct since a 4-5 year old car's value is $4,000, whereas a 2-3 year-old car's value is $6000.

19. 60 seconds = 1 minute and 60 minutes = 1 hour. Thus, 24 hours = (24)(60)(60) or (60)(60)(24) seconds.

20. We can't use millimeters in measuring milk since millimeters is a linear measurement.

21. The reading shows the average of 50 and 75 = 62.5

6 (#2)

22. Since Yvonne is shorter than both Bill and Sue, Yvonne is the shortest.

23. Statement B is assumed correct since 568 = 269 + 300 could only be true if the mileage traveled represents a straight line.

24. To find the number of bottles left, we look only for the remainder when 150 is divided b 8 (which happens to be 6).

25. 3:00 P.M. to 4:45 P.M. = 1 hour and 45 minutes = 105 minutes
Let Q = 15 minutes
105 / 15 = 7
7(15) = 105 = 7Q

EXAMINATION SECTION
TEST 1

DIRECTIONS: Each question or incomplete statement is followed by several suggested answers or completions. Select the one that BEST answers the question or completes the statement. *PRINT THE LETTER OF THE CORRECT ANSWER IN THE SPACE AT THE RIGHT.*

1. At 7:00 A.M., a student leaves his home in his automobile to drive to school 28 miles away. He averages 50 mph until 7:30 A.M., when his car breaks down. The student has to walk and run the rest of the way.
 If he wants to arrive at school at 8:00 A.M., how fast, in mph, must he travel on foot?
 A. 3   B. 4   C. 5   D. 6   E. 7   1.____

2. Express $1 + \dfrac{\frac{1}{2+1}}{1+\frac{1}{4}}$ in simplest terms.   2.____
 A. 27/28   B. 30/43   C. 1 1/9   D. 1 1/27   E. 1 13/30

3. A theater charges $5.00 admission for adults and $2.50 for children. At one showing, 240 admissions brought in a total of $800.
 How many adults attended the showing?   3.____
 A. 40   B. 80   C. 120   D. 160   E. 266

4. $\sqrt{25+?} = 5 + 8$ 4.____
 A. 8   B. 12   C. 64   D. 144   E. 169

5. The perimeter of a square is 20.
 Which of the following represents the area?   5.____
 A. 5   B. 10   C. 20   D. 25   E. 100

6. Evaluate the expression $\dfrac{1}{4} + \dfrac{3}{8} - \dfrac{6}{16} - \dfrac{8}{32}$ 6.____
 A. 7/16   B. 1/32   C. 1/8   D. 1/4   E. 0

7. Bill spent 20% of the money he initially had in his wallet on groceries and 25% on gas. He had $66.00 left.
 How much money did he have before he shopped?   7.____
 A. $85   B. $100   C. $110   D. $111   E. $120

8. Express the product $(2x+5y)^2$ in simplest form.   8.____
 A. $4x^2 + 25y^2$ B. $4x^2 + 20xy + 25y^2$ C. $4x^2 + 10y + 25y^2$
 D. $4x^2 - 20xy + 25y^2$ E. $4x + 25y$

9. A student received test grades of 83, 90, and 88.
 What was her grade on a fourth test if the average for the four tests is 84?   9.____
 A. 85   B. 80   C. 75   D. 70   E. 65

10. A rectangular room is 3 meters wide, 4 meters long, and 2 meters high. How far is it from the northeast corner at the floor to the southwest corner at the ceiling?
_____ meters.
A. $\sqrt{29}$ B. $\sqrt{11}$ C. $\sqrt{9}$ D. 9 E. 5

11. If an electron has a mass of 9.109×10^{-31} kg and a proton has a mass of 1.672×10^{-27} kg, approximately how many electrons are required to have the same mass as one proton?
A. 150,000   B. 1,800   C. 5.4×10^4
D. 5.4×10^{-4} E. 15×10^{-58}

12. The introduction of a new manufacturing process will affect a saving of $1,450 per week over the initial 8-week production period. New equipment, however, will cost 1/4 of the total savings.
How much did the equipment cost?
A. $11.600.00   B. $2,900.00   C. $725.00
D. $362.50   E. $181.25

13. If P dollars is invested at r percent compounded annually, at the end of n years it will have grown to $A = P(1+r)^n$. An investment made at 16% compounded annually. It grows to $1,740 at the end of one year.
How much was originally invested?
A. $150   B. $278.40   C. $1,461.60
D. $1,500   E. $1,700

14. What is 1/4% of 200?
A. 0.05   B. 0.5   C. 5   D. 12.5   E. 50

15. Which of the following is .5% of .95?
A. .000475   B. .00475   C. .0475   D. .475   E. 4.75

16. What is the value of (5 lbs. 1 oz.)/(3 lbs. 6 oz.) in ounces?
A. 22   B. 1.66   C. 1.5   D. 0.66   E. 0.28

17. If 1 inch = 2.56 centimeters, 3/8 centimeter equals which of the following in inches?
A. 6.77   B. .95   C. .39   D. .38   E. .15

18. If $2x + y = 7$ and $x - 4y = 4$, then x equals which of the following?
A. -15/9   B. -1/9   C. 7/15   D. 11/9   E. 32/9

19. What part of an hour is 6 seconds?
A. 1/600   B. 1/10   C. 1/360   D. 1/60   E. 1/5

20. If $1/3 + 5(x-1) = 8$, then which of the following is the value of x?
A. 8/13   B. 8/5   C. 38/25   D. 38/15   E. 38

21. Which line is perpendicular to the x-axis?
    A. x = 3   B. y = 3   C. x = y   D. x = y/3   E. y = x/3

22. If a dental hygienist at a certain office is paid H dollars a week, the dental assistant works 36 hours a week at A dollars per hour, and the receptionist works 40 hours a week and receives R dollars every other week, which of the following represents the weekly payroll for these three employees?
    A. H/3 + 36A + 40R/3
    B. H + 36A + R/2
    C. H/3 + 12A + R/6
    D. 5H + 36 + 20R
    E. H/3 + 12A + 40R

23. Company A ordered five units of anesthetic at $12.00 per unit. Company B ordered 10 units at $13.00 per unit, and Company C ordered 4 at $10.00 per unit. Since all these companies were at one address, the three orders were put on one bill.
    Approximately what percent of the total bill did Company A have to pay?
    A. 5   B. 18   C. 26   D. 36   E. 55

24. Which of the following is the value of A, if 50(A/100) = 2A^2?
    A. 25   B. 1   C. 5/2   D. 1/4   E. 1/2

25. Five-eighths of the employees in the company are single males. What percentage of the employees in the company are single males?
    A. 12.5   B. 20.0   C. 25.0   D. 32.0   E. 62.5

26. If x = 20% of y, and z = 35% of x, then z = _____ % of y.
    A. 70   B. 57   C. 7   D. 1.75   E. .07

27. Which of the following is the value of the expression $\frac{|14-3|-|7-16|}{3|(-2)+1}$?
    A. -20/3   B. -2/3   C. 0   D. 23   E. 20/3

28. A tank can be filled by a pipe in 30 minutes and emptied by another pipe in 50 minutes.
    How many minutes will it take to fill the tank if both pipes are open?
    A. 45   B. 60   C. 75   D. 80   E. 100

29. If (4/5)x = (2/5)y, then which of the following is equal to y/x?
    A. 1/2   B. 2/5   C. 25/8   D. 2   E. 3

30. Which of the following would NOT result in a straight line? x =
    A. 1/y   B. 2y + 5   C. (y+6)/(2)   D. 5 – y   E. 4(x+3y)

31. $\frac{5}{4} + \frac{4}{5} + \frac{3}{2}$ - _____ = a positive integer.
    A. 10/20   B. 11/20   C. 71/20   D. 3/20   E. 4/20

32. If $\frac{2}{x} + \frac{3}{5} = \frac{4}{3}$, then which of the following is the value of x?   32.____
    A. 30/11   B. 30/29   C. 11/30   D. -11/6   E. -5/2

33. Optometry school applicants decreased by 25% during a 4-year period. During the same time, the number of first-year openings in optometry school increased by 12%.   33.____
    If the ratio of applicants to first-year student openings had been 3 to 1, then which of the following would be the APPROXIMATE ratio at the end of the 4-year period?
    A. 1.5 to 1   B. 2 to 1   C. 3 to 2   D. 4 to 3   E. 6 to 5

34. If then which of the following is the value of x?   34.____
    A. 4   B. 27   C. 29   D. 40   E. 729

35. Two cars start at the same point and travel north and west at the rate of 24 and 32 mph, respectively.   35.____
    How far apart are they at the end of 2 hours?
    A. 63   B. 80   C. 112   D. 116   E. 100

36. Right triangle ABC with right angle C and AB = 6, BC = 3, find AC.   36.____
    A. 3   B. 6   C. 27   D. 33   E. $3\sqrt{3}$

37. When each of the sides of a square is increased by 1 yard, the area of the new square is 53 square yards more than that of the original square.   37.____
    What is the length of the sides of the original square?
    A. 25   B. 26   C. 27   D. 52   E. 54

38. Evaluate: $3(2)^2 + \sqrt{25} - (-2)^3$.   38.____
    A. 9   B. 24   C. 25   D. 33   E. 76

39. Which of the following is the length of the line segment BC if AB = 14, AD = 5, and angle BAD = 30°?   39.____
    A. $\sqrt{221}$
    B. $\sqrt{171}$
    C. $7\sqrt{3}$
    D. 7
    E. 9

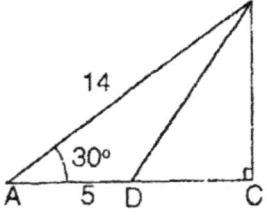

40. A bowl contains 7 green and 3 red marbles.   40.____
    What is the probability that two marbles selected at random from this bowl without replacement are both red?
    A. 1/15   B. 9/100   C. 21/100   D. 47/90   E. 6/10

41. If x pens cost 75 cents and y pencils cost 57 cents, then which equation below can be used to find the cost of 2 pens and 3 pencils?
    A. 2(75/x) + 3(57/y)   B. 3x/75 + 2y/57   C. 75/2x + 57/3y
    D. 2(x/75) + 3(y/57)   E. 3(75/x) + 2(57/y)

42. Maria has a number of dimes and quarters whose total value is less than $9.00. There are twice as many dimes as quarters.
    At most, how many quarters could she have?
    A. 14   B. 15   C. 19   D. 20   E. 35

43. The number (1, 2, 3, 6) have an average (arithmetic mean) of 3 and a variance of 3.5.
    What is the average (arithmetic mean) and variance of the set of numbers (3, 6, 9, 18)?
    A. 9, 31.5   B. 3, 10.5   C. 3, 31.5   D. 6, 7.5   E. 9, 27.5

44. A fence encloses a triangular-shaped region whose sides are 20 feet, 20 feet, and 10 feet in length.
    If the number of inches between fence posts (centers) is 30 inches, how many posts will be needed?
    A. 17   B. 20   C. 21   D. 22   E. 23

45. A ceiling 6 feet by 7 feet can be painted for $52.
    Find the cost of painting a ceiling 18 feet by 21 feet, all things equal except the dimensions.
    A. $104   B. $126   C. $156   D. $378   E. $468

46. Three consecutive odd numbers have a sum of 51.
    What is the LARGEST of these numbers?
    A. 15   B. 17   C. 18   D. 19   E. 21

47. It takes 5 hours for a qualified typist to complete a report. Coffee break begins at 10:15 A.M. It is now 9:55 A.M.
    How much of the task can the typist be expected to complete by coffee break?
    A. 1/8   B. 1/25   C. 1/3   D. 1/6   E. 1/15

48. A container in the form of a rectangular solid is 10 feet long, 9 feet wide, and 2 feet deep. The container is filled with a liquid weighing 100 pounds per cubic foot.
    A. 90   B. 180   C. 1,800   D. 9,000   E. 18,000

49. The value of cost ($\pi/3$) equals the value of
    A. $-\cos(2\pi/3)$ B. $\cos(2\pi/3)$ C. $\cos(6\pi/3)$
    D. $-\cos(5\pi/3)$ E. $\cos(4\pi/3)$

50. If $5 \leq x \leq 12$ and -2y9, then is as large as possible when x = _____ and y = _____.
    A. 12; 9   B. 12; 0   C. 12; -2   D. 0; 0   E. 0; 0

KEY (CORRECT ANSWERS)

1. D	11. B	21. A	31. B	41. A
2. E	12. B	22. B	32. A	42. C
3. B	13. D	23. C	33. B	43. A
4. D	14. B	24. D	34. C	44. B
5. D	15. B	25. A	35. B	45. E
6. E	16. C	26. C	36. E	46. D
7. E	17. E	27. D	37. B	47. E
8. B	18. E	28. C	38. C	48. E
9. C	19. A	29. D	39. D	49. A
10. A	20. D	30. A	40. A	50. B

SOLUTIONS TO PROBLEMS

1. Let x = rate of walking/running. Then, $(50)(1/2) + (x)(1/2) = 28$. Simplifying, $1/2x = 3$. Solving, $x = 6$.

2. $3 + \frac{1}{4} = 3\frac{1}{4}$, $1/3 \cdot \frac{1}{4} = \frac{4}{13}$, $2 + \frac{4}{13} = 2\frac{4}{13}$, $1/2 \cdot \frac{4}{13} = \frac{13}{30}$
   Finally, $1 + \frac{13}{30} = 1\frac{13}{30}$

3. Let x = number of adults, 240-x = number of children.
   Then, $5x + 2.50(240-x) = 800$. Simplifying, we get $5x + 600 - 2.50x = 800$. This reduces to $2.50x = 200$. Solving, $x = 800$

4. $\sqrt{25 + x} = 13$ squaring both sides, $25 + x = 169$. So, $x = 144$.

5. If the perimeter of a square is 20, each side must be 5. The area is $5^2 = 25$.

6. Changing to a denominator of 32, we get $8/32 + 12/32 + 12/32 - 12/32 - 8/32 = 0/32 = 0$

7. Let x = original amount. 100% - 20% - 25% = 55%. Then, $\$66 = .55x$. Solving, $x = \$120$

8. $(2x+5y)^2 = 4x^2 + 10xy + 25y^2 = 4x^2 + 20xy + 25y^2$

9. Let x = grade on her 4th test. Then, $(83+90+88+x)/4 = 84$. This becomes $(261+x)/4 = 84$. Further reduction leads to $261 + x = 336$, so $x - 75$.

10. The required distance is $\sqrt{3^2 + 4^2 + 2^2} = \sqrt{9 + 16 + 4} = \sqrt{29}$

11. $(1.672 \times 10^{-27}) \div (9.1109 \times 10^{-31})$. $1836 \times 10^4 \approx 1800$

12. Total savings is $\$1450)(8) = \$11,600$. Equipment costs $(1/4)(\$11,600) = \$2900$.

13. $\$1740 = P(I+.16)'$. Then, $P = \$1740 \div 1.16 = \$1500$.

14. 1/4% of 200 is $(.0025)(200) = .5$

15. .5% of .95 is $(.005)(.95) = .00475$

16. 5 lbs. 1 oz. = 81 oz. and 3 lbs. 6 oz. = 54 oz. Then, 81 oz. ÷ 54 oz. = 1.5

17. 3/8 cm = 3/8 ÷ 2.54 = .375 ÷ 2.54 ≈ .1476 ≈ .15 inch.

18. From equation 1, $y = 7 - 2x$. Substituting into equation 2, $x - 4(7-2x) = 4$. Simplifying, $x - 28 + 8x = 4$. This reduces to $9x = 32$, so $x = 32/9$

19. Since there are 3600 seconds in 1 hour, 6 seconds would represent 6/3600 = 1/600 of an hour.

8 (#1)

20. 1/3 + 5(x-1) = 8. Simplify to 1/3 + 5x – 5 = 8. This will reduce to 5x = 12 2/3, so x = 38/15.

21. A line perpendicular to the x-axis must have an undefined slope. The equation must be x = constant. The only choice fitting this format is x = 3.

22. The receptionist works 40 hours at R/2 dollars per week. Thus, the weekly payroll for all three workers is H + 36A + R/2. (The 40 hours is not used in computing.)

23. The total bill was (5)($12) + (10)($13) + (4)($20) = $230. Company A's bill was $60. Thus, $60/$230 ≈ 26.1% ≈ 26%.

24. 50(A/100) = 2A^2 becomes A/2 = 2A^2. Simplifying further, we get A = 4A^2. Simplifying further, we get A = 4A^2 or A(4A-1) = 0. The two values of A are 0 and 1/4.

25. The number of single males is represented as (5/8)(1/5)(100)% = 12.5%

26. z = .35x and x = .20y. Thus, z = (.35)(.20)y = .07y.

27. The numerator is |11| - |-9| = 11 - 9 = 2. The denominator is 3|-1| = 3. Thus, the fraction = 2/3.

28. Let x = required number of minutes. Then, 1/30x – 1/50x = 1. Multiplying by 150, 5x – 3x = 150. Solving, x = 75.

29. $\frac{4}{5}x = \frac{2}{5}y$. Then, $\frac{y}{x} = \frac{4}{5} \div \frac{2}{5} = 2$

30. $x = \frac{1}{y}$ becomes xy = 1, which represents a hyperbola.

31. $\frac{5}{4} + \frac{4}{5} + \frac{3}{2}$ = (25+16+30)/20 = 71/20. If 71/20 – x = a positive integer, then the only correct values of x are 11/20, 31/20, 51/20.

32. Multiplying the equation by 15x, we get 30 + 9x = 20x. Then, 30 = 11x, so x = 30/11.

33. Let 3x = number of applicants, x = 1st year student openings. Over the 4-year period, the number of applicants dropped to .75(3x) = 2.25x and the number of openings rose to 1.12x. Now, 2.25x ÷ 1.12x ≈ 2 to 1.

34. $\sqrt{x - 25}$ = 2. Squaring both sides, x – 25 = 4, so x = 29.

35. At the end of 2 hours, their individual <u>distances</u> are 48 miles and 64 miles. Their distance apart is = 80 miles.

36. AC^2 + 3^2 = 6^2. This simplifies to AC^2 = 27. Thus, AC = $\sqrt{27}$ = 3$\sqrt{3}$

9 (#1)

37. Let x = original length of each side, so that x + 1 = new length of each side of the square. Then, $(x+1)^2 - x^2 + 53$. This simplifies to $x^2 + 2x + 1 = x^2 + 53$. Then, $2x + 1 = 53$, so x = 26.

38. $3(2)^2 + \sqrt{25} - (-2)^3 = 12 + 5 + 8 = 25$.

39. Sine 30° = BC/14 1/2 = BC/14, so BC = 7.

40. Probability of 2 red marbles being drawn without replacement is (3/10)(2/9) = 1/15.

41. Each pen costs 75/x cents and each pencil costs 57/y cents. Then, 2 pens and 3 pencils cost 2(75/x) + 3(57/y).

42. Let x = number of quarters, 2x = number of dimes. Then, .25x + .10(2x) < 9.00. Solving, x < 20, so x = 19.

43. The new set of numbers is 3 times as large as the original set. Therefore, the mean is 3 times as big, which is 9, and the variance is 3^2 or 9 times as big, which is (9)(3.5)= 31.5.

44. Using the diagram shown at the right, for the fence $\overline{BC}$, we'll need 5 posts whose distance from each other is 12 1/2'. (This includes a post at B and a post at C.) Now along $\overline{AB}$, since AB = 20' and $20 \div 2\frac{1}{2} = 8$, we'll need 8 posts (including a post at A). Finally, starting at A and ending at C, we need to place only 20 ÷ 2 1/2 – 1 = 7 posts since a post already exists at A and at C. Thus, the total number of posts is 5 + 8 + 7 = 20.

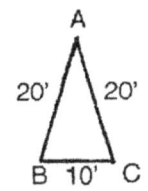

45. (6')(7') = 42 square feet costing $52, which means $52/$42 or $(26/21) per square foot. Now a ceiling 18 ft. by 21 ft. is 378 square feet and will cost (26/21)(378) = $468.

46. Let x, x+2, x+4 represent the three odd numbers. Then, x + x+2 + x+4 = 51. This reduces to 3x + 6 = 51, from which x = 15. The three numbers are 15,17, 19 and so the largest is 19.

47. From 9:55 A.M. to 10:15 A.M. represents 20 minutes. Then, 20 minutes/5 hours = 20 minutes/300 minutes, which reduces to 1/15.

48. Volume is (10)(9)(2) = 180 cu. ft. The weight of the liquid is (100)(180) = 18,000 lbs.

49. Cosine $\frac{\pi}{3}$ = .5, which is also the value of -Cosine $\frac{2\pi}{3}$.

50. To make $(3x-4)(4+5y^2)$ as large as possible, we maximize the numerator and minimize the denominator. Given the restriction $5 \leq x \leq 12$, use x = 12. Given the restriction use y = 0. (Note carefully that y = 0 yields a smaller value of $4 + 5y^2$ than y = -2)

ABSTRACT REASONING

COMMENTARY

The mathematical or quantitative ability of the candidate is generally measured through the form of questions and/or problems involving arithmetical reasoning, algebraic problem solving, and the interpretation of visual materials—graphs, charts, tables, diagrams, maps, cartoons, and pictures.

A more recent development, which attempts to assay facets of quantitative ability not ordinarily discernible or measurable, is the nonverbal test of reasoning of the type commonly designated as the figure analogy. Figure analogies are novel and differentiated measures of non-numerical mathematics reasoning.

Since intelligence exists in many forms or phases and the theory of differential aptitudes is now firmly established in testing, other manifestations and measurements of intelligence than verbal or purely arithmetical must be identified and measured.

Classification inventory, or figure classification, involves the aptitude of form perception, i.e., the ability to perceive pertinent detail in objects or in pictorial or graphic material. It involves making visual comparisons and discriminations and discerning slight differences in shapes and shading figures and widths and lengths of lines.

One aspect of this type of nonverbal question takes the form of a *positive* requirement to find the COMPATIBLE PATTERN (i.e., the one that *does* belong) from among two (2) sets of figure groups. The prescription for this question-type is as follows:

A group of three drawings lettered A, B, and C, respectively, is presented, followed on the same line by five (5) numbered alternative drawings labeled 1, 2, 3, 4, and 5, respectively.

The first two (2) drawings (A, B) in each question are related in some way.

The candidate is then to decide what characteristic *each* of the figures labeled A and B has that causes them to be related, and is then to select the one alternative from the five (5) numbered figures that is related to figure C in the same way that drawing B is related to drawing A.

Leading examples of presentation are the figure analogy and the figure classification. The Section that follows presents progressive and varied samplings of this type of question.

FIGURE ANALOGIES

Figure analogies are a novel and differentiated measure of non-numerical mathematics reasoning.

This question takes the form of, and, indeed, is similar to, the one-blank verbal analogy. However, pictures or drawings are used instead of words.

SAMPLE QUESTIONS AND EXPLANATIONS

DIRECTIONS: Each question in this part consists of 3 drawings lettered A, B, C, followed by 5 alternative drawings, numbered 1 to 5. The first 2 drawings in each question are related in some way. Choose the number of the alternative that is related to the third drawing in the same way that the second drawing is related to the first, and mark the appropriate space on your answer sheet.

1.

The CORRECT answer is 3. A vertical line has the same relationship to a horizontal line that a rectangle standing on its end has to a rectangle lying on its side.

2.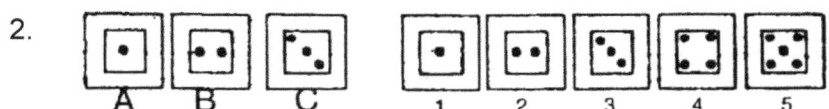

The second square has one more dot than the first square. Therefore, the CORRECT answer is alternative 4, which has one more dot than the third square.

3.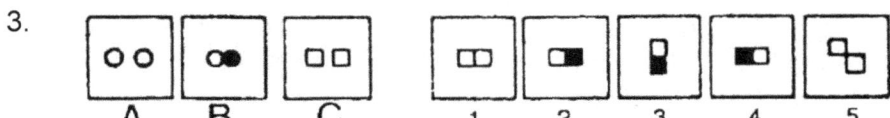

In the second drawing, the circles are moved together and the circle on the right darkened. Therefore, the CORRECT answer is 2, in which the squares are moved together and the right-hand square darkened.

4.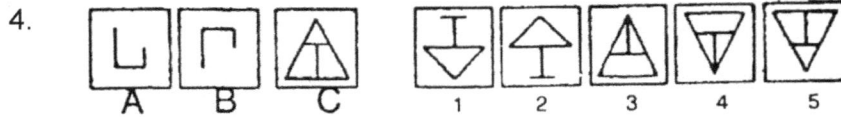

The CORRECT answer is 5. The second drawing is the inverted version of the first; alternative 5 is the inverted version of the third drawing.

5.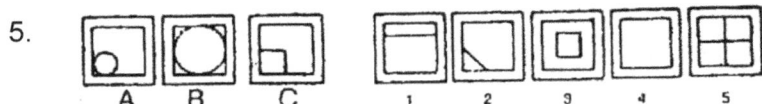

The CORRECT answer is 4. Drawing A has a small circle within a square; drawing B contains a circle completely filling the square. Drawing C has a small square within a square; in alternative 4, this small square has been magnified to its complete size within the outline of only one square.

6.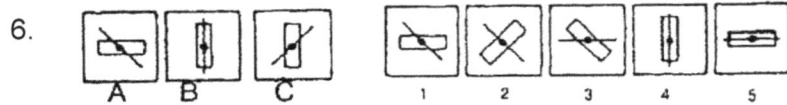

The CORRECT answer is 5. Drawing A appears in a horizontal position, with a diagonal line drawn through the center dot; drawing B appears in a vertical position, with a straight line drawn through the center dot. Drawing C is similar to drawing A, except that it appears in a vertical position; drawing 5 is similar to drawing B, except that it appears in a horizontal position. Our analogy may, therefore, be verbally expressed as

A : B : C : 5.

SUGGESTIONS FOR ANSWERING THE FIGURE ANALOGY QUESTION

1. In doing the actual questions, there can be little practical gain in rationalizing each answer that you attempt. What is needed is a quick and ready perceptive sense in this matter.

2. The BEST way to prepare for this type of question is to do the "Tests" in figure analogies that follow. By this method, you will gain enough functional skill to enable you to cope successfully with this type of question on the Examination.

SAMPLE TEST

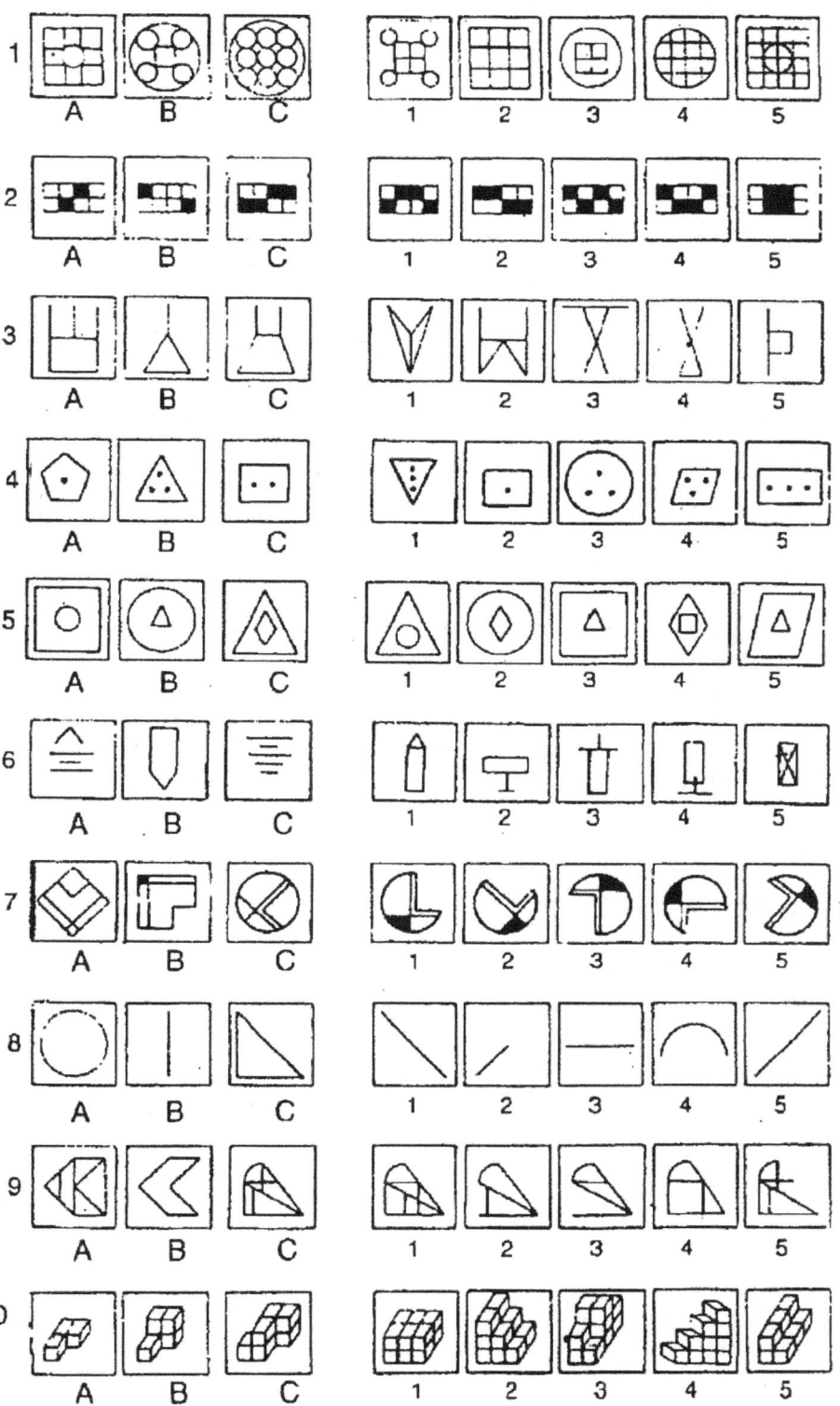

6

KEY (CORRECT ANSWERS)

1.	2	5.	4
2.	2	6.	3
3.	4	7.	3
4.	1	8.	2

EXPLANATION OF ANSWERS

1. In the second figure, the squares are changed to circles and the circles to squares.

2. In the second figure, the upper darkened area has moved two squares to the left, the lower, two squares to right.

3. The second figure has a flat base, like the first.

4. The sum and sides and dots in the second figure equals that of the first.

5. The outside part of the second figure is the inside part of the first.

6. The second figure is constructed from the lines given in the first.

7. The second figure is obtained from the first by rotating it 135° clockwise, darkening the smaller area and deleting the larger.

8. The second figure is the bisector of the area of the first.

9. The second figure is obtained from the first by deleting all the vertical lines.

10. The second figure contains two blocks more than the first.

FIGURE ANALOGIES
EXAMINATION SECTION
TEST 1

DIRECTIONS: Each question in this part consists of three drawings lettered A, B, C, followed by five alternative drawings, numbered 1 through 5. The first two drawings in each question are related in some way. Choose the number of the alternative that is related to the third drawing in the same way that the second drawing is related to the first and mark the appropriate space on your answer sheet.

TEST 2

DIRECTIONS: Each question in this part consists of three drawings lettered A, B, C, followed by five alternative drawings, numbered 1 through 5. The first two drawings in each question are related in some way. Choose the number of the alternative that is related to the third drawing in the same way that the second drawing is related to the first and mark the appropriate space on your answer sheet.

TEST 3

DIRECTIONS: Each question in this part consists of three drawings lettered A, B, C, followed by five alternative drawings, numbered 1 through 5. The first two drawings in each question are related in some way. Choose the number of the alternative that is related to the third drawing in the same way that the second drawing is related to the first and mark the appropriate space on your answer sheet.

TEST 4

DIRECTIONS: Each question in this part consists of three drawings lettered A, B, C, followed by five alternative drawings, numbered 1 through 5. The first two drawings in each question are related in some way. Choose the number of the alternative that is related to the third drawing in the same way that the second drawing is related to the first and mark the appropriate space on your answer sheet.

TEST 5

DIRECTIONS: Each question in this part consists of three drawings lettered A, B, C, followed by five alternative drawings, numbered 1 through 5. The first two drawings in each question are related in some way. Choose the number of the alternative that is related to the third drawing in the same way that the second drawing is related to the first and mark the appropriate space on your answer sheet.

KEY (CORRECT ANSWERS)

TEST 1
1. 2   6. 2
2. 4   7. 1
3. 1   8. 3
4. 5   9. 3
5. 3   10. 5

TEST 2
1. 3   6. 2
2. 1   7. 1
3. 5   8. 4
4. 2   9. 4
5. 3   10. 1

TEST 3
1. 1   6. 2
2. 3   7. 1
3. 2   8. 4
4. 4   9. 5
5. 5   10. 3

TEST 4
1. 2   6. 5
2. 5   7. 4
3. 1   8. 3
4. 3   9. 5
5. 2   10. 4

TEST 5
1. 1   6. 5
2. 3   7. 3
3. 5   8. 1
4. 2   9. 4
5. 2   10. 4

FIGURE ANALOGIES/*INCOMPATIBLE PATTERN*

A form of the figure classification question is the nonverbal question which takes the form of finding the INCOMPATIBLE PATTERN from among two (2) sets of figure groups. The prescription for this question-type is as follows:

Two groups of four (4) figures each, labeled 1 and 2, are presented side by side. Then follows on the same line a third group of five (5) figures, labeled A, B, C, D, and E, respectively. The candidate is then to decide what characteristics EACH of the figure in group 1 has that NONE of the figures in group 2 has. Then select the lettered answer figure that has this characteristic.

SAMPLE QUESTIONS AND EXPLANATIONS

DIRECTIONS: Each of these problems consists of two groups of figures, labeled 1 and 2. These are followed by five (5) lettered answer figures. For each problem you are to decide what characteristic EACH of the figures in group 1 has that NONE of the figures in group 2 has. Then select the lettered answer figure that has this characteristic.

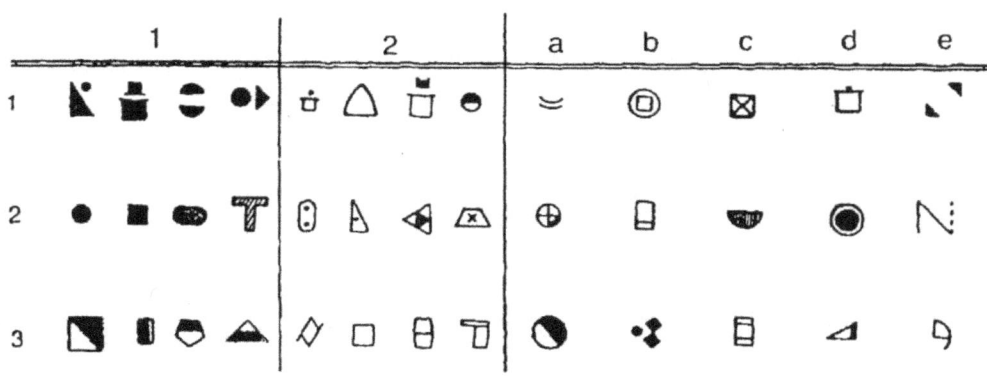

KEY
EXPLANATION OF ANSWERS

1. e Two figures completely blacked in.
2. c Shaded figure.
3. a A figure composed of solid line, partially shaded (blacked in).

TEST 1

TEST 2

TEST 3

TEST 4

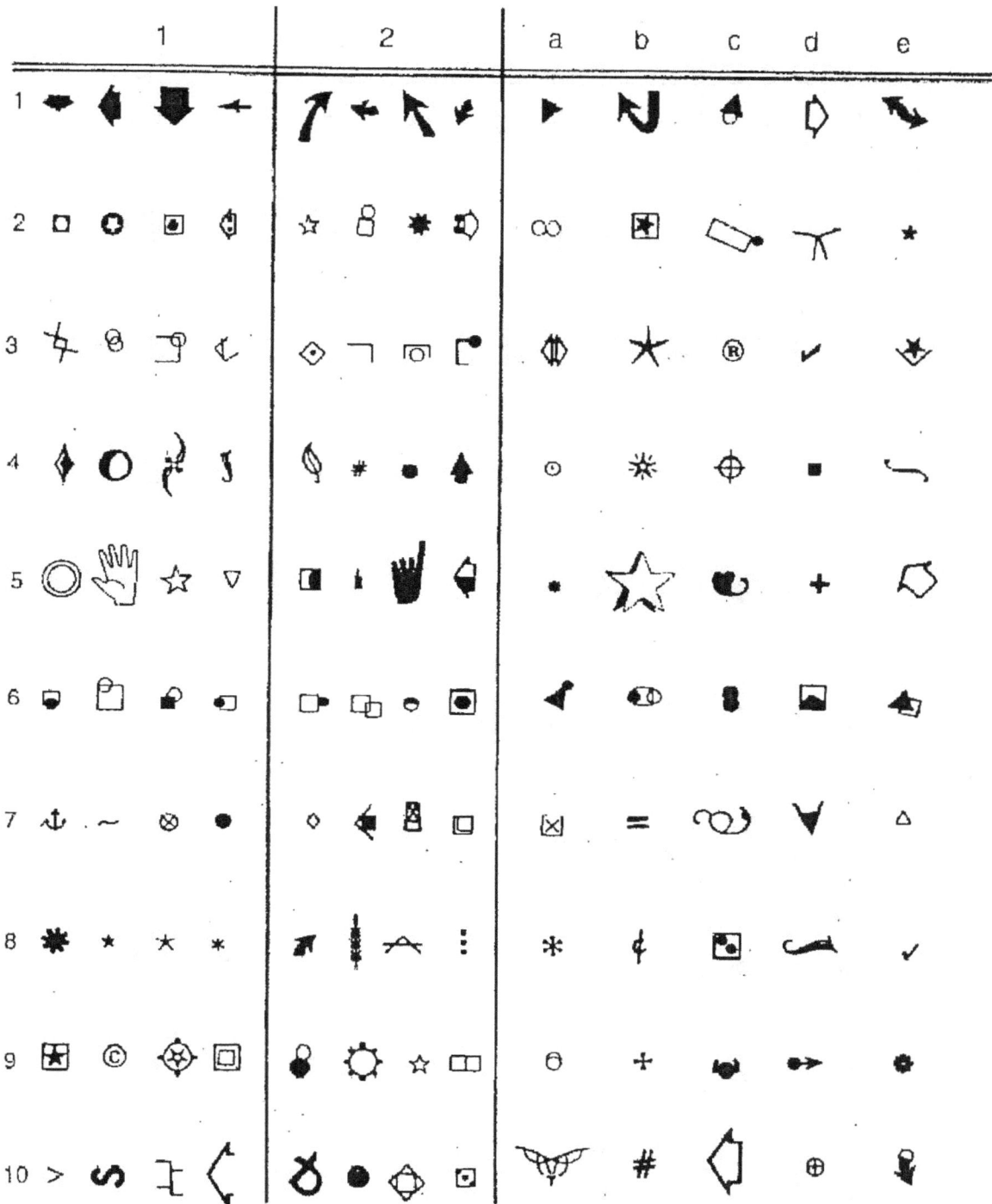

TEST 5

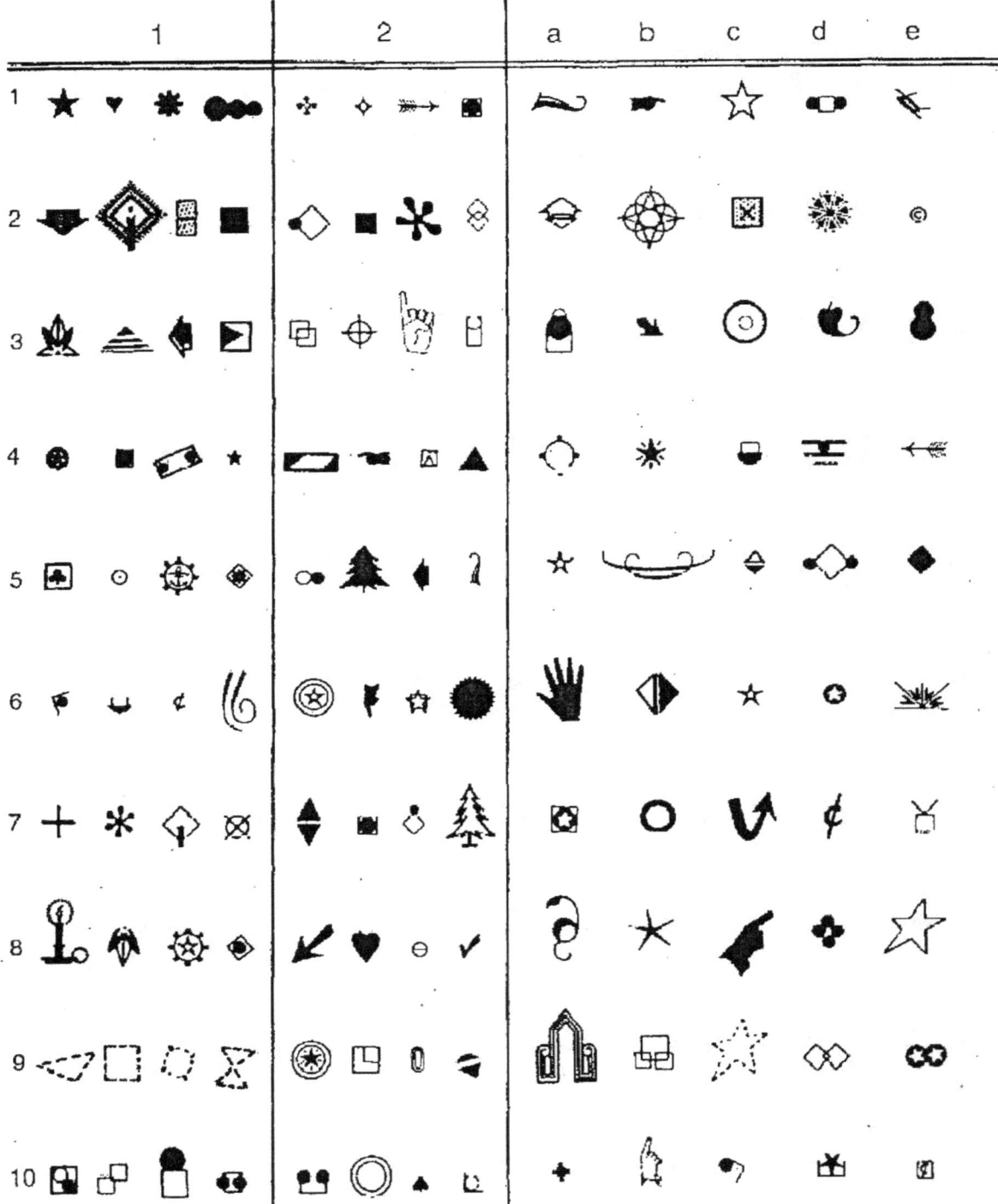

KEY (CORRECT ANSWERS)

EXPLANATION OF ANSWERS

TEST 1
1. e Solid circle
2. b Figure within a figure
3. c Square within a square, not filled in
4. e Dot within a figure
5. e Dot within a figure
6. c Open sided figure
7. e Open sided figure
8. a Overlapping figure
9. e Line extending from shape
10. b Shape within a shape

TEST 2
1. e Three-sided figure
2. d Completely broken-line figure
3. d Lines touch, but do not cross
4. a. Circular figure, half shaded
5. a Dot and straight line, not touching
6. b. Circular figure, partially shaded
7. d Triangular figure with dot inside
8. b Straight line figure
9. d Figures touch or overlap
10. c Two different figures, overlapping.

TEST 3
1. c Shaded (or lined) figure
2. a Completely broken outline with solid line center
3. c Smaller figure in conjunction with larger figure
4. d Three-sided figure
5. a Completely open figure
6. b Put together it makes a four-sided figure
7. e Cross ("X") inside of figure
8. d Shape made up of triangles
9. c Rounded (dotted) ends on star
10. e Part of center filled in solid

TEST 4
1. a Arrow with straight stem (not curved)
2. b Figure within a figure
3. a Overlapping lines
4. b Figure partially blacked in
5. e Complete line shape, not blacked in
6. b Circle and square overlapping
7. c Figure with curved line
8. a Star-shaped figure
9. e Figure within a figure
10. b Open-sided figure

TEST 5
1. b Completely blacked in figure
2. c Shaded figure
3. a Partially blacked in figure
4. d Dot within figure
5. a Figure within a figure
6. e Open-sided figure
7. d Figure with lines crossing
8. a Partially blacked in figure
9. c Broken line figure
10. e Figure with square

ABSTRACT REASONING

SPATIAL RELATIONS/TWO DIMENSIONS

COMMENTARY

Since intelligence exists in many forms or phases and the theory of differential aptitudes is now firmly established in testing, other manifestations and measurements of intelligence than verbal or purely arithmetical must be identified and measured.

The spatial relations test, including that phase designated as spatial perception, involves and measures the ability to solve problems, drawn up in the form of outlines or pictures, which are concerned with the shapes of objects or the interrelationship of their parts. While, concededly, little is known about the nature and scope of this aptitude, it appears that this ability is required in science, mathematics, engineering, and drawing courses and curricula. Accordingly, tests of spatial perception involving the reconstruction of two-dimensional patterns, are presented in this section.

It is to be noted that the relationships expressed in spatial tests are geometric, definitive, and exact. Keeping these basic characteristics in mind, the applicant is to proceed to solve the spatial perception problems in his own way. There is no set method of solving these problems. The examinee may find that there are different methods for different types of spatial problems. Therefore, the BEST way to prepare for this type of test is to TAKE and study the work-practice problems in two-dimensional patterns provided in this section.

ABSTRACT REASONING
SPATIAL RELATIONS/TWO DIMENSIONS

The tests of spatial relations that follow consist of items which involve the visualization of two dimensions.

Each of the items of these tests consists of a line of figures—a complete figure on the left and four lettered alternatives of component parts on the right, only one of which can be fitted together exactly to form the complete figure on the left.

The candidate is then required to select that choice of component parts which could be fitted together to form the complete figure given at the left.

SAMPLE QUESTIONS AND EXPLANATIONS

DIRECTIONS: The items in this part constitute a test of spatial relations involving two dimensions. Each item consists of a line of figures. The first figure is the complete figure. This is followed by four lettered choices of component parts, only one of which can be fitted together exactly to form the first (complete) figure.

Rules To Be Followed:
1. The lettered choice of component parts selected as the answer must have the same number of parts as the first (complete) figure.
2. The parts must fit exactly.
3. The parts may be turned around but may not be turned over.

1.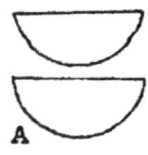

The correct answer is D. When the two parts of D are completely closed, they form the complete figure on the left.

2.

The correct answer is B. When the two parts of B are reversed in position, they form the complete figure on the left.

244

TEST 1

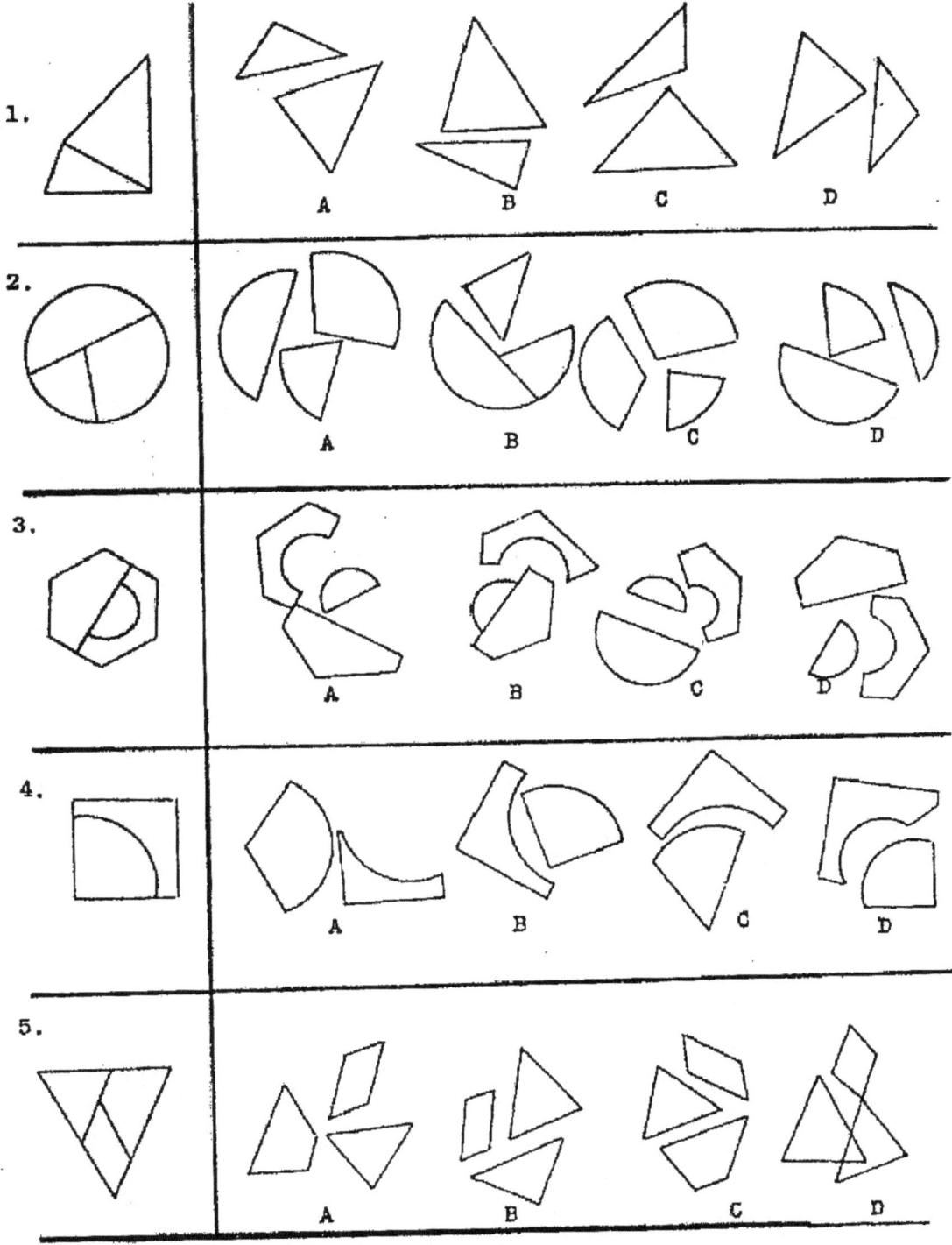

TEST 2

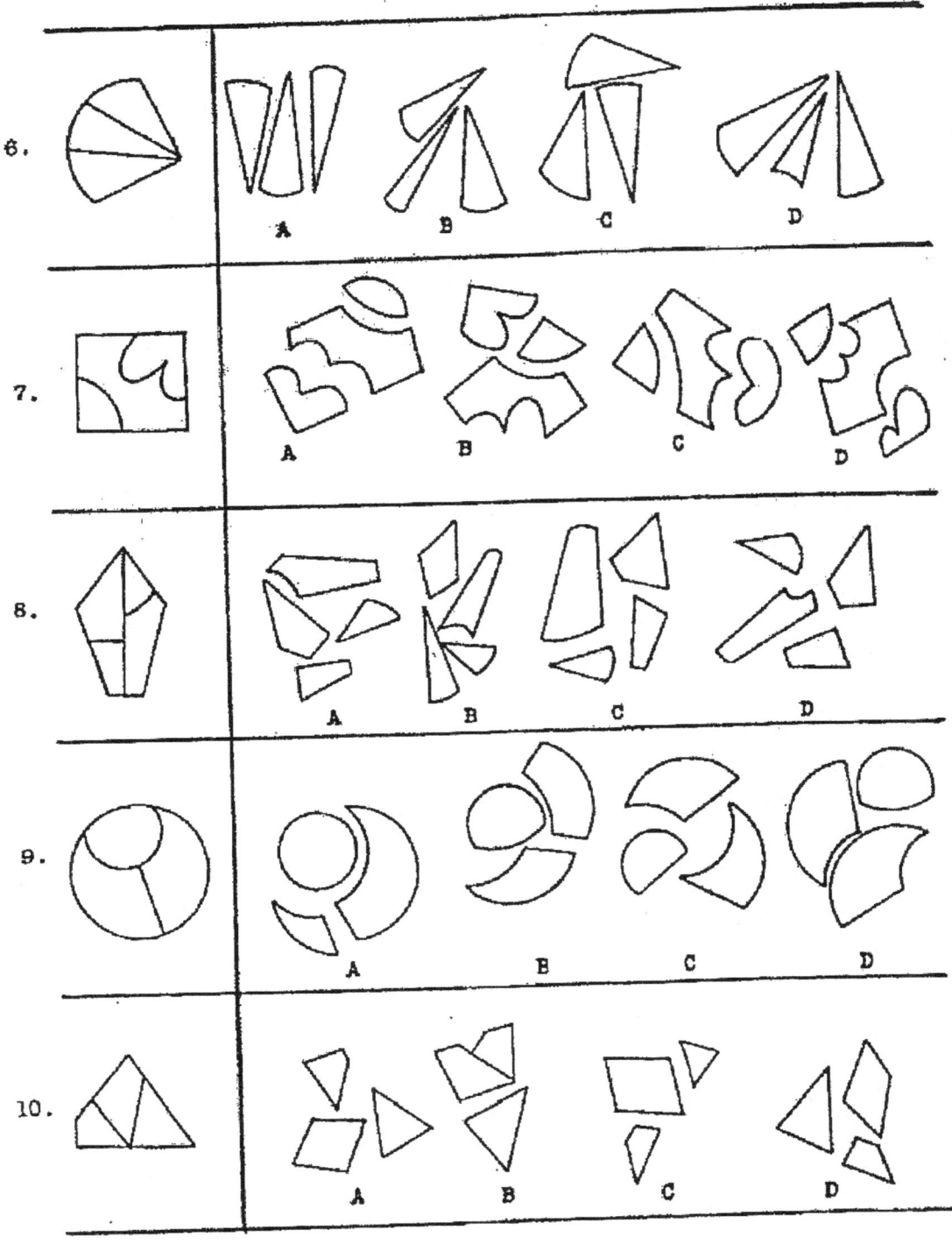

TEST 3

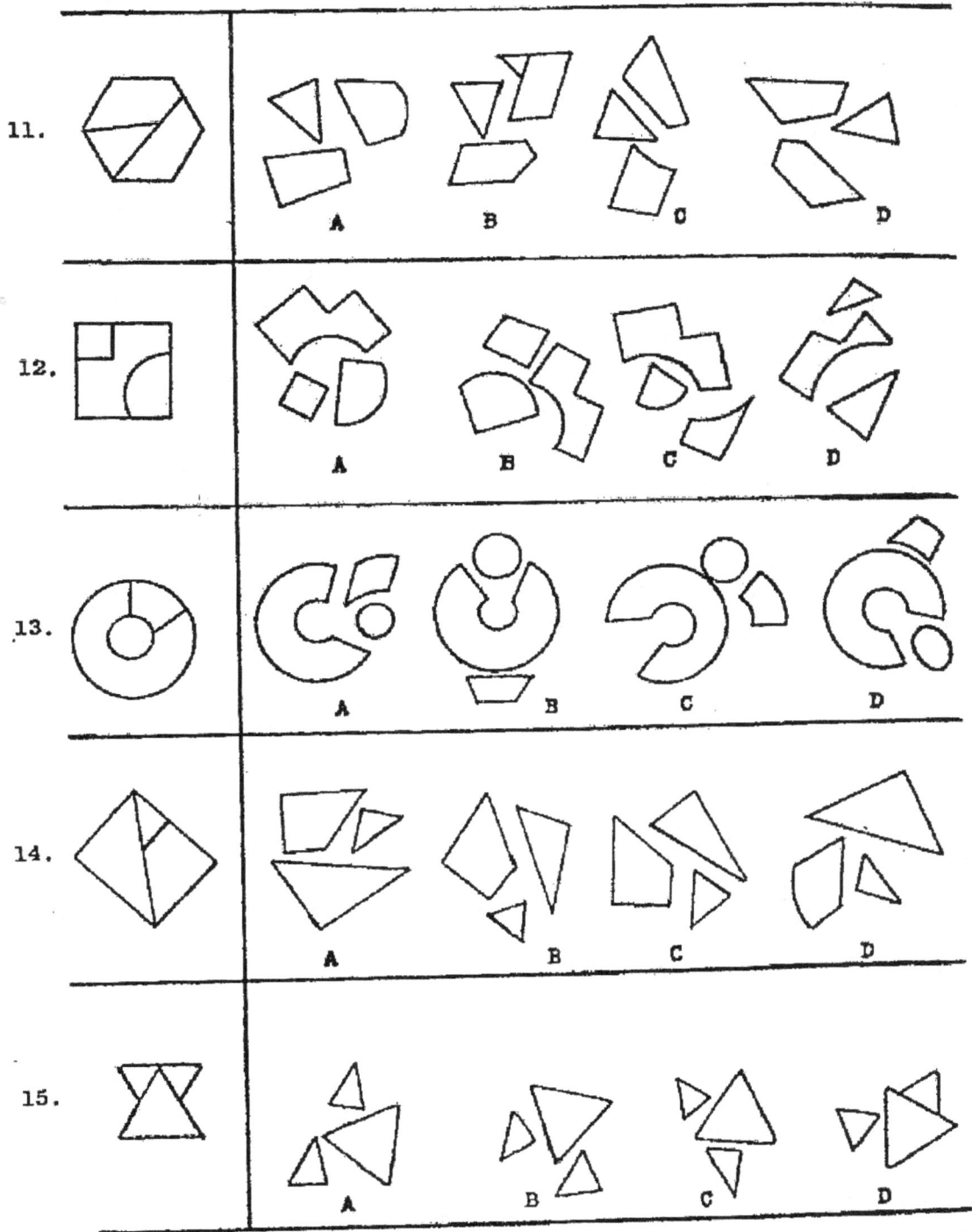

TEST 4

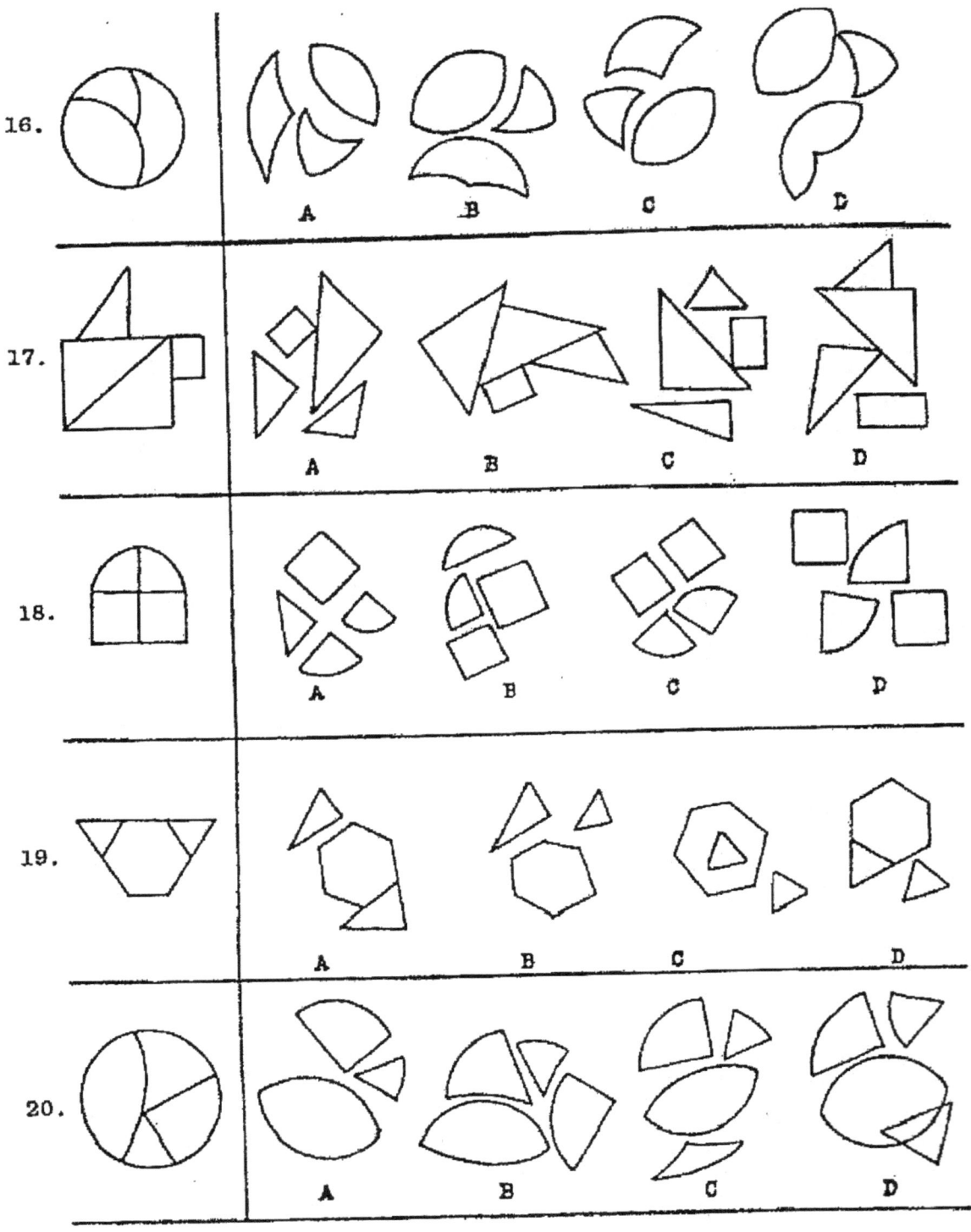

TEST 5

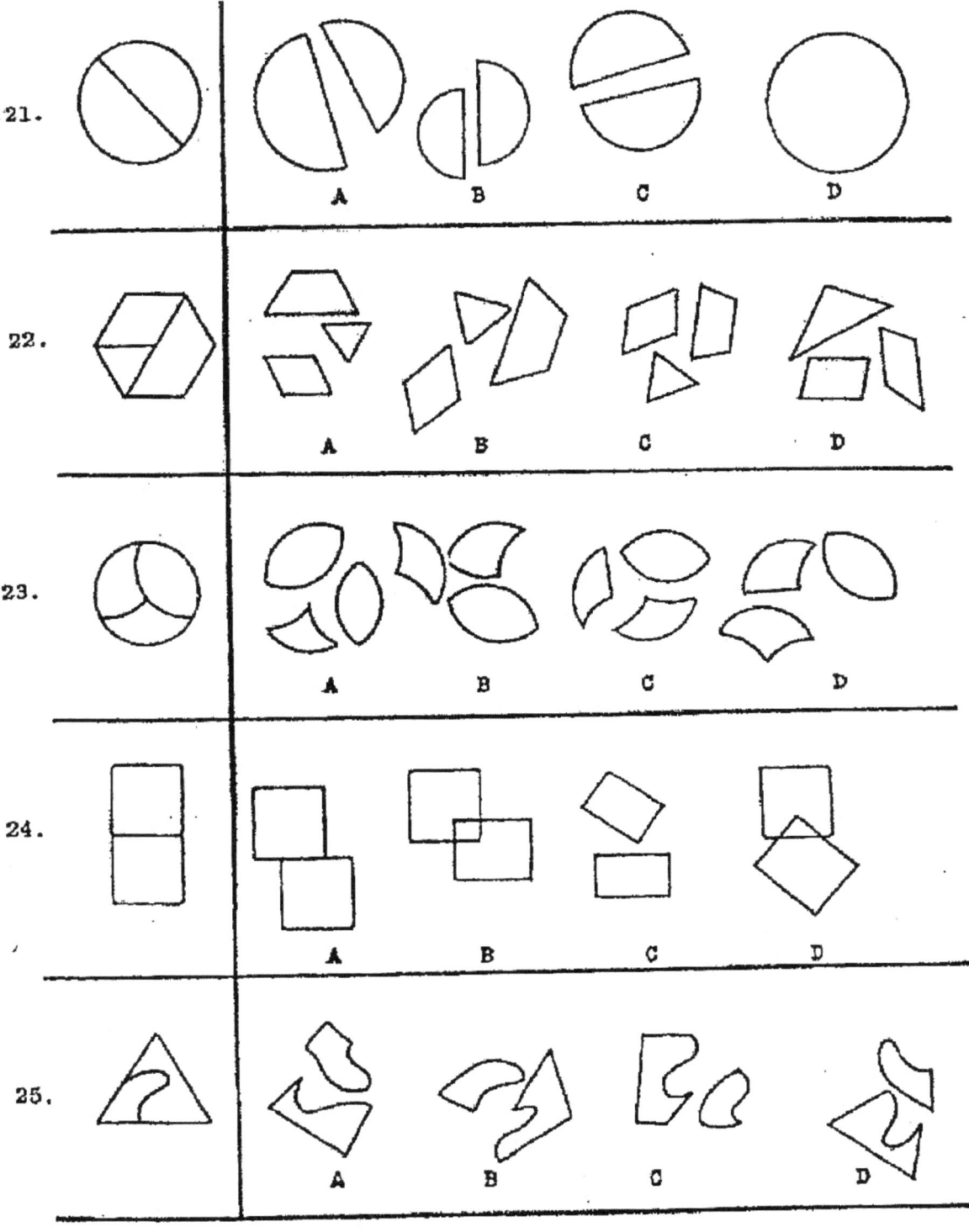

KEY (CORRECT ANSWERS)

TEST 1
1. B
2. A
3. D
4. B
5. C

TEST 2
6. C
7. B
8. A
9. D
10. B

TEST 3
11. D
12. A
13. C
14. A
15. D

TEST 4
16. B
17. B
18. C
19. D
20. B

TEST 5
1. C
2. B
3. B
4. A
5. D

SPATIAL RELATIONS
EXAMINATION SECTION
TEST 1

DIRECTIONS: In each of Questions 1 to 11 the front and top views of an object are given. Of the views labeled 1, 2, 3, and 4, select the one that CORRECTLY represents the right side view of each object for third angle projection.

1.
A. 1 B. 2 C. 3 D. 4

1.____

2.
A. 1 B. 2 C. 3 D. 4

2.____

3.
A. 1 B. 2 C. 3 D. 4

3.____

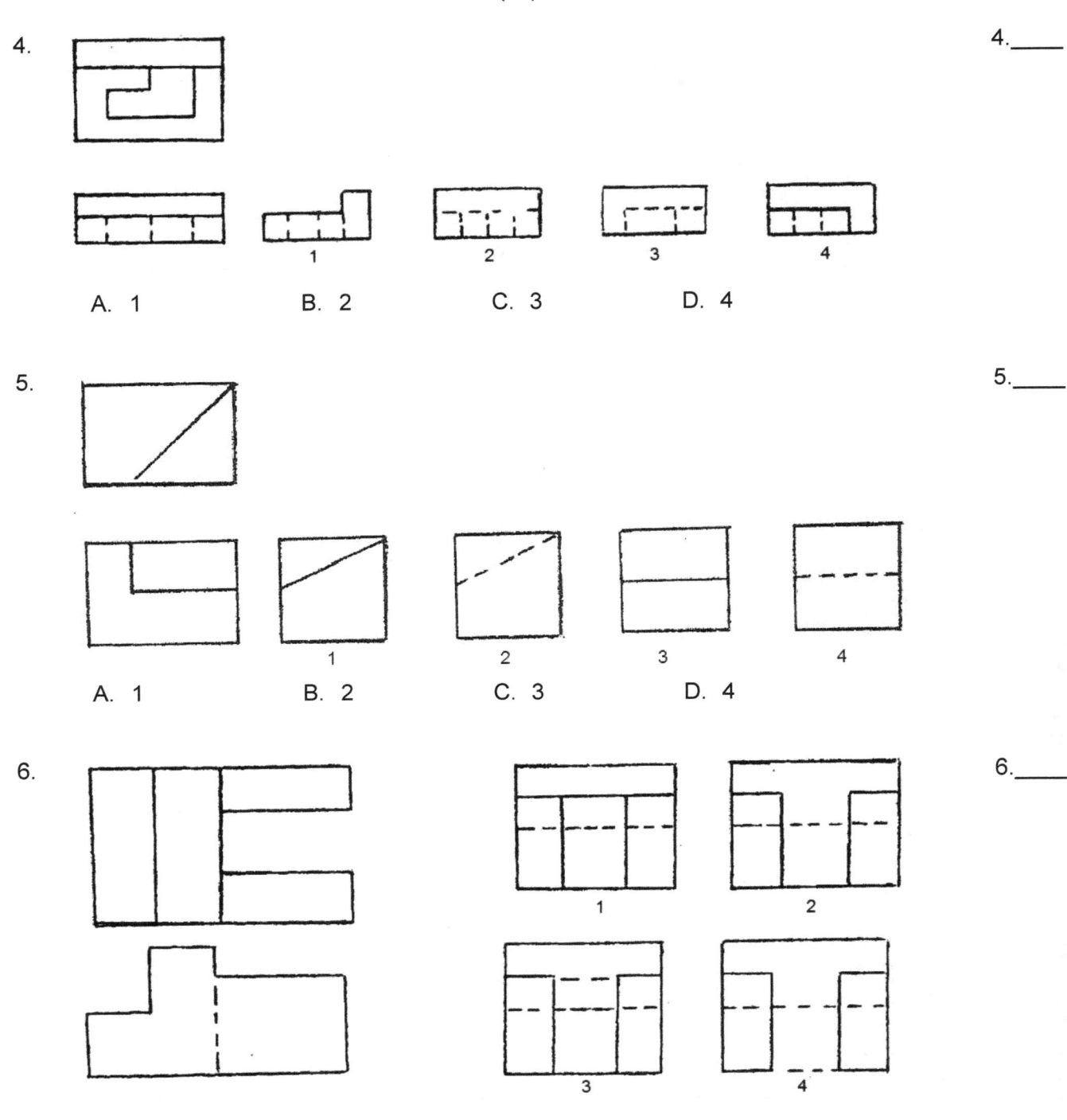

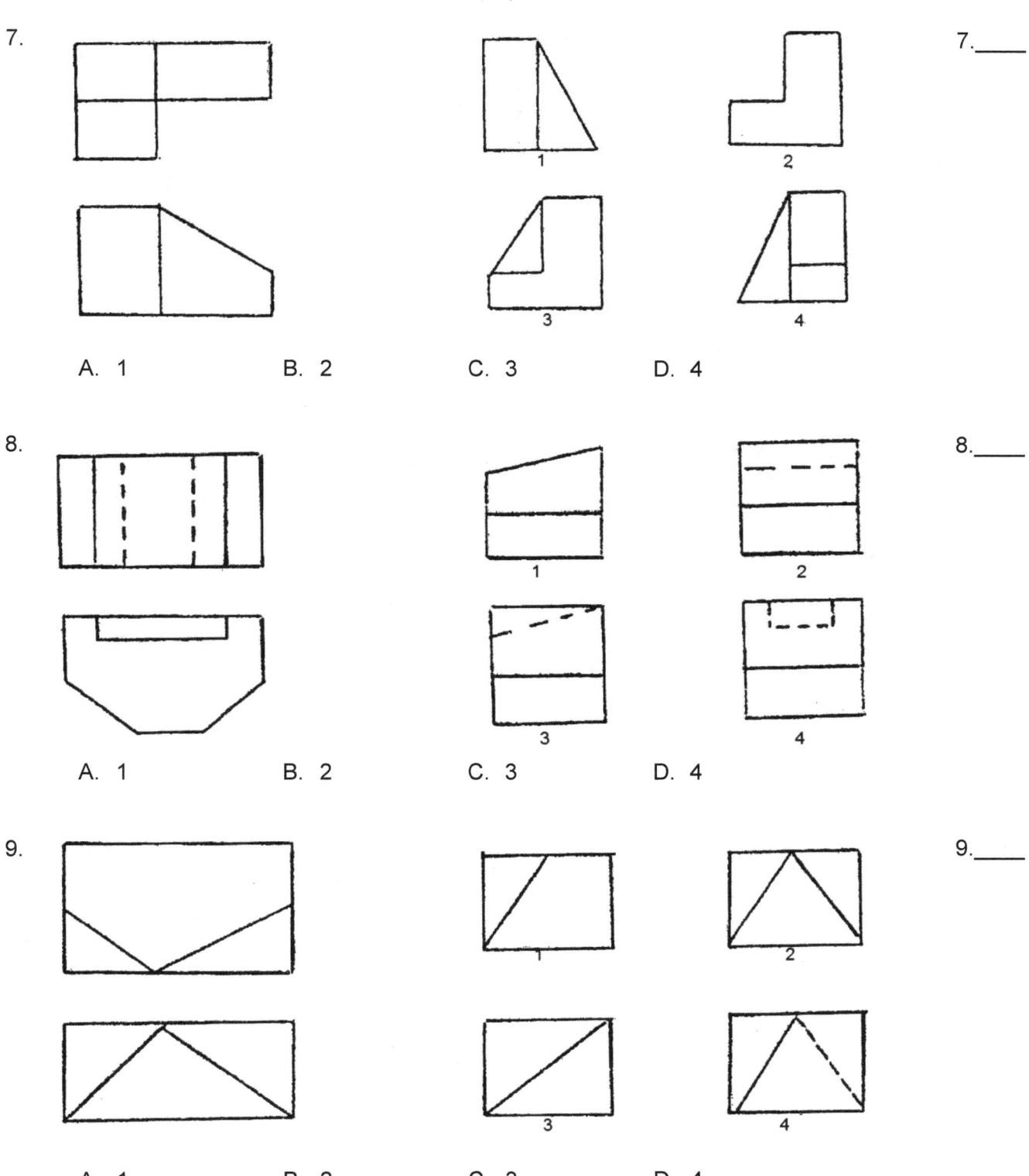

7. A. 1 B. 2 C. 3 D. 4

8. A. 1 B. 2 C. 3 D. 4

9. A. 1 B. 2 C. 3 D. 4

7. ___
8. ___
9. ___

10. 10.____

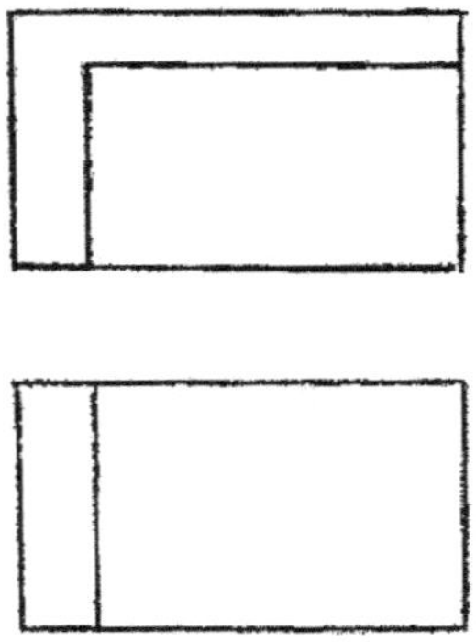

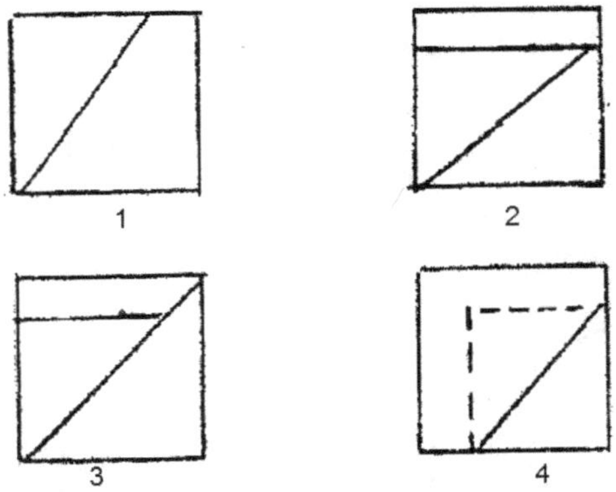

A. 1 B. 2 C. 3 D. 4

11. 11.____

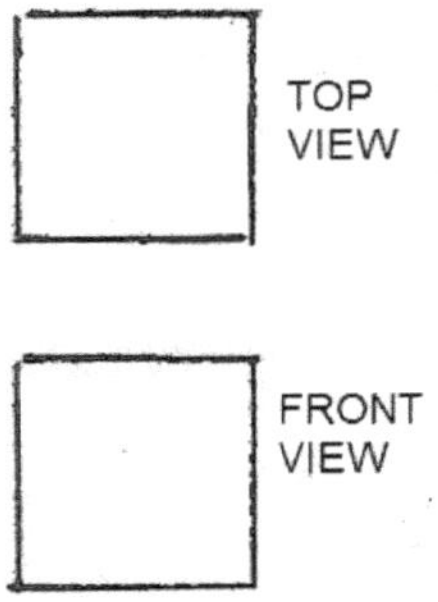

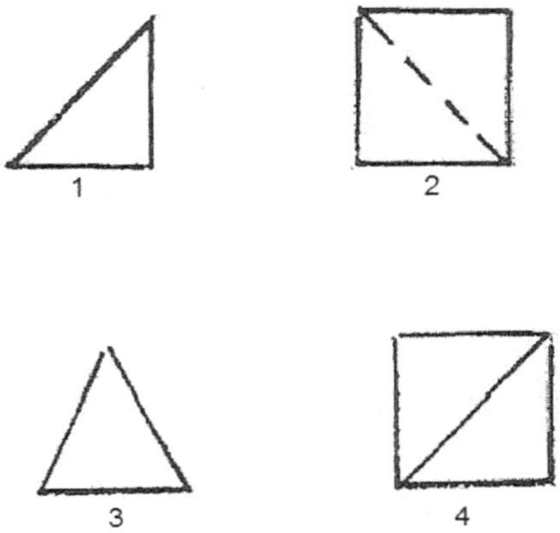

A. 1 B. 2 C. 3 D. 4

Questions 12-16.

DIRECTIONS: In each of Questions 12 to 25 inclusive, two views of an object are given. Of the views labeled 1, 2, 3, and 4, select the one that CORRECTLY represents the right side view of each object.

12. 12.____

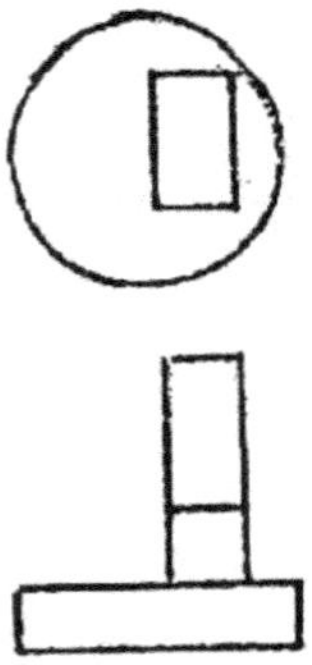

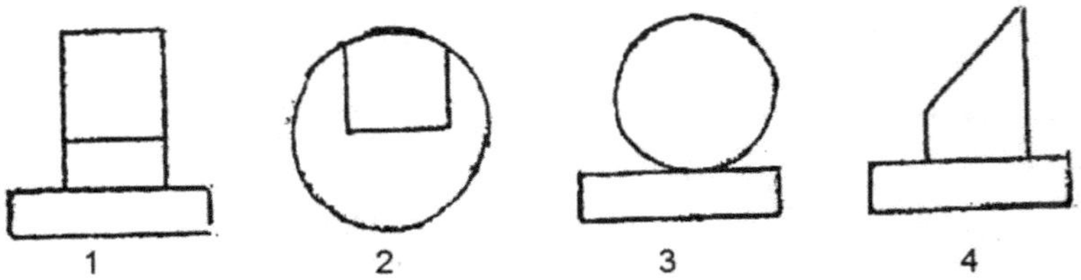

A. 1 B. 2 C. 3. D. 4

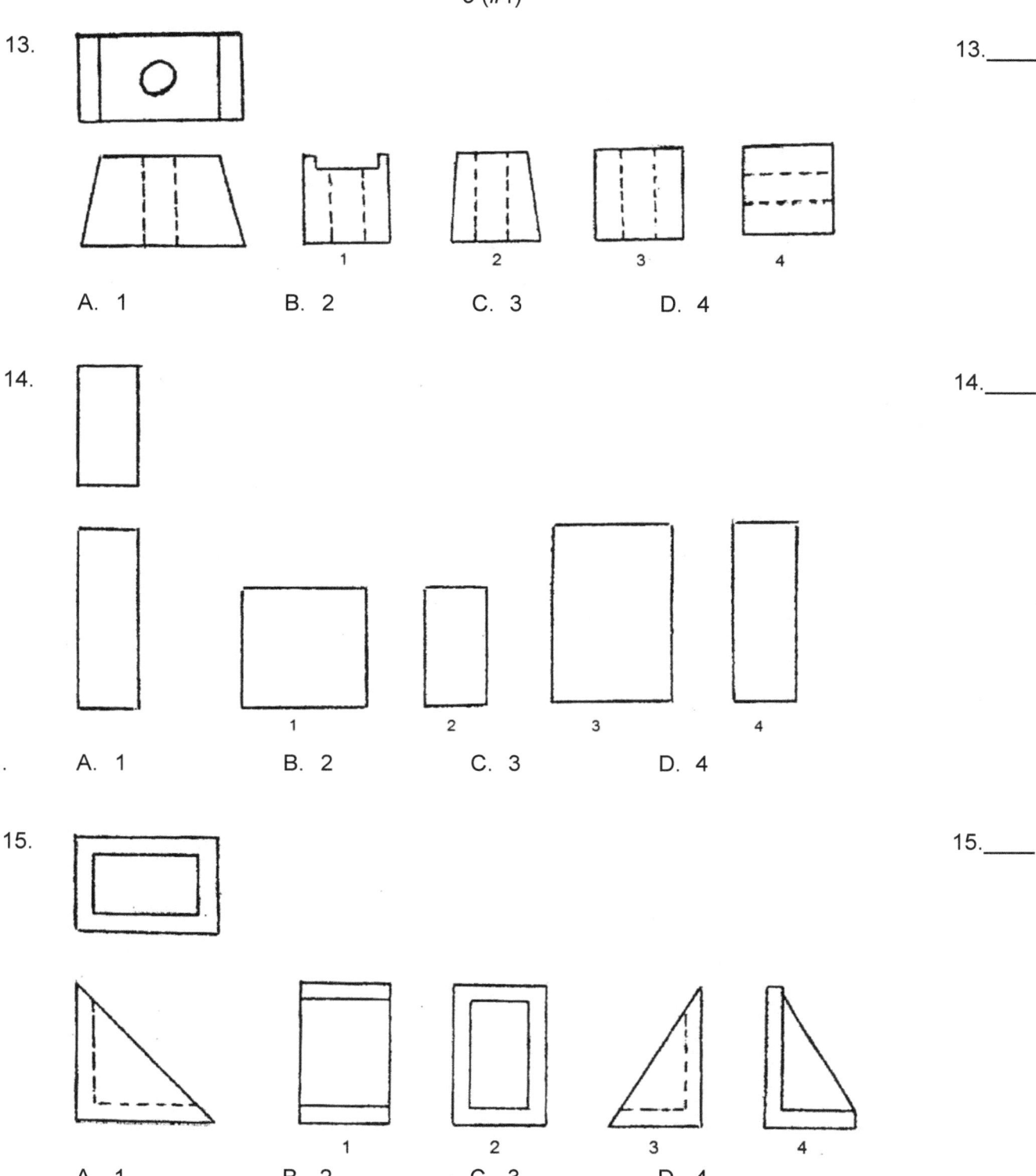

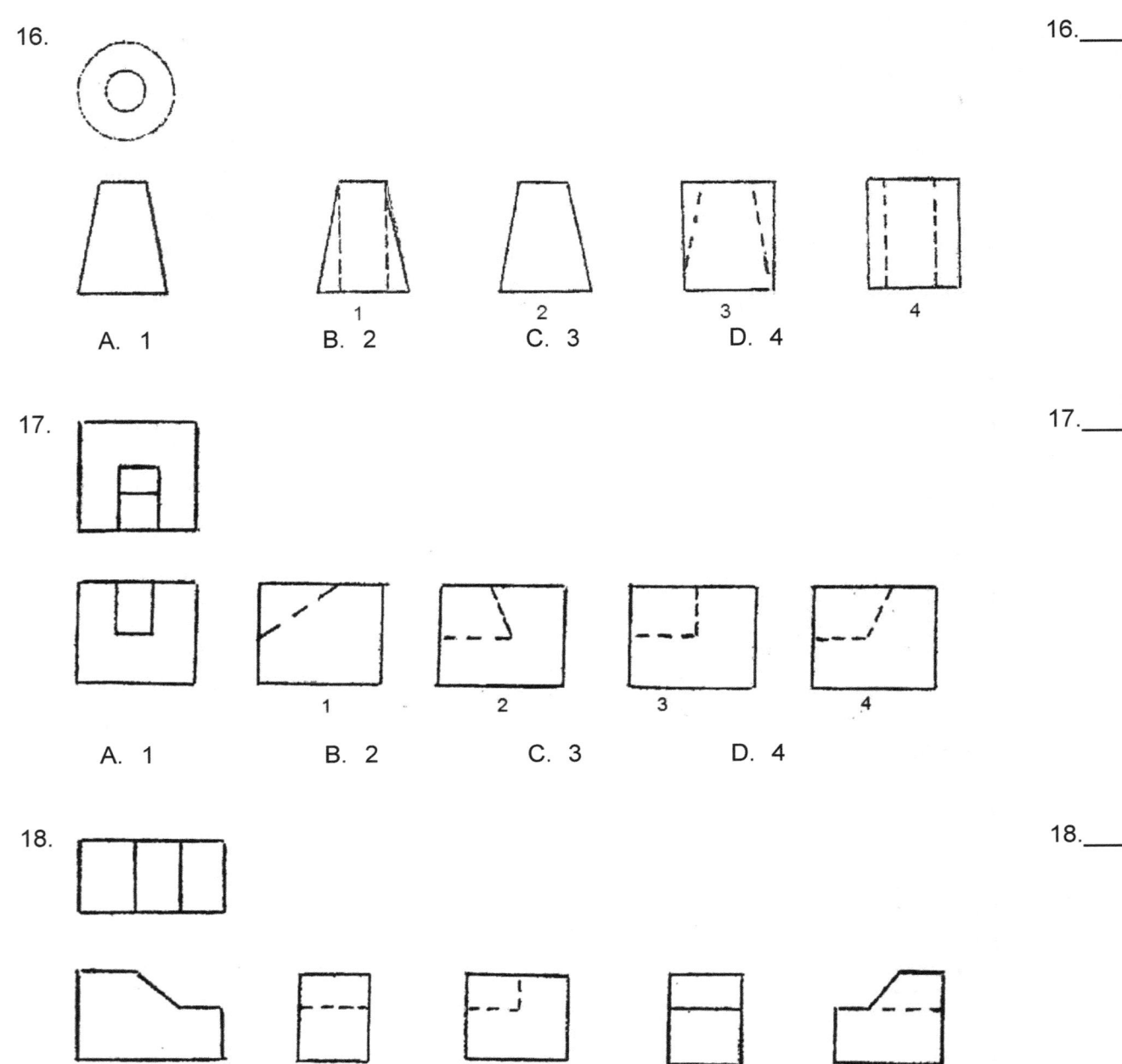

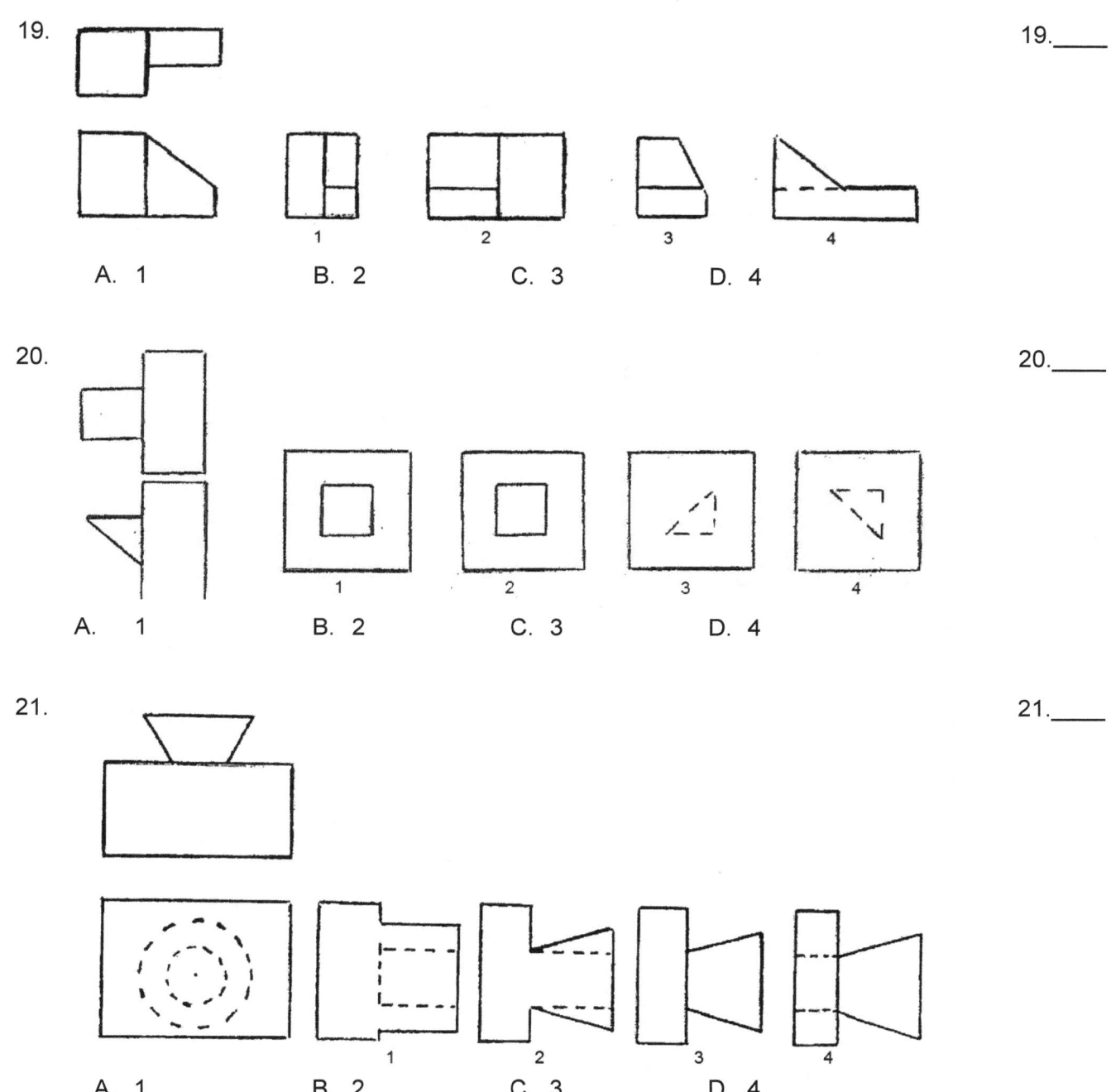

19. _____

20. _____

21. _____

22.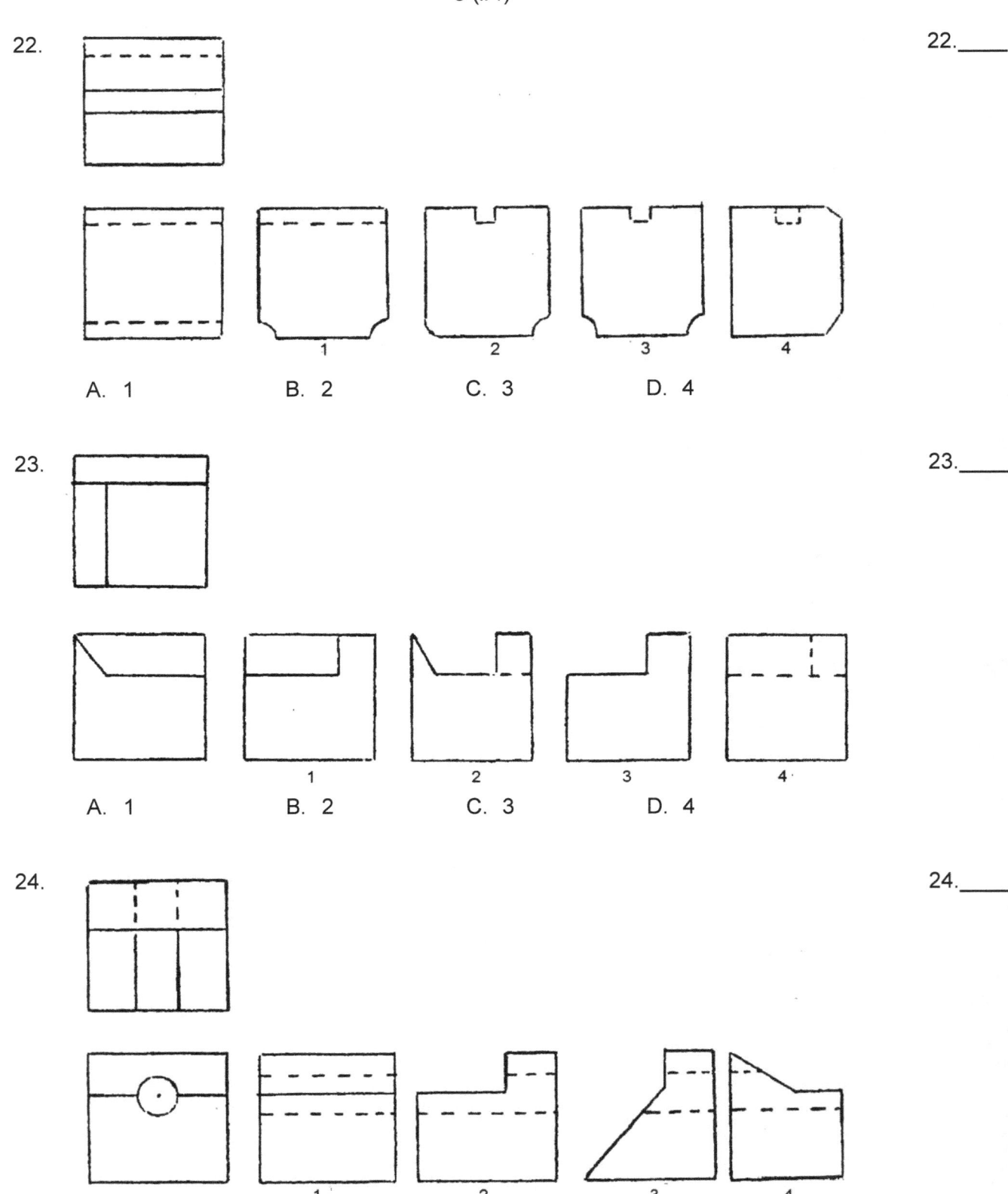

A. 1   B. 2   C. 3   D. 4

23.

A. 1   B. 2   C. 3   D. 4

24.

25.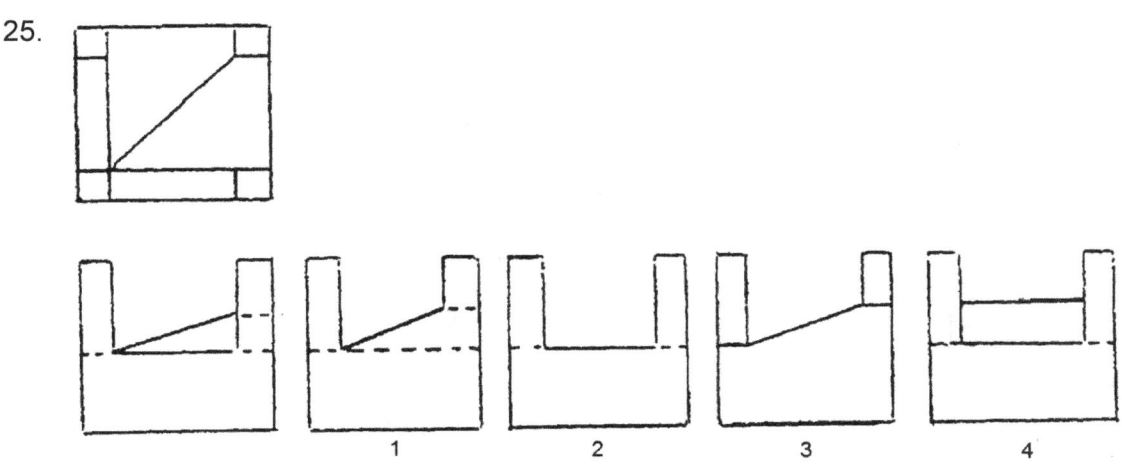

A. 1   B. 2   C. 3   D. 4

Questions 26-30.

DIRECTIONS: In Questions 26 through 30 which follow, the plan and front elevation of an object are shown on the left, and on the right are shown four figures, one of which and only one represents the right side elevation. Mark in the space at the right the letter which represents the right side elevation. In the sample below, which figure correctly represents the right side elevation?

SAMPLE QUESTION

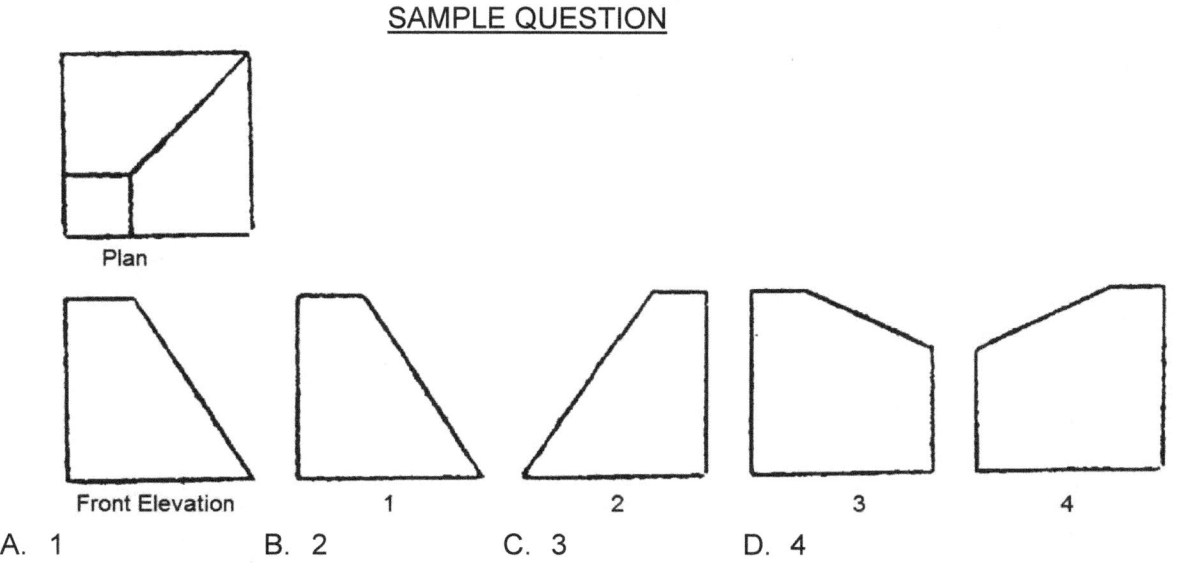

A. 1   B. 2   C. 3   D. 4

The correct answer is A.

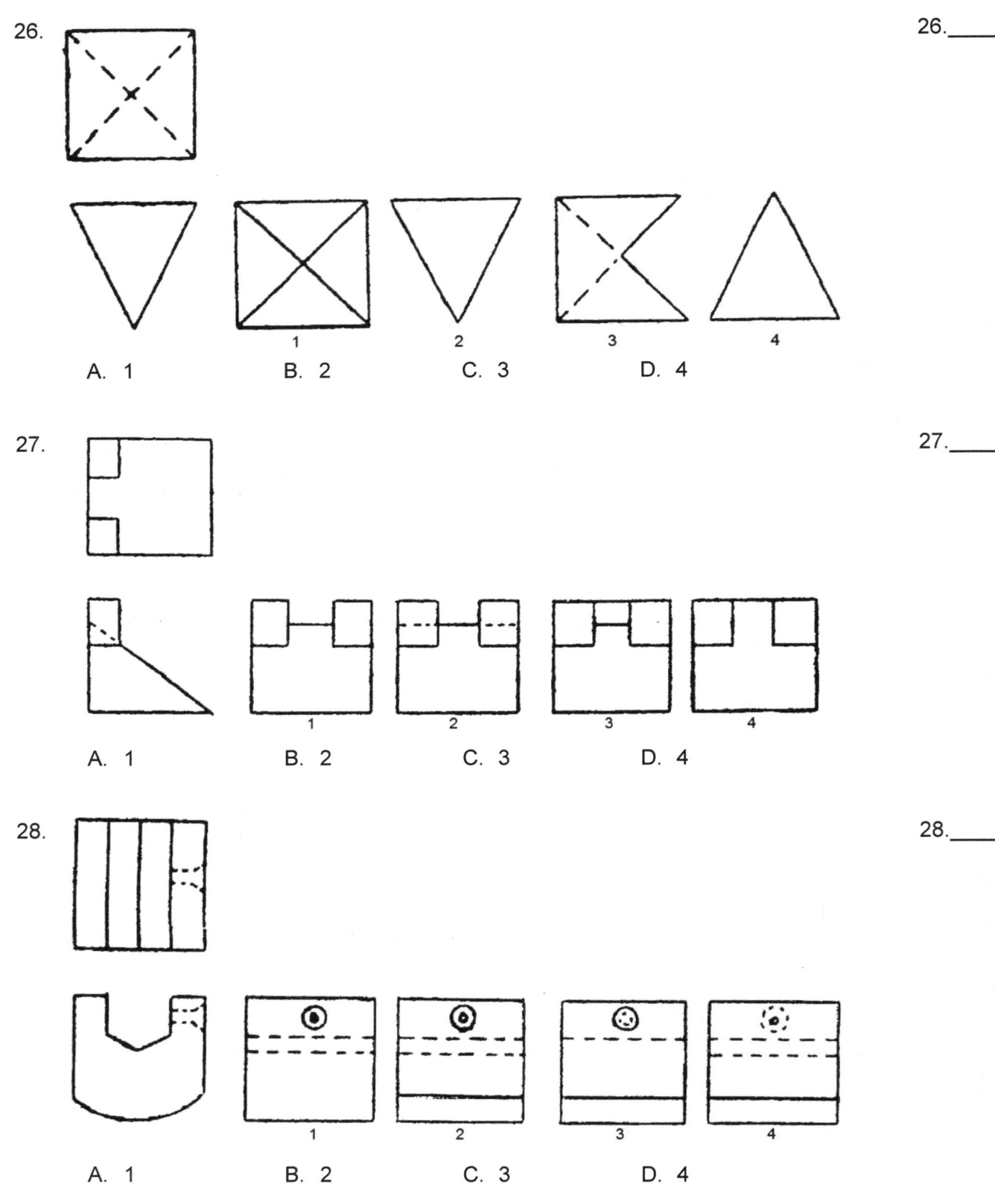

29.

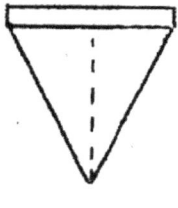 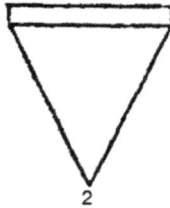 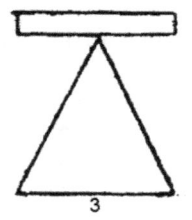 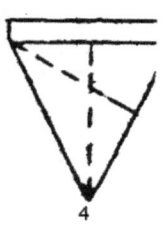

A. 1   B. 2   C. 3   D. 4

30.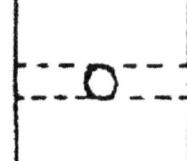

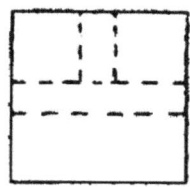 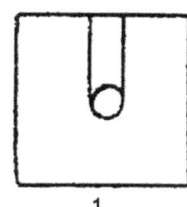 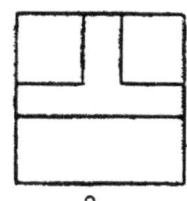 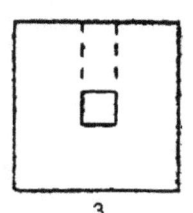 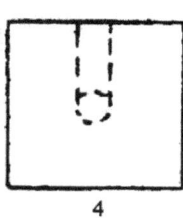

A. 1   B. 2   C. 3   D. 4

KEY (CORRECT ANSWERS)

1.	B	11.	A	21.	C
2.	D	12.	D	22.	B
3.	A	13.	C	23.	A
4.	A	14.	C	24.	B
5.	C	15.	B	25.	A
6.	B	16.	B	26.	B
7.	D	17.	D	27.	A
8.	C	18.	C	28.	B
9.	A	19.	A	29.	A
10.	A	20.	B	30.	C

TEST 2

Questions 1-10.

DIRECTIONS: Questions 1 through 10 deal with relationships between sets of figures. For each question, select that choice (A, or B, or C, or D) which has the SAME relationship to Figure 3 that Figure 2 has to Figure 1.

SAMPLE: Study Figures 1 and 2 in the Sample. Notice that Figure 1 has been turned clockwise 1/4 of a turn to get Figure 2. Taking Figure 3 and turning it clockwise 1/4 of a turn, we get choice A, the correct answer.

Questions 11-16.

DIRECTIONS: Questions 11 through 16 show the top view of an object in the first column, the front view of the same object in the second column and four drawings in the third column, one of which correctly represents the RIGHT side of the object. Select the CORRECT right side view.

As a guide, the first one is an illustrative example, the correct answer of which is C.

11. _____

12. _____

13. _____

14. _____

15. _____

16. _____

Questions 17-20.

DIRECTIONS: In each of the following groups of drawings, the top view and front elevation of an object are shown on the left. At the right are four drawings, one of which represents the end elevation of the object as seen from the right. Select the drawing which represents the correct end elevation and print the letter in the space at the right.

The first group is shown as an example only.
The correct answer in this group is C.

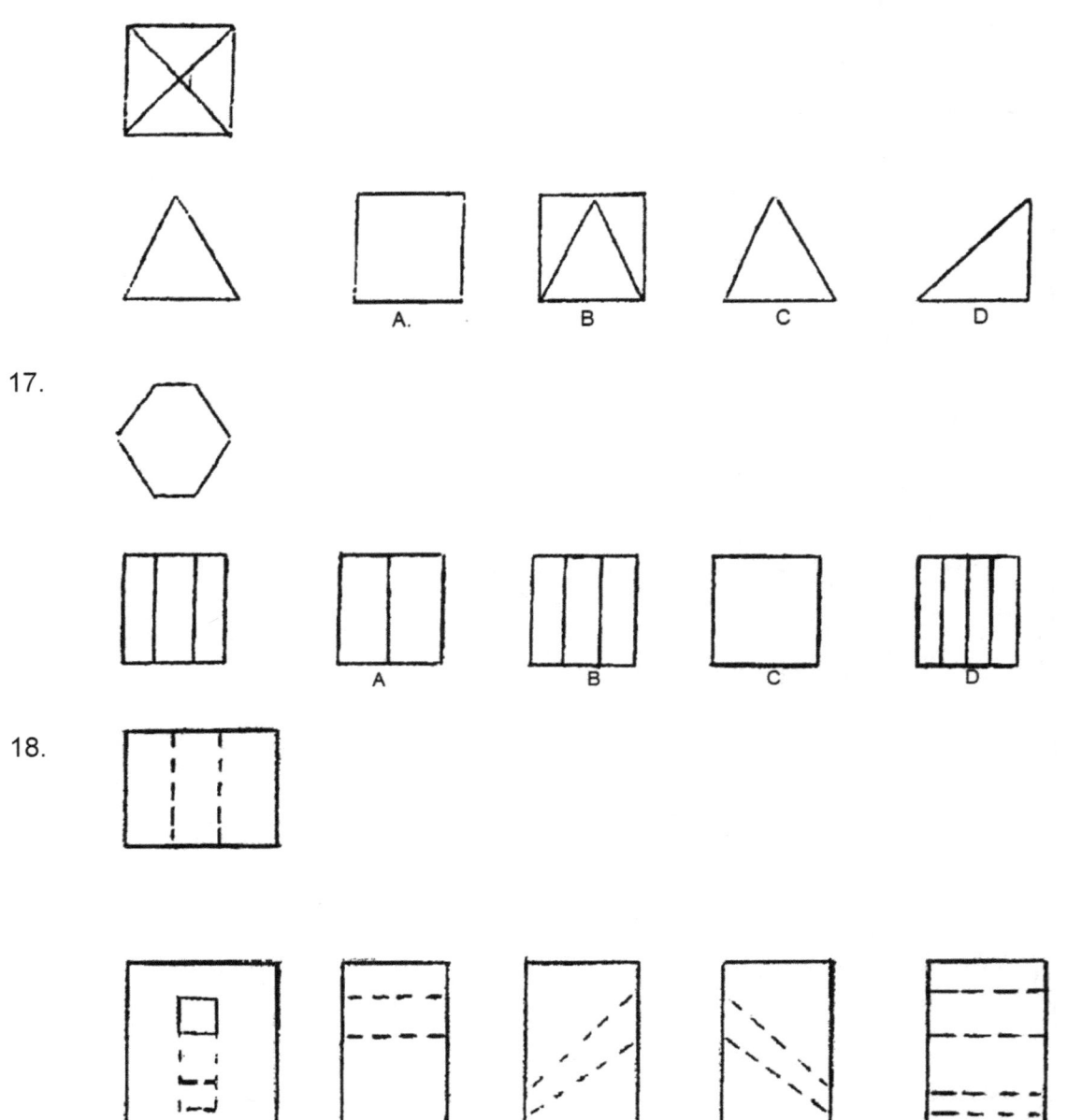

17. ____

18. ____

19. 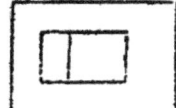 19.____

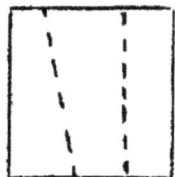   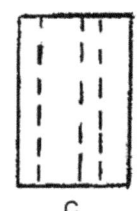 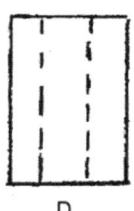
A B C D

20.  20.____

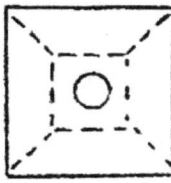 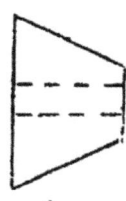 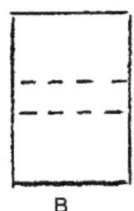 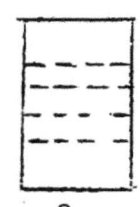 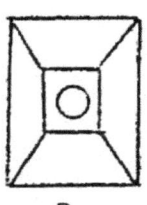
A B C D

KEY (CORRECT ANSWERS)

1.	C	6.	C	11.	C	16.	C
2.	B	7.	A	12.	A	17.	A
3.	D	8.	B	13.	C	18.	C
4.	A	9.	B	14.	B	18.	D
5.	B	10.	D	15.	B	19.	A

ABSTRACT REASONING

CLASSIFICATION INVENTORY SECTION
INCOMPLETE PATTERNS (NINE FIGURES)

The tests of incomplete patterns that follow consist of items which involve the visualization of nine figures arranged in sequence.

An incomplete pattern only is given. The candidate is to select from the five-lettered choices the correct figure for the last or ninth space.

DIRECTIONS: Each item in this test consists of an incomplete pattern. The complete pattern would be made up of nine figures arranged in sequence. The candidate is to determine the correct figure for the last or ninth space from the five-lettered choices given

SAMPLE QUESTIONS AND EXPLANATIONS

QUESTIONS

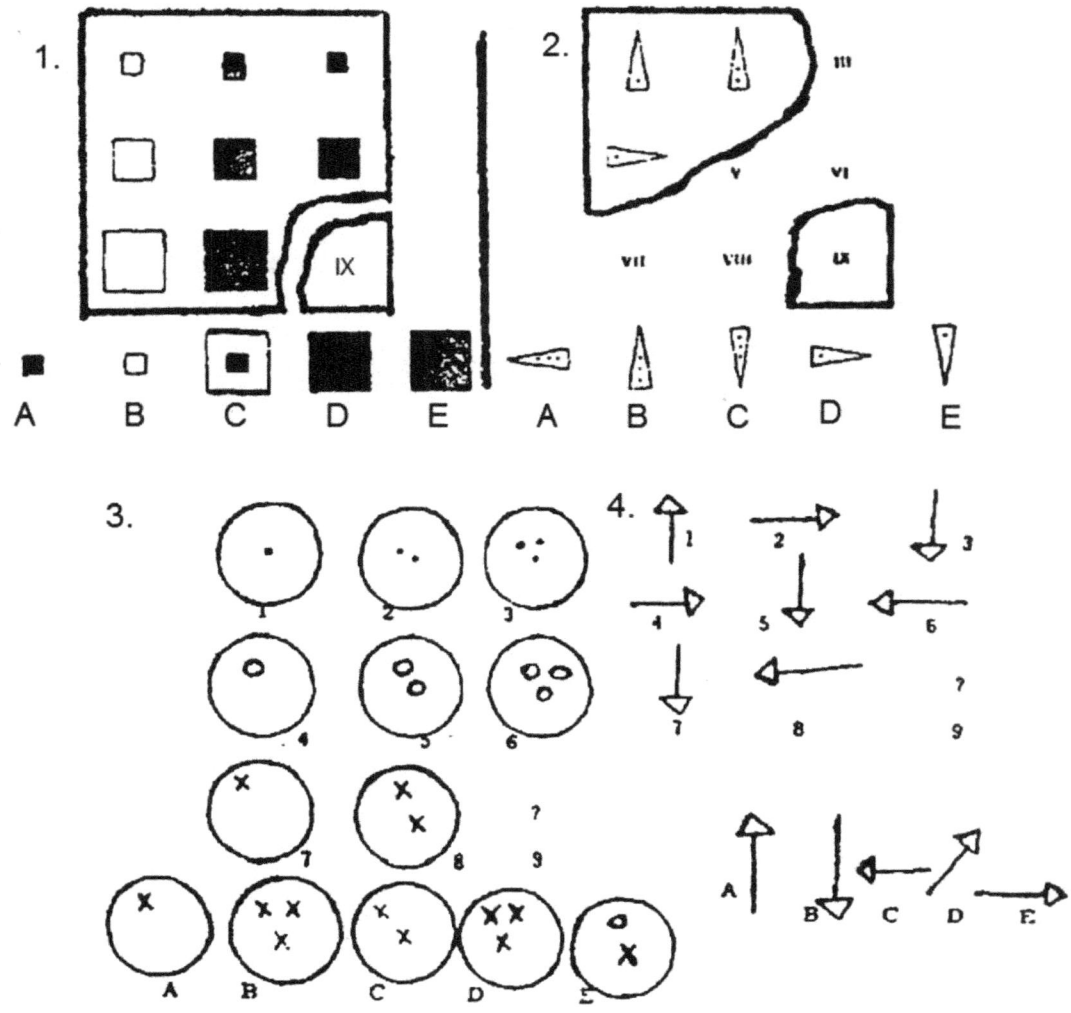

EXPLANATIONS: In Question 1, notice how the figures change as they go across each row of the pattern. They become darker. As they go down, the figures become larger. Therefore, the CORRECT figure for space IX is large is large and dark. Answer choice D is the CORRECT answer.

In Question 2, the figures acquire more dots as they go across the top row. As they go down, the point of the figure is rotated a quarter of a turn to the right. Therefore, the CORRECT answer figure for space IX has three dots and its point is directed downward toward the bottom of the page. Answer choice C is the CORRECT answer.

3. The correct answer is D. Each of the rows of circles has, exclusively, a number of ., o, or x's om ascending order. (Note that B is incorrect since the circle is larger than the given circles.)

4. The correct answer is A. Note that in row 1, two of the arrows (1,2) are turned to the right and one (3) is turned to the left. In row 2, one of the arrows (4) is turned to the right, and two (5,6) are turned to the left. In row three, two arrows are turned to the left (7,8). Therefore, one arrow (9) must be turned to the right in a similar way (answer A).

TESTS IN INCOMPLETE PATTERNS

TEST 1

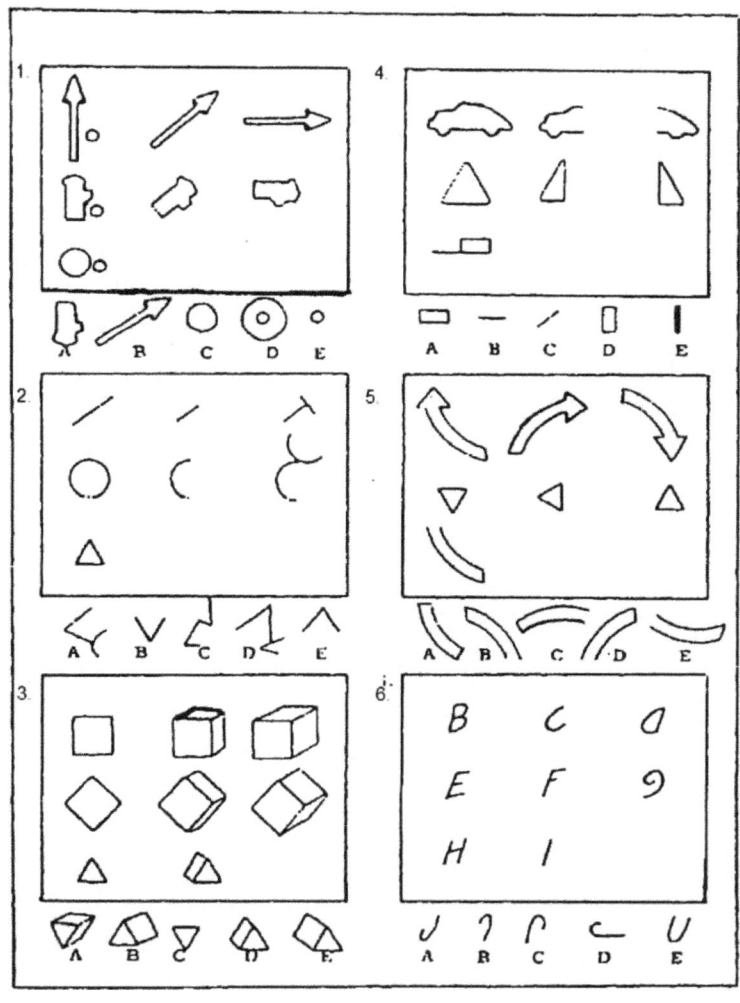

KEY (CORRECT ANSWERS)

1. C
2. C
3. E
4. A
5. B
6. C

TEST 2

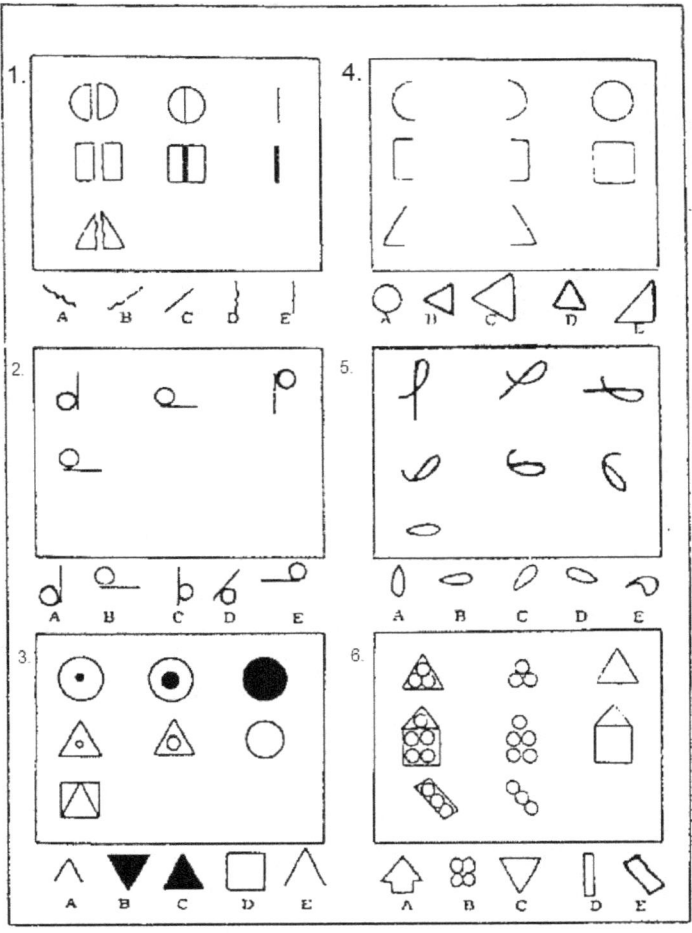

KEY (CORRECT ANSWERS)

1. D
2. A
3. E
4. C
5. A
6. E

TEST 3

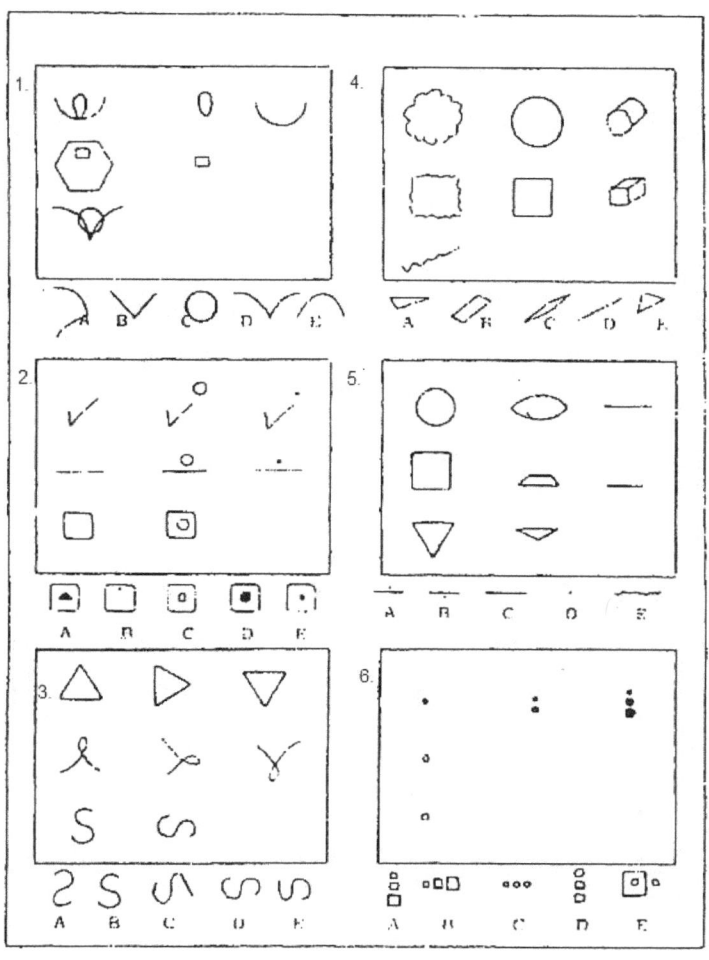

KEY (CORRECT ANSWERS)

1. D
2. E
3. B
4. C
5. C
6. A

TEST 4

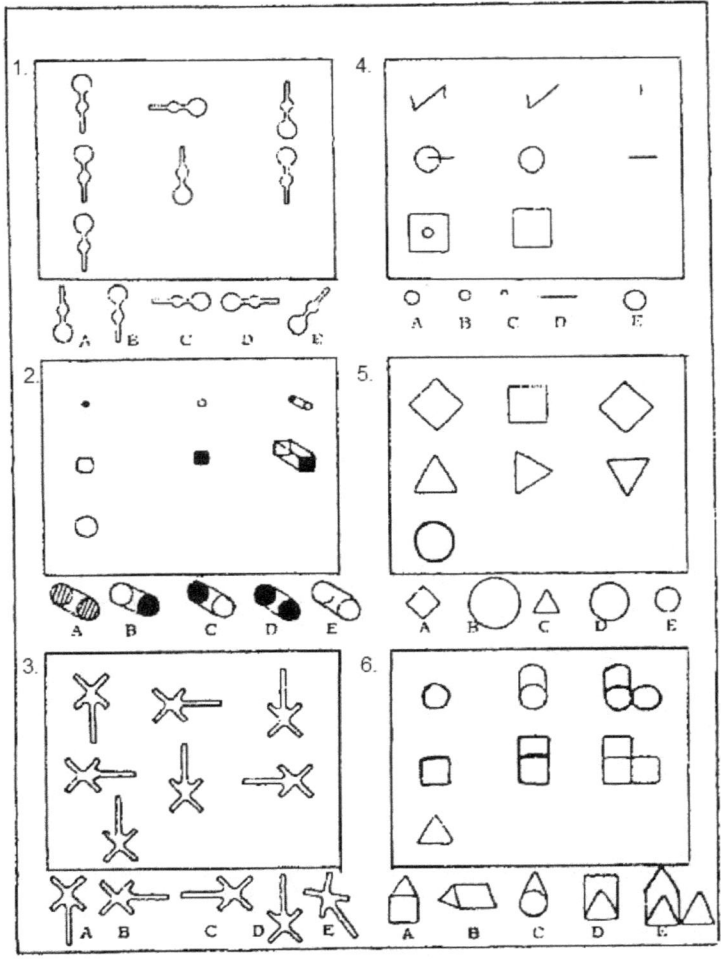

KEY (CORRECT ANSWERS)

1. A
2. B
3. A
4. B
5. D
6. E

TEST 5

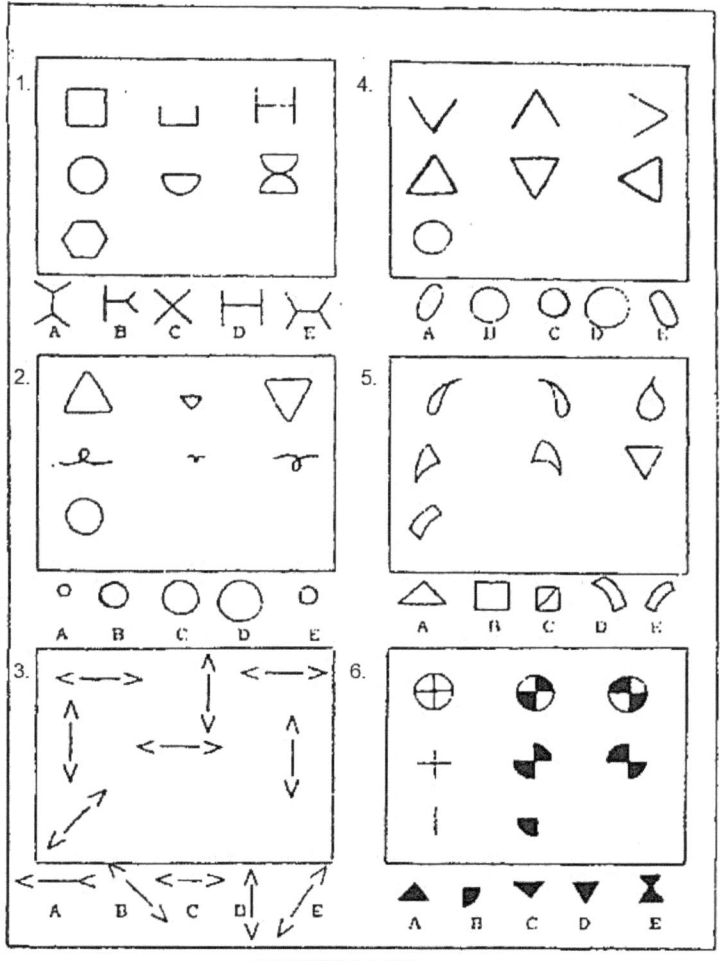

KEY (CORRECT ANSWERS)

1. E
2. C
3. E
4. B
5. B
6. B

PATTERN ANALYSIS (RIGHT SIDE ELEVATION
SAMPLE QUESTION

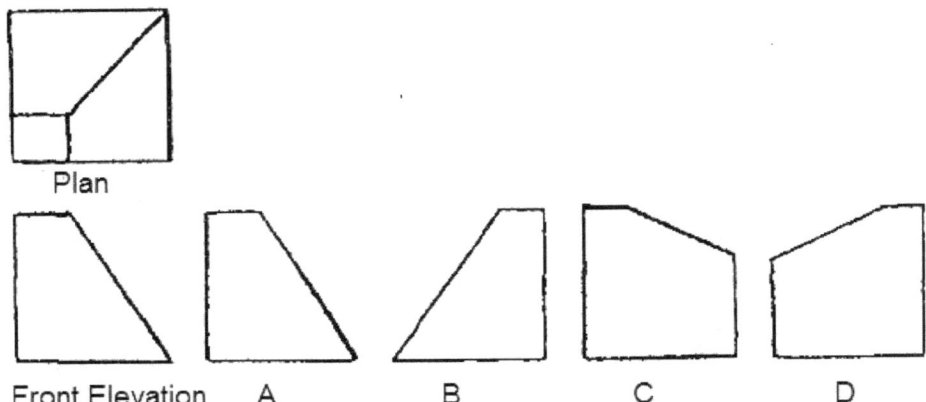

5. In the sample shown above, which figure CORRECTLY represents the right side elevation?

   1. A   2. B   3. C   4. D

5.____

The correct answer is 1.

TEST 1

Questions 1-5.

DIRECTIONS: In Questions 1 through 5 which follow, the plan and front elevation of an object are shown on the left, and on the right are shown four figures, one of which, and ONLY one, represents the right side elevation. Mark your answer in the space at the right the number which represents the right side elevation.

1. A 2. B 3. C 4. D

1.   1.____

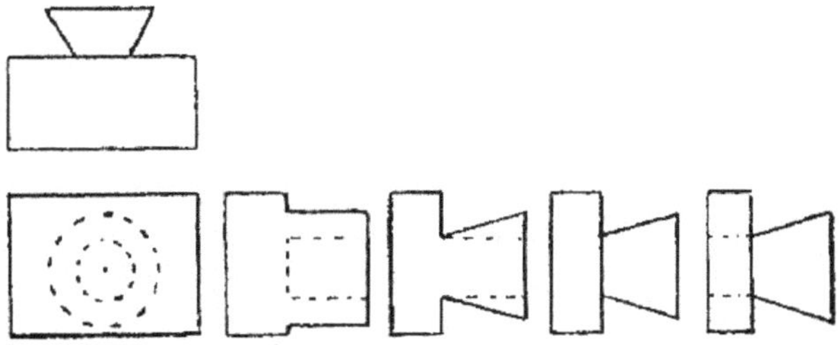

2.   2.____

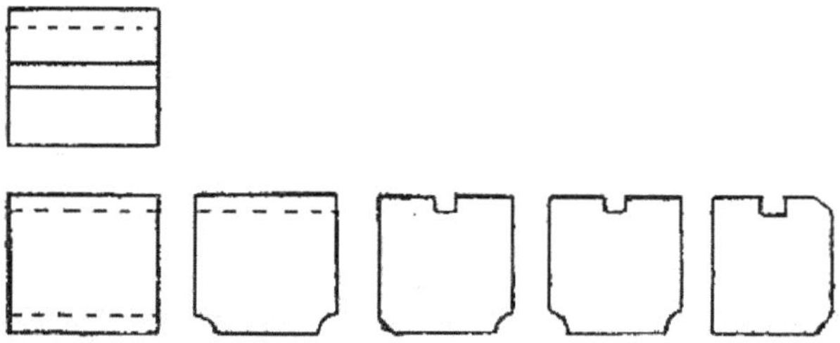

3.   3.____

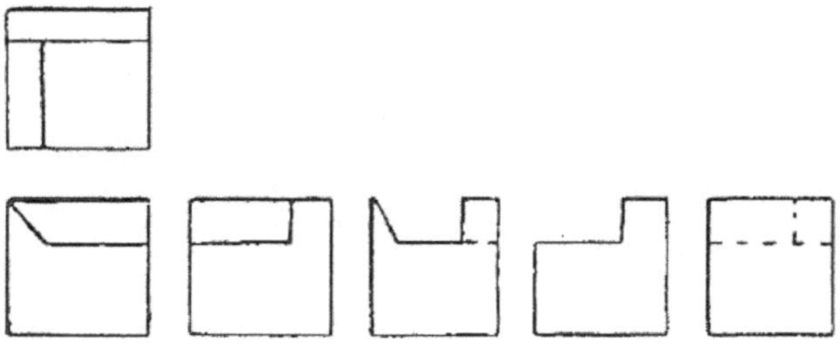

4. ____

5. ____

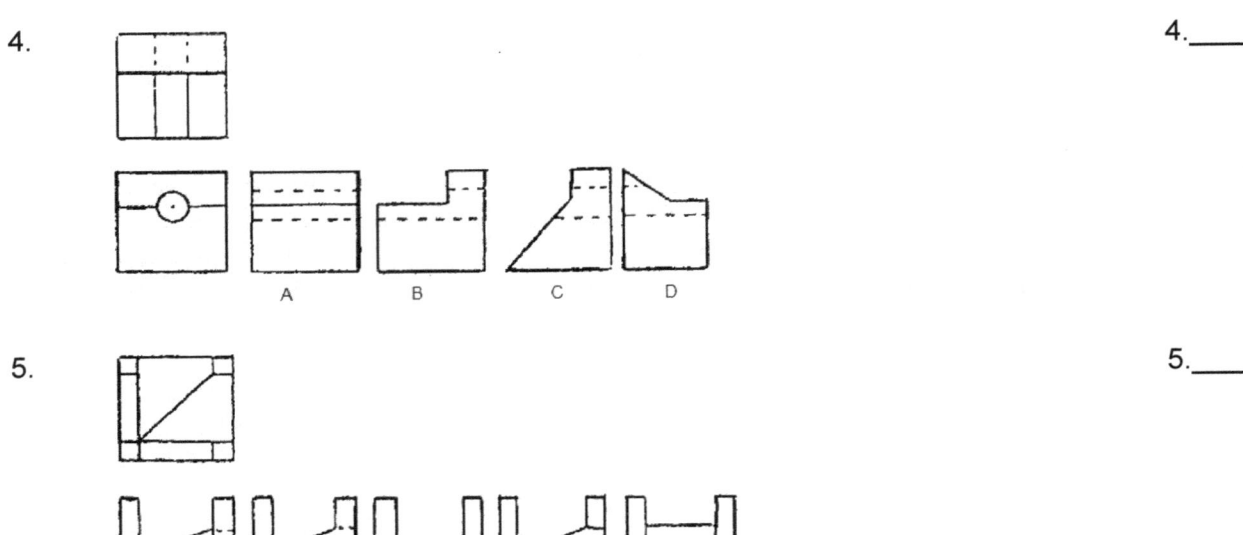

KEY (CORRECT ANSWERS)

1. 4
2. 3
3. 3
4. 2
5. 2

PATTERN ANALYSIS (END ELEVATION)

Questions 1-5.

DIRECTIONS: In each of the following groups of drawings, the top view and front elevation of an object are shown at the left. At the right are four drawings, one of which represents the end elevation of the object as seen from the right. Select the drawing which represents the CORRECT end elevation. The first group is shown as a sample ONLY.

SAMPLE QUESTION

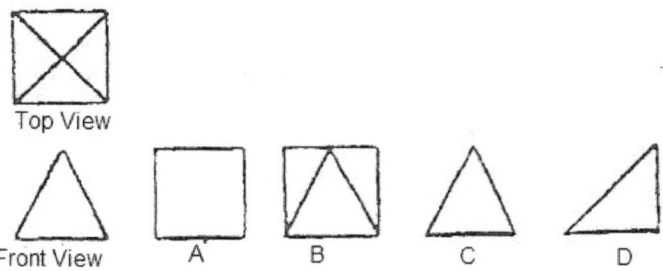

Which drawing represents the CORRECT end elevation?
1. A 2. B. 3. C 4. D

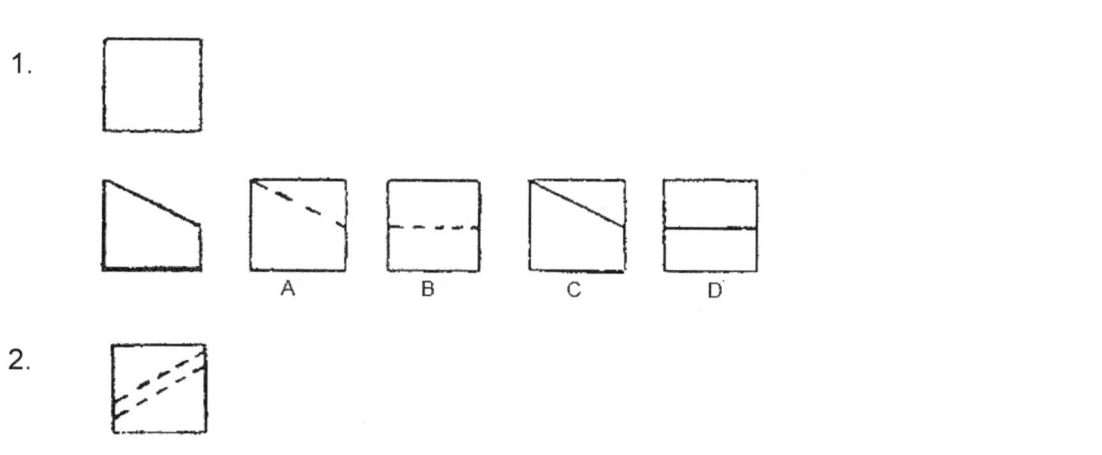

1.____

12

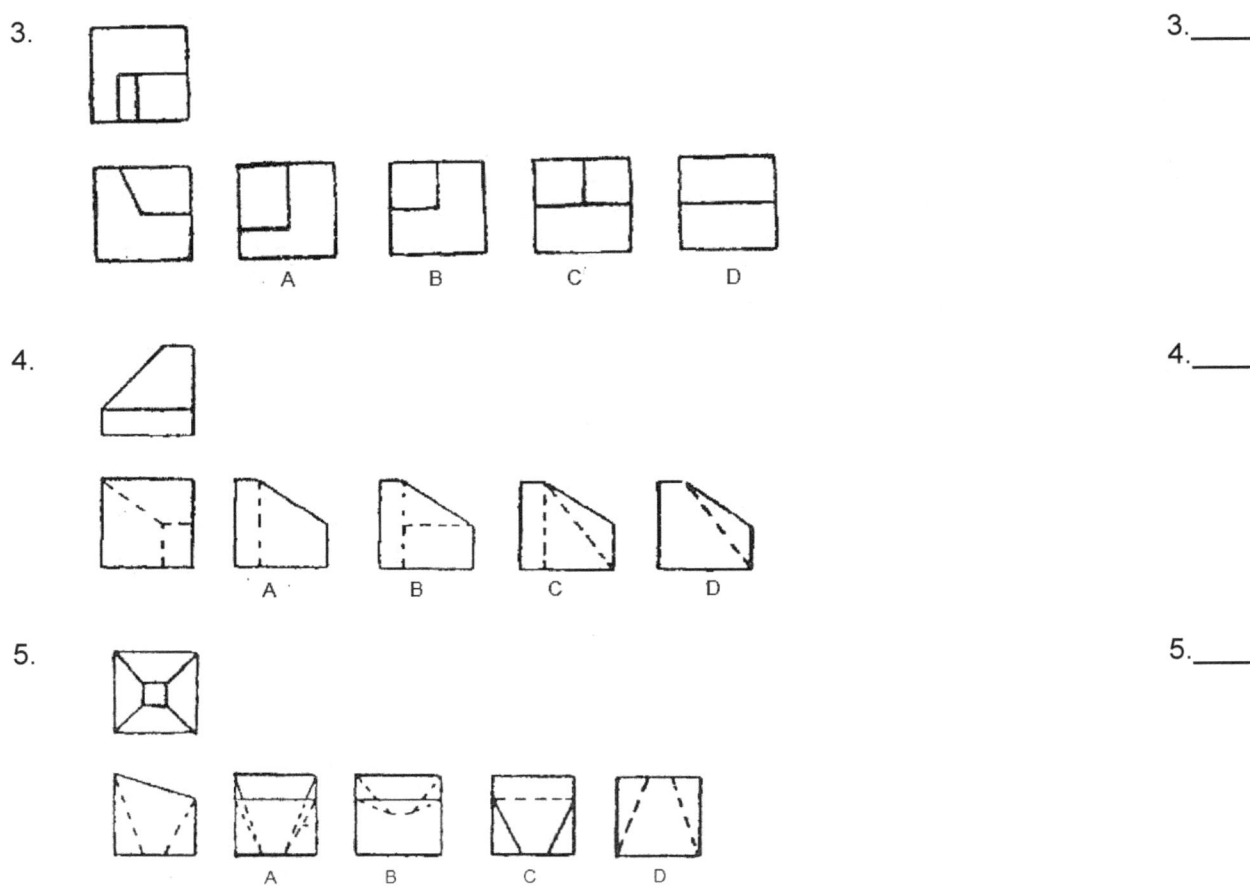

KEY (CORRECT ANSWERS)

1. 4
2. 3
3. 2
4. 1
5. 1

PATTERN ANALYSIS (RIGHT SIDE VIEW)

TEST 1

Questions 1-5.

DIRECTIONS: In each of Questions 1 to 5, inclusive, two views of an object are given. Of the views labeled A, B, C, and D, select the one that CORRECTLY represents the right side view of each object.

Which view represents the right side view?   1. A; 2. B; 3 C; 4. D.

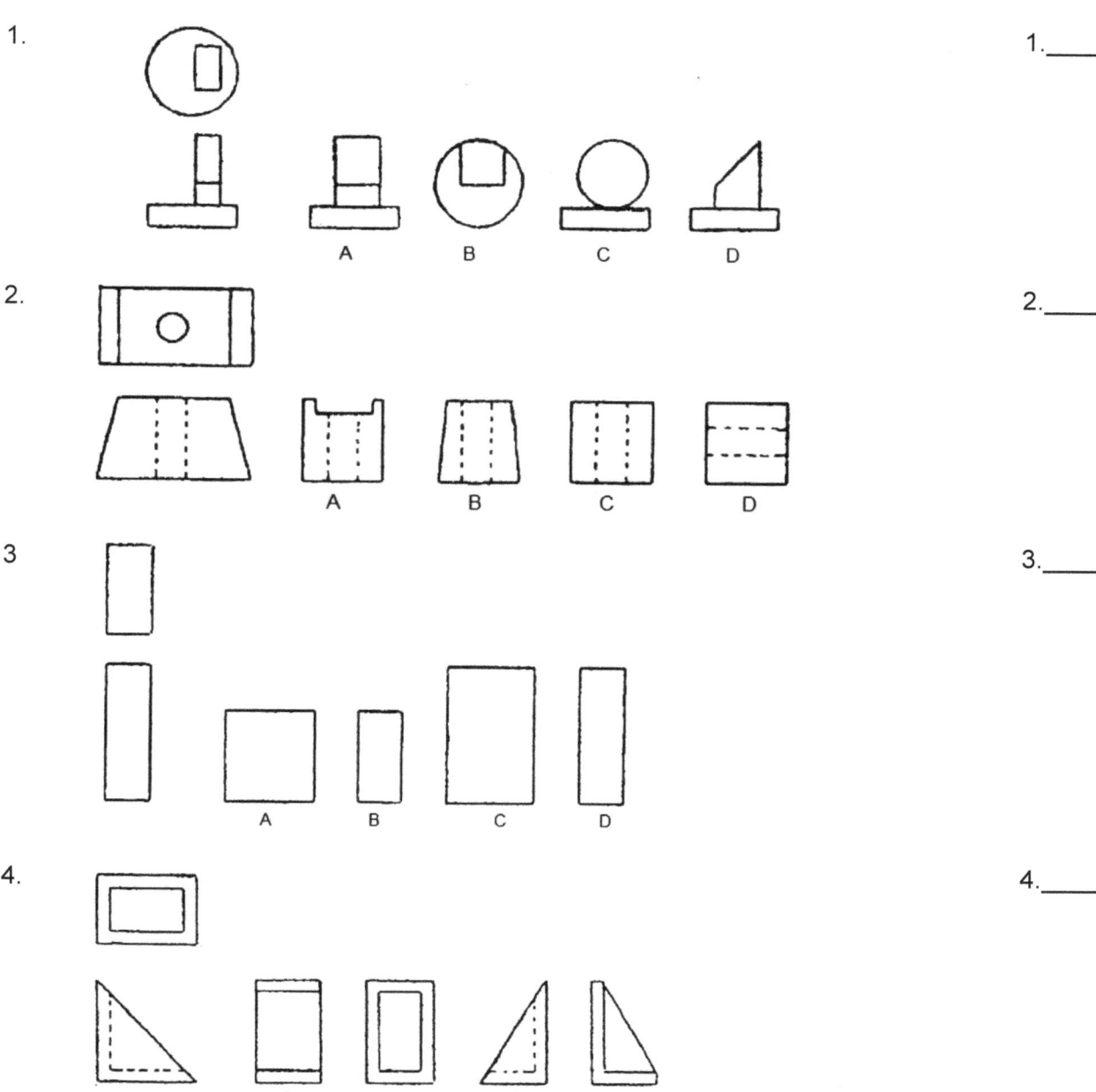

1.____

2.____

3.____

4.____

5.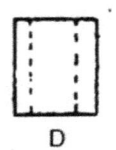

A. B. C. D.

5.____

KEY (CORRECT ANSWERS)

1. 4
2. 3
3. 3
4. 2
5. 2

15

SURVEY OF OTHER TYPES OF PATTERN ANALYSIS QUESTIONS

SOLID FIGURE TURNING

Questions 1-3.

DIRECTIONS: The following questions represent figures made up of cubes or other forms glued together. Select the ONE of the four figures lettered A, B, C, D which is the figure at the left turned in a different position and print the letter of the answer in the space at the right. (Note: You are permitted to turn over the figures, to turn them around and to turn them both over and around.)

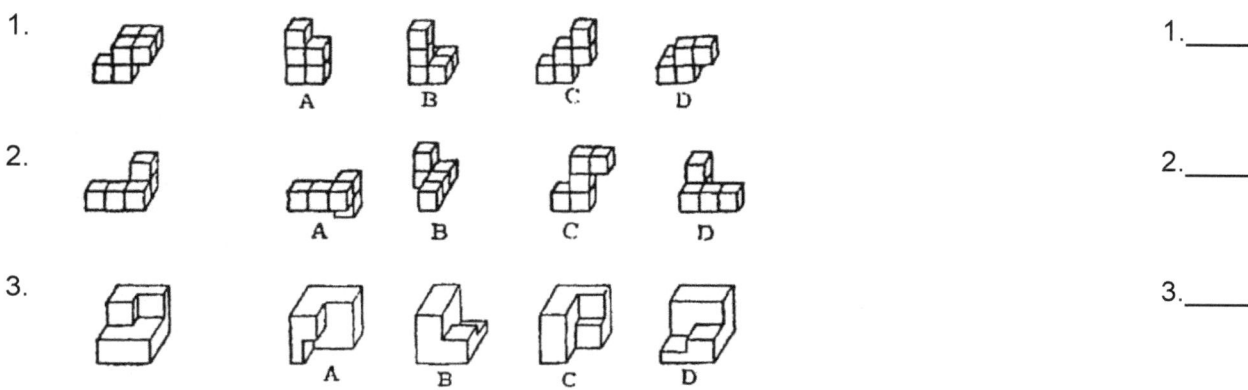

1.____

2.____

3.____

TOUCHING CUBES

Questions 4-7.

DIRECTIONS: Questions 4 and 5 are based on the group of touching cubes at the left, and Questions 6 and 7 on the group at the right.

All the cubes are exactly the same size, and there are only enough hidden cubes to support the ones you can see. The question number is on a cube in the group. You are to find how many cubes in that group touch the numbered cube. Note: A cube is considered to touch the numbered cube if ANY part, EVEN A CORNER, touches. Mark the answer in the space at the right to show how many cubes touch the numbered cube
- A. if the answer is 1 or 6 or 11 cubes
- B. if the answer is 2 or 7 or 12 cubes
- C. if the answer is 3 or 8 or 13 cubes
- D. if the answer is 4 or 9 or 14 cubes
- E. if the answer is 5 or 10 or 15 cube

4.

5.

6.

7.

Questions 8-9.

DIRECTIONS: In each of the following questions, the drawing at the left represents a cube. There is a different design on each of the six faces of the cube. At the right are four other drawings of cubes lettered A, B, C, and D.

Select the ONE of the four which is actually the cube on the left turned to a different position and print the CORRECT answer in the space at the right. (Note: The cube at the left may have been turned <u>over,</u> it may have been turned may have been turned <u>around</u>, or it may have been turned <u>both</u> over and around, and faces not seen in the drawing on the left may have become visible.)

8.   A   B   C   D   6.____

282

9.
   A   B   C   D

7.____

CUBE COUNTING

Questions 10-15.

DIRECTIONS: In each of the following questions, count the number of boxes or cubes represented in the drawing and print the letter of the correct answer in the space at the right.

10.

A. 16   B. 26   C. 40   D. 22

10._____

11.

A. 22   B. 16   C. 27   D. 24

11._____

12.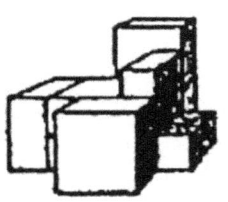

A. 7   B. 8   C. 9   D. 10

12._____

13.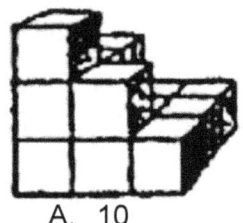

A. 10   B. 13   C. 12   D. 14

13._____

14.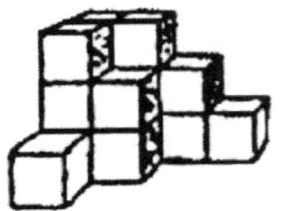

A. 15   B. 13   C. 12   D. 1-

14.____

15.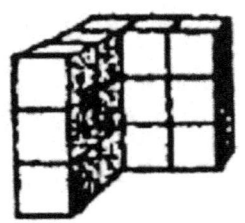

A. 16   B. 12   C. 10   D. 15

15.____

KEY (CORRECT ANSWERS)

1.	D	6.	B(7)	11.	A
2.	B	7.	E(10)	12.	B
3.	D	8.	B	13.	.D
4.	C(3)	9.	A	14	A
5.	A(6)	10.	C	15.	A